In accordance with the latest syllabus prescribed by the Council for the Indian Certificate of Secondary Education Examination, New Delhi.

A TEXT BOOK OF
ICSE ECONOMIC APPLICATIONS

CLASS IX

Authors

A. GHOSH   A. BANERJEE

Advisory Member
Chetan Tiwari
M. Com., M.Sc., B.Ed.,
Principal St. Anthony's School, Kurseong

OSWAL PUBLISHERS
1/12 Sahitya Kunj, M. G. Road, Agra-282 002

No part of this book can be reproduced in any form or by any means without the prior written permission of the publisher.

Edition : 2021

ISBN : 978-93-90278-76-3

OSWAL PUBLISHERS

Head office : 1/12, Sahitya Kunj, M. G. Road, Agra-282 002
Phone : (0562) 2527771-4, +91 75340 77222
E-mail : contact@oswalpublishers.com
Website : www.oswalpublishers.com
Printed at : Upkar Printing Unit, Agra

Preface

We feel immense pleasure in introducing the latest thoroughly revised edition of 'ICSE Economic Applications' text book for class IX. This edition strictly adheres to the latest syllabus prescribed by the Council for the Indian School Certificate Examinations, New Delhi.

Economics by its very nature is considered both—as Art and Science. Often it has to deal with abstract ideas which need to be related to practical experiences. Economics has become imperative in the current national and international dynamics and is being applied in the arenas of business, engineering, planning, marketing, social sciences and various other fields, thus, making it a critical component of the curriculum. The students must, therefore, equip themselves with the basic principles of Economics and must understand the manner in which economic decisions affect the progress the development of society. This book is designed to achieve this goal.

Salient features of this Revised Edition of the Book
- Specially designed to meet the requirements of ICSE students.
- Based on new examination pattern
- Up-to-date study material incorporating the most reliable and latest data taken mostly from government journals and publications relating to the Indian Economy.
- Comprehensive coverage of the prescribed course.
- Project work given at the end of the text book has been designed to give students a first hand experience in applying the principles of economics in real life.

The subject matter has been presented in a very simple, lucid and interesting manner and every attempt has been made to relate theoretical knowledge with actual life. The Exercises at the end of each chapter are designed to test students' understanding of the text and to stimulate further study. The Exercises include both Short Answer Questions and Long Answer Questions.

We do hope that we have taken steps in the right direction towards guiding young minds into the realms of this vast yet beautiful discipline viz. Economics.

Constructive suggestions and comments will be appreciated and thankfully acknowledged.

—**PUBLISHER**

SYLLABUS CLASS IX
ECONOMIC APPLICATIONS

There will be **one** theory paper of **two hours** duration of 100 marks and Internal Assessment of 100 marks.

The paper will consists of Part I and Part II.

Part I (compulsory) will contain short answer questions on the entire syllabus.

Part II will consist of questions that will require detailed answers. There will be a choice of questions.

Theory—100 Marks

1. **Basic Concepts of Economics**

    (i) Meaning and Definition of Economics; Economic entities: Consumer, Producer, Households and Government. The importance of these economic entities. The meaning of an economy and role of the economic entities.

    A basic understanding of the concepts of economics. The definitions of economics with reference to allocation of resources and scarcity resources (Robbins, Samuelson). Basic explanation of the role of consumer, producer, government and household in an economy.

    (ii) Three major problems of an economy: What to produce? How to produce? For whom to produce? Efficient use of resources; basic understanding of the terms: economic growth and economic development.

    A brief introduction to the basic problems of an economy-what to produce? How to produce? For whom to produce? Needs to be emphasized irrespective of the type of an economy. Manner in which economics as a subject helps us to allocate scarce resources in an efficient way needs to be explained. The concept of economic growth and economic development should be explained.

    (iii) The nature and classification of an economy: developed, underdeveloped and developing economy; Capitalistic, Socialistic, Mixed economies; main features.

    A basic understanding of the features of capitalistic, socialistic and mixed economies is required. Meaning and classification of economies into developing and developed should be explained.

2. **An Overview of Indian Economy**

    The nature of Indian economy: the main sectors of Indian economy– Agriculture, Industry and Services. Role of these sectors in Indian economy and their interrelationship. The sectors according to ownership- private and public; the sectors according to type of economy–rural and urban.

    Role of Argiculture in India and its problems.

    Impact of Agricultural practices on the Ecosystem.

    Construction of dams—loss of habitat species.

    Loss of top soil and desertification.

Indiscriminate use of fertilizers and pesticides.

Measures to check the ecosystem.

Governmental initiatives: not building large dams for generating hydroelectric power which leads to less land being submerged and less displacement of people.

Alternative cropping for checking loss of topsoil and desertification. Plantation and conservation of grasslands to check soil erosion. Use of manure, bio-fertilizers and bio-pesticides green manuring, compost. These are eco-friendly alternatives to pesticides and fertilizers.

Role of Industries in the Indian Economy.

Impact of industrial practices on the ecosystem.

Mining, industries, energy generation, automobiles, urbanisation leading to defacement of land, deforestation, deterioration of hydrological resources.

Industrial waste : mining operations, cement factories, oil refineries, construction unit.

Spoilage of landscape, pollution, health hazards, effect on terrestrial, aquatic (fresh water and marine) life.

Measures to check the ecosystem.

Improving efficiency of existing technologies and introducing new eco-friendly technologies.

Methods of safe disposal of waste– segregation, dumping, composting, drainage, treatment of effluents before discharge.

Abatement of pollution

Air: *setting standards and implementing them, using technical devices to reduce pollution.*

Importance of Service Sector— National Income, Employment and Regional Development (in brief, no statistical data required). Interdependence of all three sectors (Primary, Secondary and Tertiary).

Meaning of Private and Public sector with examples. Meaning of Rural and Urban sector with examples.

3. **Infrastructure of the Indian Economy**

Economic and social infrastructure of Indian economy. Social infrastructure-education, health, family welfare and housing.

A basic understanding of the economic and social infrastructure and its role in India's economic development. The problems pertaining to lack of such infrastructure and their adverse impact on the economy to be discussed.

4. **Consumer Awareness**

Ways in which consumer is exploited. Reasons for exploitation of consumers. Growth of consumer awareness; consumer behaviour in the market; consumer rights. Legal measures available to protect consumers from being exploited (COPRA, RTI).

Understanding the importance of educating consumers of their rights - awareness of food adulteration and its harmful effects.

5. **Globalisation**

Meaning and factors enabling Globalisation, WTO, impact of Globalization.

Meaning of Globalisation, Factors enabling globalisation—technology and liberalisation (removal of trade barriers). WTO (main objectives), favourable impacts of the globalization—starting of MNC's and benefits to Indian companies.

Note : It is suggested that case studies may be discussed on the following topics:

- Globalization
- Consumer Awareness
- Bhopal Gas Tragedy
- Chernobyl Disaster

INTERNAL ASSESSMENT   100 Marks

Candidates will be required to do a minimum of **four** assignments during the year, as assigned by the teacher.

Suggested list of assignments:

1. Identify 100 consumers of major brands of edible oils in a locality/area where you live. Draw up the pattern of their monthly expenditure on this product and compare it with the other household expenditure. Make a presentation of your findings in class.

2. Identify the major brands of bathing soaps that are available in the market in your area. Select a sample of 10 shops/department stores that sell these brands and collect the sales of these brands over a period of one week at these shops. Identify the brands that sell the most and make a presentation for your class.

3. Make a presentation on the central problems an economy faces. Explain these with reference to the Indian economy.

4. Take a developed country such as the USA and a developing country such as India. Analyze the main characteristics of these economies.

5. Outline the main modes of transport in the district/city you live. What problems do you and other citizens face pertaining to the availability of public transport ? Analyze.

6. Take a table of food grain production in India from any textbook on Indian economy or any other secondary source such as internet. Interpret the changes in the production over a given period of time.

7. Given a table of population growth for period between 1971 and 2001 and table of contribution of agriculture, industry and services sector for the same period, compare the two tables and present your findings in the form of a presentation.

8. Make a presentation of the major trading partners of India in the last 15 years. Specify the major changes that have taken place in the last five years.

9. What are the major items of export and imports from India in the last five years? Use secondary data sources and make out the changes that have taken place in this context.

CONTENTS

1.	Definitions of Economics	9 – 18
2.	Concept of Economics	19 – 27
3.	Basic Problems of an Economy	28 – 37
4.	Type of Economies	38 – 53
5.	An Overview of Indian Economy	54 – 59
6.	Sectors in Indian Economy	60 – 80
7.	Public and Private Sectors in Indian Economy	81 – 90
8.	Environment and Agriculture	91 – 100
9.	Measures to Check Ecosystem	101 – 106
10.	Impact of Industrial Practices on the Ecosystem	107 – 115
11.	Impact of Industrial Wastes & Its Accumulation	116 – 125
12.	Eco-friendly Technologies	126 – 131
13.	Waste Disposal Methods	132 – 136
14.	Abatement of Pollution	137 – 140
15.	Infrastructure of Indian Economy	141 – 169
16.	Consumer Awareness	170 – 187
17.	Globalisation	188 – 196
18.	World Trade Organisation (WTO) and Multinational Corporations (MNCs)	197 – 203
	• Case Study	204 – 206
	• Project Work	207 – 210
	• Glossary	211 – 214

01 Definitions of Economics

The word *Economics*, derived from Greek words *Oikos* (a house) and *Nomos* (management) means the prudent management of one's household affairs. But, now it means the study of those activities which are related to production, exchange, consumption, etc., that satisfy the economic needs of the people.

Man is a social being. He lives in a society. His actions are influenced by the actions and reactions of other living beings in a society and in turn also influence them. Human activities are so diverse and pervasive that a single science cannot handle all such activities. Different branches of social sciences like politics, ethics, civics, etc., deal with different and distinct aspects of human behaviour in a society. Economics being one of the social sciences; deals with the study of human activities in a society in relation to income and wealth *i.e., how man earns them and how he spends them.* Economics is concerned with the utilization of scarce means, having alternative uses, for achieving multiple ends.

OVERVIEW

The concept of 'ECONOMICS' and its DEFINITION has changed from classical view of 'Wealth-Oriented' approach to the modern 'Growth-Oriented' view. Since it covers almost all 'Human Activities' related to 'Progress of Wealth'; it is equally useful to individuals, businessmen, industrialists, labourers, social reformers, statesmen and politicians, society and the country as a whole.

Economics explains how to use scarce goods to one's best advantage or how to economise. A man has only a limited amount of cash, housing accommodation and other things. With the limited amount of cash, he wants to buy so many things, but he cannot buy them all. He must, therefore, choose what to buy and what not to buy. *Thus, "Economics is a science of choice when faced with scarce means against unlimited ends."*

As pointed out earlier, the definition of Economics has been modified from time to time, depending upon the scope covered and inclusion of various human motives. Different definitions were given by different economists. Some of the important ones will be studied and reviewed here, so that the nature, scope or subject matter of Economics becomes clearer to the learners.

Mr. Jacob Viner described Economics in very simple words by saying, *"Economics is what Economists do."* A lot can be discussed on this simple but vague definition, as it leads directly to the study of the subject covered by economists and the methods used by them. But this definition also suggests that the scope of the subject changes in accordance to the range of activities considered by the economists. However, this definition is inadequate and incomplete as it does not give a clear understanding of the fundamental concept of economics.

In earlier periods, the desire to earn money and accumulation of wealth was considered to be the primary motive, which subsequently changed to welfare of the society. With the economic development, the scarcity and then the growth was considered to be primary motives of economics. The definition of Economics was also modified accordingly, but none of the definitions is complete in itself. The plethora of various definitions display that there is no unanimity. Thus, these definitions can be divided in the following categories depending upon various inherent motives :

- Wealth-oriented definition [**Adam Smith, J.S. Mill, F.A. Walker,** etc.]
- Welfare-oriented definition [**Marshall, Pigou, Beveridge, Cannan,** etc.]
- Scarcity-oriented definition [**Robbins, Keynes,** etc.]
- Growth-oriented definition [**Samuelson,** etc.]

The study of all above definitions will give an idea to the readers about the progress of the economic development also, because a modification in definitions and fundamental concepts directly reflects as to what was the economic approach prevailing at that time which led to the modification in the definition itself.

ADAM SMITH'S DEFINITION: WEALTH-ORIENTED DEFINITION

The economists of early stages of development of Economics considered *'earning money'* as a fundamental motive behind all economic activities and described economics as *"The Science of Wealth"*.

Adam Smith—the founding father of Economics—defined Economics as, *"The study of nature and causes of the wealth of nations."* According to him, it is a subject related with producing wealth and using it. Many eminent thinkers and writers also supported his views.

- *"The science which treats of wealth."* —**J.B. Say**
- *"The subject treated by political economists is not happiness, but wealth."*—**W.N. Senior**

J. S. Mill, F.A. Walker and few others also supported the above view. While defining *'Economics'*, these economists paid attention and importance only to wealth because in their opinion wealth was everything. The human happiness, for which wealth is meant, was ignored totally.

In the ordinary language, by "wealth", we mean money, but in economics, wealth refers to those goods which satisfy human wants. But we should remember all goods which satisfy human wants are not wealth. For example, air and sunlight are essential for us. We cannot live without them. But they are not regarded as wealth because they are available in abundance and unlimited in supply. We consider only those goods which are relatively scarce and have money value as wealth.

Main Features of Adam Smith's Definition

The main features of **Adam Smith's** wealth-oriented definition are as follows:

Study of Wealth: Economics deals with the study of wealth only. Therefore, it is concerned with the activities of man related to production, consumption, exchange and distribution of goods.

Only Material Commodities: This definition conveys the feeling that wealth constitutes only material commodities while it ignores non-material goods such as services, air and water.

Stress on Wealth: Economy gives more stress on production, augmentation of nation's wealth, not anything else.

Causes of Wealth: Economics is considered as study of causes of wealth accumulation which brings economic development. In order to increase wealth, production of material goods will have to be increased.

Economic Man: This definition is basically based on the man who is always aware of his 'self-interest' that leads him to material gains.

CRITICISM

The definition of Economics as a science of wealth cannot be regarded as being a correct one as it is criticised on various grounds *viz.* too much emphasis on wealth, narrow view of wealth, secondary place to man, etc.

Over Importance to Wealth: In this definition, attention was exclusively paid to wealth as if wealth was everything. Therefore, men of letters like **Carlyle** and **Ruskin** criticized the economists who propagated the wealth-oriented concept. According to these eminent thinkers, Economics was considered to teach selfishness and they described it as a *"Dismal Science"*.

Importance to Material Goods Only: Subsequently, the great thinkers and philosophers of early part of the 19th century also criticized the approach of considering economics as the science which attached an undue importance to only material or tangible goods constituting wealth, excluding non-material goods and services such as health and education, etc. Actually, such definitions restricted the scope of Economics and because of this limitation, such approach was exposed to condemnation. **Ruskin** has remarked, *"The science of getting rich is a bastard science."*

During the later part of the 19th century, the economists started realizing the humanistic character of economics. It was visualized that wealth is only a means to an end, the end being human welfare. The attention and importance of economics now distinctly shifted from wealth to human welfare.

MARSHALL'S DEFINITION: WELFARE-ORIENTED DEFINITION

Alfred Marshall was the first Economist who lifted the science of Economics from the morass into which it had fallen towards the close of 19th century. He shifted his emphasis from 'wealth' to 'welfare'.

Alfred Marshall was inspired by the criticism of social thinkers and made a thorough study of original writings of Adam Smith and then came to a conclusion that *"Wealth for its own sake is of no use, but when placed in the hands of man, it gains the importance."* The concept of 'welfare' was included in the definition of Economics in his famous book, *'Principles of Economics.'*

- *"Economics is a study of mankind in the ordinary business of life. It examines that part of individual and social actions, which is most closely connected with the attainment and the use of material requisites of well-being. Thus, it is, on one side, a study of wealth, and on the other and more important side, a part of the study of man."* —**Marshall**

Marshall, at another place, writes, *"Economics is a study of man's actions in the ordinary business of life. It inquires how he gets his income and how he uses it."*

Thus, we see that through his definition of Economics, **Marshall** has given preference to man over wealth. According to him, the main and the fundamental aim of Economics is to promote human welfare. As such Economics acquired a great social importance and it no more remained as a *"Dismal Science"* or the *"Science of Selfishness".*

Main Features of Marshall's Definition

The main features of Marshall's welfare-oriented theory, which gave primary importance to man and his welfare are as below :

Study of Mankind:
Economics deals with ordinary men and women, who have feelings of love, affection, friendship and do not get motivated merely by the desire of availing themselves of the maximum monetary benefits. He believed that wealth is not an end in itself but it is only means to human welfare, giving study of man a primary place in study of economics.

Causes of Material Welfare: Economics is concerned with the causes of material welfare. It ignores non-material aspects and their causes.

Promotion of Welfare: The most important feature is that wealth is not considered as the 'be-all' and 'end-all' of all economic activities. The primary importance and greater emphasis is on human welfare. The money and wealth are simply the means for human welfare.

Study of Social Science: Economics is a social science, which attempts to study the ordinary business of life of the persons living in society and influencing each other. That ordinary business of a person refers to the activities of earning and spending the income for the welfare of human beings.

Use of Money: This definition considers material or economic welfare as a part of social welfare which can be easily measured with the measuring rod of money.

Marshall's view of Economics was held to be the best and most correct for many years and because of this, a good number of Economists became his supporters and followers. The following definitions of several other Economists also represent the same view (material welfare view) as propounded by **Marshall.**

- *"Economics is the study of economic welfare, which can be brought, directly or indirectly, into relationship with the measuring rod of money."* —**A.C. Pigou**
- *"Economics is the study of general methods by which men cooperate to meet their material needs."* —**William Beveridge**
- *"The aim of political economy is the explanation of the general causes on which the material welfare of human beings depends."* —**E. Cannan**

Criticism

In 1932, **Prof. Lionel Robbins** of London School of Economics wrote his famous book *'An Essay on Nature and Significance of Economic Science'* and pointed out certain flaws to **Marshall's** definition. The concept by **Robbins**, however, can be considered as an improvement over **Marshall's** views. In fact, the basic concept of Economics propounded by both these economists; are almost the same with minor variations.

The important objections raised by **Prof. Robbins** will now be described.

Impractical: The distinction made by Marshall between economic and non-economic activities was not accepted by **Robbins**. His contention was that all human activities have some degree of economic aspects and significance. No activity can be classified purely as non-economic. **Robbins** was of the view that *'Economics'* does not deal with economic activities only, but it deals with all kinds of human activities from an economic point of view. According to him, a man going to temple, has to spend some of his money either in the form of conveyance expenses (if distance is more), or in the form of donations besides spending his time in going and coming from temple. Thus, both time and money are spent and this activity cannot be said to be purely non-economic. Therefore, he expressed that *"Every human activity has an economic aspect."*

Welfare Approach: The *'Welfare Approach'* was not accepted by **Robbins** because there are certain goods and commodities which do not promote any human welfare but have monetary value and satisfy human wants. For example, wine and opium. On the other hand, there are many aspects like love, affection, patriotism, religious feelings, etc., which are highly conducive to human welfare, but have no monetary value in Economics.

Eliminate the Word 'Welfare': **Robbins** also objected to the use of word 'welfare' because in his opinion, the concept of welfare differs from country to country and from time to time and varies from person to person, *i.e.,* it is a subjective thing. Moreover, 'Welfare' is an entity in itself and cannot be divided into material or non-material welfare. The 'welfare' cannot be precisely and accurately measured by any means or by any method. Also, the material welfare cannot be exactly separated from total welfare.

Only Materialistic Aspect: **Robbins** pointed out, *"Whatever Economics is concerned with, it is not concerned with the causes of material welfare as such."* Robbins has criticised welfare definition on the ground that it includes in its orbit only material things excluding non material goods and services (such as services of doctors, teachers, singers, dancers, etc.) which also satisfy human wants and promote welfare.

Robbins gave scarcity-oriented definition that was free from the shortcomings which he had pointed out in **Marshall's** definitions.

ROBBINS' DEFINITION: SCARCITY-ORIENTED DEFINITION

In view of the above limitations of welfare definition, *Prof. Robbins* based his definition on the clear-cut concept that human wants are unlimited and any person, however best he may try; cannot satisfy all his wants because the means to satisfy human wants are limited (or scarce) and the time also is limited at his disposal. Besides the limited availability of means, there are many alternative uses of each item. All these circumstances compel a man to make a proper choice of satisfying his wants depending upon the priorities.

Prof. Lionel Robbins defined economics in the following words:

"Economics is the science which studies human behaviour as a relationship between ends and scarce means which have alternative uses."

Main Features of Robbins' Definition

Economics as a Science:

Prof. Robbins has raised economics to the status of science. By science he meant that economics possess all the features of science, *i.e.,* it establishes relationship between cause and effect and it helps in the analysis of the events which have economic repercussions.

Man has Innumerable Wants: By *'ends'*, it meant, human wants. These human wants are various and unlimited. When one want is satisfied, another want arises. When that, too, is satisfied, the next one immediately appears. There is, thus, a chain of wants one after the other.

Wants can be Arranged in Order of their Importance: However, all wants are not equally important. Some are more important and urgent than others. Thus, a man's want can be arranged in diminishing order of importance or priority. This is possible because the importance of each of them can be compared to make an appropriate choice. It means that wants can be graded.

Scarcity of Means: Whereas wants are unlimited, the means to satisfy them are relatively limited. The means refer to goods and services or the resources which are used to satisfy wants. Means, which are scarce, may involve time, energy, money, manpower, material and other productive resources, that are at our disposal. If these means were abundant, there would be then no economic problem. Since means are scarce, therefore one is forced to postpone some of his wants according to priorities.

Means have Alternative Uses: Our means are not only limited but also have many uses. They can be used for satisfying any of our many wants. Our means are, thus, capable of alternative uses. For instance, land can be used for the construction of a house or a factory, a shop, a school, etc. Similarly, all the economic means and resources can be put to alternative uses.

Choice: Unlimited wants and limited means with alternative uses give rise to the problem of choice. People have to make choice in allocating their scarce resources in producing different commodities.

CRITICISM

Like the *'Welfare'* definition, the *'Scarcity'* definition is also not free from objections which have emerged on account of rapid economic progress and increasing scope of economic aspects. The main points of criticism are discussed below, which led to further modifications in the definition of Economics.

Welfare Concept: It is generally pointed out that **Robbins** has said much against the welfare but it is a fact that the concept of *'welfare'* is implicit in the definition of Economics given by him. The very theme of 'maximum satisfaction' (or 'welfare') is present in the scarcity definition also.

Limited Scope of Definition: The narrowness and neutral attitude of scarcity definition, toward ends, is not acceptable to some economists who support **Marshall's** views.

Makes Economics a Pure Science: **Robbins'** definition transforms the Economics into a pure science which has nothing to do with practice. Pure science is a science that is concerned with formulation of economic laws only but not with the solution of economic problems. But as a matter of fact, most of the economists of modern period have started realizing that Economics must not only teach how to make a tool, but also how to use it. In other words, an Economist should not only be a tool-maker, but also a tool-user.

Abundance an Economic Problem: According to **Robbins'** definition, scarcity is considered as a cause of economic problem. But it is a fact that even the abundance may cause an economic problem. The *'Great Depression'* during the *'thirties'* of this century is a good example of economic crisis which was not because of scarcity, but due to surplus of goods.

Static View: The definition given by **Robbins** has taken an entirely static view of the scarcity problem, as it deals with the adjustments of given scarce resources with unlimited ends ignoring the possibility of increase in resources and increase in efficiency over time. This is a static and rigid approach to a dynamic problem.

Non-economic Aspects: According to **Robbins**, each activity has an economic aspect. But many economists do not agree to it. In their opinion, the economic criterion does not apply to all kinds of human activities. In fact, there are certain activities where the economic criterion does not apply but such an attempt to do so is positively harmful and detrimental. An example will make it more clear. Suppose that a student wants to pass his examination with first division. There are two different ways to accomplish it. The normal method is to make a thorough study of the subjects using maximum available literature and devoting maximum possible time and energy. Another speedy or rather say economic method (minimum devotion of time and energy) is to resort to guide books, etc., so as to secure only required passing marks in the examination but then the knowledge of the subject acquired by him may not be adequate.

Thus, there are certain human activities where the economic criteria are not applicable in the true sense.

Samuelson's Definition: Growth-Oriented Definition

The definition of economics had taken a static view of the dynamic problems until Samuelson removed this defect. The greatest merit of **Samuelson's** definition is that it recognizes the dynamic changes taking place, both in the *means* (resources) and *ends* (wants) with the passage of time. The progress or changes occurring from time to time also affect the whole concept of the related developments in economic world. That is the reason of describing it as a growth-oriented definition.

Samuelson's definition is known as a modern definition of economics.

According to **Samuelson,** *"Economics is the study of how people and society end up choosing with or without the use of money, to employ scarce productive resources that could have alternative uses to produce various commodities over time and distributing them for consumption, now or in the future, among various persons or groups in society. It analyses costs and benefits of improving patterns of resource allocation."*

MAIN FEATURES OF SAMUELSON'S DEFINITION

Because of dynamic and wider coverage of scope, the definition of economics given by **Samuelson** is the most appropriate. The main features of **Samuelson's** definition are given below:

Efficient Allocation of Resources: There is a great deal of similarity between the approaches of **Samuelson** and **Robbins.** Both have stressed the problem of scarcity of *means* (resources) in relation to the unlimited *ends* (wants). Besides scarcity of means, there are many alternative uses of each commodity (means or resources).

Dynamism: **Samuelson** has included dynamism in the definition of Economics by incorporating the time element. The problem of growth has been included in the purview of the definition, thereby building up a new edifice on the foundation provided by **Robbins.**

Problem of Choice: The greatest feature of the **Samuelson's** definition is that it takes into account the problem of choice in its dynamic framework of Economics.

Barter System: Besides being dynamic in nature, the definition given by **Samuelson** covers the *barter system* also, in which *money* occupies a conspicuous position because of its absence. Thus, making problem of allocation of resources a universal problem found in both barter as well as monetary exchange economies.

Improvement in Resource Allocation: Economics analyse the costs and benefits of improving the pattern of resource allocation. Improvement of resource allocation and better distributive justice are synonymous with economic development. Thus, issue of development of a less developed economy has also been made subjects of the study of Economics.

Distribution: The modern definition also concerns itself with the distribution for the consumption among various persons and groups in a society. Thus, while the problem of distribution is implicit in the earlier definitions; the modern definition makes it explicit, thus giving a broader perspective to the definition of economies.

We have studied, in brief, about how the concepts about *Economics* has gradually changed and various modifications made from time to time by great economists. All this was necessary to clearly understand, 'What actually Economics is ?' and 'What does it cover ?' In this context, it can be very rightly concluded that **Samuelson's** definition is the most appropriate and satisfactory, as it accounts for the growth and development of economy with the passage of time.

LESSON AT A GLANCE

Economics: Economics explains how to use scarce goods to one's best advantage or how to economise. In other words, Economics is a science of choice when faced with scarce means against unlimited ends.

Definitions of Economics:

Adam Smith's or Wealth-Oriented Definition: Economics is the study of nature and causes of nation's wealth. It is a subject related with producing wealth and using it.

Features: (i) Study of wealth; (ii) Only material commodities; (iii) Stress on wealth; (iv) Causes of wealth; (v) Economic man.

Criticism: (i) Over importance to wealth, (ii) Importance to Material Goods Only:

Alfred Marshall's or Welfare-Oriented Definition: Economics is a study of mankind in the ordinary business of life. It examines that part of individual and social actions, which is most closely connected with the attainment and the use of material requisites of well-being. Thus, it is on one side, a study of wealth and on the other and more important side, a study of man.

Features: (i) Study of mankind; (ii) Causes of material welfare; (iii) Promotion of welfare; (iv) Study of social science; (v) Use of money.

Criticism: (i) Impractical; (ii) Welfare approach; (iii) Eliminate the word 'welfare'; (iv) Only materialistic aspect.

Robbins' or Scarcity-Oriented Definition: Economics is a science which studies human behaviour as a relationship between ends and scarce means which have alternative uses.

Features: (i) Economics as a science; (ii) Man has innumerable wants; (iii) Wants can be arranged in order of their importance; (iv) Scarcity of means; (v) Means have alternative uses; (vi) Choice.

Criticism: (i) Welfare concept; (ii) Limited scope of definition; (iii) Makes economics a pure science; (iv) Abundance—an economic problem; (v) Static view, (vi) Non-economic aspects.

Prof. Samuelson's or Growth-Oriented definition: Economics is the study of how people and society end up choosing with or without the use of money, to employ scarce productive resources that could have alternative uses to produce various commodities over time and distributing them for consumption, now or in the future, among various persons or groups in society. It analyses costs and benefits of improving patterns of resource allocation.

Features: (i) Efficient allocation of resources; (ii) Dynamism; (iii) Problem of choice; (iv) Barter system; (v) Improvement in resource allocation; (vi) Distribution.

QUESTIONS

A. Short Answer Questions

1. From where is the word 'Economics' derived?
2. Give Adam Smith's definition of Economics.
3. Explain welfare definition of Economics given by Prof. Marshall.
4. Give the difference between Adam Smith's and Marshall's definition of Economics.
5. Give three main features of Robbins' definition of Economics.
6. What are 'scarce means' according to Robbins?
7. Give two definitions regarding material welfare.
8. Mention any two features of the wealth centered definition of Economics.
9. Give any scarcity-oriented definition of Economics.
10. (a) Explain briefly the contribution of Prof. L. Robbins to Economics.
    (b) Explain briefly the contribution of Prof. Marshall to Economics.
11. State briefly the shortcomings in the definition of Economics, as given by the early economists.
12. Mention any two features of growth-oriented definition of Economics.
13. Why is Samuelson's definition of Economics, regarded as the most accepted definition? Give two reasons.
14. Define the problem of scarcity of resources.

B. Long Answer Questions

1. Critically examine Adam Smith's definition of Economics.
2. Explain wealth-oriented (Marshall's) definition of Economics.
3. State the main features of Prof. Marshall's definition of Economics.

4. Discuss Prof. Robbins' definition of Economics and what are its shortcomings?

    OR

    Discuss scarcity definition of Economics given by Prof. Robbins and its criticism.
5. Point out the salient features of Robbins' definition of Economics.
6. Explain clearly the difference between Marshall's and Robbins' approach to Economics.
7. Explain Prof. Samuelson's definition of Economics.

    OR

    Explain Growth-oriented definition of Economics.
8. Explain the following features of Marshall's definition:
    (a) Study of mankind
    (b) Promotion of welfare

02
Concept of Economics

We find different people engaged in different activities to earn their living. These activities are concerned with the production and exchange of goods and services. Farmers, workers, shopkeepers, manufacturer, teachers, doctors, lawyers, chartered accountants, etc., carry out various types of activities to earn their livelihood through providing goods and services to others. Similarly, all of us also have to carry out one or the other activity to earn certain sum of money, so that we can fulfill the necessities for ourselves and other members of our families. All such activities which are paid (remunerated in Economic terminology), are called economic activities. These activities are concerned with producing goods and services which satisfy human wants. Economy, in this way, is the sum total of all economic activities of the society.

Economy consists of all agricultural, industrial, manufacturing, construction, mining, business and other productive activities. It also includes services in private institutions and Government departments. Professionals like doctors, lawyers, singers, nurses and managers, etc., are also the members of economy. In the nutshell, every activity which has economic motive and is legal, constitutes part of economy. According to **Brown**, *"Economy is the system of earning livelihood."* It also consists of the consumers generating demand for the finished goods and services and households providing factor services to industry and government.

The basic functions of an economy are production, consumption and investment. Production means creation of and addition to utilities. Utility means capacity to satisfy human wants. Every goods and services which satisfies human wants is said to have utility. Consumption means the demand of final goods and services for using and deriving utility out of them for satisfaction of wants. Investment is the creation of new equipment and machines to produce goods and services. Economy is, therefore, concerned with the production, consumption, distribution and investment of, goods and services of a country or other area.

OVERVIEW

An economy consists of all agricultural, industrial, manufacturing, construction, mining, business and other productive activities taking place in a country.

Consumers, producers, government and households are the various entities that are part of an economy and bear several responsibilities towards it. All these entities have certain rights and duties.

Government is the regulatory organ of the economy. It plays a significant role in the development of the economy.

Consumers and producers are complementary to each other. Their role in the economy is to move the circle of production in the economy.

Household is also an important element of an economy. Its role is to provide all the factors of production to the industry and government.

"A total system comprising farms, factories, mines, shops, roads, railways, offices, schools, colleges, hospitals, etc., are all looked upon as growing institutions which provide various types of goods and services to the people; is called an Economy."

BASIC ECONOMIC ENTITIES

Basic economic entities in an economy are the consumers, the household, the producers and the Government. They are regarded as the basic economic entities or units because they perform the basic economic activities of production and consumption in an economy. An economic entity refers to those institutional units who independently undertake the economic activities like acquiring assets, incurring liabilities, undertaking transactions with other economic entities, etc. The economic activities performed by these economic agents or economic units are the pre-requisite for the continuous and smooth functioning of an economy.

(I) CONSUMERS–MEANING AND ITS ROLES

The consumers are the basic economic entities in an economy. Generally consumers refer to individuals who use goods and services generated within the economy. Their objective is to maximize their utility from the consumption of such goods and services. Typically, when business people and economists talk of *consumers* they are talking about individual as consumer. But in practice consumers consist of institutions, individuals, household and groups of individuals. For example, various educational institutions are the consumers of black boards, chalks and dusters. The students are the consumers of school dresses, textbooks, exercise books, pencils, etc. The consumption pattern of any particular individual depends on his or her own desires or wants and income as well. However, in any household, the members may take 'group decisions' regarding the consumption of any commodity such as T.V., car, fridge, etc. Such 'group decisions' are based on some compromise between individual wants within the household.

The Importance of the Consumers

Create Demand for Various Goods: Production of any commodity requires the existence of sufficient demand for that commodity. Consumers create the demand for various commodities, particularly the consumption goods such as food grains, bread, butter, vegetables, cotton and non-cotton clothes, shoes, socks, pencils, table lamps, books, journals, etc.

Encourage Product Diversification: Preference patterns of different consumers are also different. Some consumers of music DVDs prefer classical music, while some others prefer modern music; some consumers prefer T-shirts, while others prefer short-sleeved shirts; etc. As a result, the producers are encouraged to diversify their productive activities, *i.e.*, they start producing goods of different designs and colours.

Expand the Market for Consumer Goods: With an increase in the number of consumers, the markets for various durable consumer goods (*e.g.*, T.V., washing machines, air-conditioners, motor-cycles, etc.), semi-durable consumer goods (*e.g.*, shoes, T-shirts, socks, etc.) and perishable consumer goods (*e.g.*, bread, milk, butter, vegetables, etc.) get expanded. Such expanded market encourages the producers to undertake large-scale production of various consumer goods.

Expands the demand for various service items : The consumers also consume different service goods like transport service, tele-communication service, banking and insurance service, medical service, tourism service, educational service, etc. Thus, the service sector in an economy grows with an increase in the number of consumers of such services.

(II) PRODUCERS–MEANING AND ITS ROLES

Producer is a person who produces different goods. The firms are 'production units'. They collect and employ different factors of production and produce different types of commodities. They play a dual role :

- They produce and sell different products in exchange of product–prices.
- They purchase different factors of production, *e.g.,* labour, machines, raw materials, etc. They purchase these factors by paying factor–prices to the owners of those factor services.

Thus, the firms create a supply of different products in the market. On the other hand, they create a demand for different factors of production.

The Importance of Producers

Organizing Business Activities: Proper co-ordination among different factors of production such as land, labour and capital is necessary for the smooth progress of business activities. The producers take the responsibility of employing these factors in an appropriate proportion and organise the business activities.

Supply of Various Goods and Services: The supply of various goods and services becomes possible in any country through the business activities or productive activities of the producers. Since, the firms are production units, so an increase in the number of firms would mean an increase in the supply of various goods and services.

Efficient Utilization of Different Factors of Production: Different factors of production and economic resources in a country (such as forest resources, mineral resources, water resources, etc.), can be efficiently utilised for producing various goods and services only under the initiative of these producers. For example, the producers of the North-eastern region of India, who are engaged in the production of various handicrafts items, help in the efficient utilisation of forest resources in that region.

Expand the Demand for Various Factors of Production: The producers, through their productive activities, expand the demand for various factors of production such as skilled and semi-skilled labour, raw materials, machines, land, etc. They also create expanded demand for different services such as electricity service, transport service, tele-communication service, banking and insurance service, etc.

Help in Creating Employment and Income Opportunities: When the producers expand the scale of production (say, from small-scale production to medium-scale, and then to large-scale production), the employment and income opportunities will also get increased within the economy. A large number of people get employment in several firms.

Help in Raising the Export Income of a Country: Different firms are engaged in producing exportable goods. So, with the expansion of such firms, the amount of exports and the export income of the country can be increased to a great extent.

Determines Level of Investment: The producers create demand for investment to produce goods and services. Higher the level of production, more will be the investment demand. Thus, these are producers who increase the level of investment, increasing the rate of capital formation.

(III) GOVERNMENT–MEANING AND ITS ROLES

Government is the regulatory authority that looks after administration and law and order situations of the economy.

It includes all units belonging to and under direct control of the Government at all levels—central, state and local. It includes public agencies, Government bodies and other such organisations such as the cabinet, central bank, the police force, legislative bodies, the law courts, revenue collecting departments, social welfare departments, etc. These units are engaged in general administration, provision of social services as well as regulation and promotion of economic activities. The main roles of the Governemnt are:

(i) Government frames different economic policies such as tax policy, import and export policy, industrial policy, etc. for the smooth running of economy.
(ii) Government provides health and education facilities for the benefit of common people by opening schools and hospitals.
(iii) Government regulate monopolies and promote healthy competition.
(iv) Government takes various steps to ensure full employment, price stability and economic growth in the country.
(v) Government regulates supply of money in an economy.
(vi) Government makes investment expenditure for helping the process of capital accumulation in the economy.

Importance of Government

In this category, there is a direct and indirect participation or involvement of the Government in economic matters. Usually, these matters include the participation of Government in the sectors in which private entrepreneurs are not interested either because of the paucity of funds or low profitability or long gestation period or the involvement of Government is considered beneficial. But the socio-economic considerations are the main motives behind state's participation in various economic activities.

Regulating the Functioning of Economy: The Government intervenes in a variety of ways to overcome the flaws of free enterprise economy. It regulates the number of producers, sets standards for ensuring product quality, regulates monopoly power to create healthy and competitive market environment. The Government is also engaged in maintaining economic stability. This improves the functioning of the economy.

Social and Economic Overheads: These overheads include infrastructural facilities like irrigation, power, transport, communication, ports, etc. The private entrepreneurs are not generally interested in developing such facilities because of huge investments involved, while the returns are low and take a long time. Hence, it becomes the duty of the State to undertake such projects.

The development of human capital is also equally important, because the labour force becomes more efficient through education, training and good health services. Private entrepreneurs are least interested in this sphere and it is only for the Government to make all such facilities available for speedy economic development.

Agricultural Development: In almost all the underdeveloped countries, agriculture is the basic means of livelihood of the people and most of the people depend upon it. Hence, it becomes very important for a Government to develop this sector and provide all the necessary infrastructure facilities like electricity, irrigation, storage houses, transportation, credit facilities, mandis, fertilizers, good seeds, etc., so that the functioning of this sector can be ensured and improved. Therefore, the role of Government becomes all the more important to develop this basic and fundamental sector of the economy.

Industrial Development: For accelerating industrial progress, the basic industries like iron and steel, cement, heavy engineering, fertilizers, etc., are very essential. Also, for the efficient utilization of natural resources, a country should be industrially self-reliant. But all these basic industries require heavy capital (money) investment, which only a Government can afford. The Government must also make proper arrangements for technical training, industrial research, innovating new techniques of production and improving the quality of the products.

Removal of Socio-economic Inequalities: With the progress of economic development, the disparities in income and wealth also increases. As a matter of fact, in the initial stages of economic progress, there may be some increase in the disparities of income and wealth, but continuous increase in disparities year after year, is harmful for the nation. Thus, at this stage, the Government is required to take appropriate measures to reduce the inequalities of income and wealth and to achieve equitable distribution among the people. Some measures which the Government can adopt are to impose *progressive tax* on income, wealth and luxury items. The poor masses can be benefited through public expenditure on social facilities like subsidised food, education and health facilities, etc. Other possible measures include reforms in inheritance laws, regulation of competition, control on monopolies and ensuring equal opportunities for all. These steps can help in achieving economic development.

Allocation of Resources and Creation of Full Employment: The optimum utilization of economic resources is very important for any country to achieve proper economic progress. In an underdeveloped country, there should be a properly planned process in which the priorities of developments in different sectors are decided and followed. The overall planning should aim at maintaining balanced growth between all the regions, so that greater employment opportunities are created throughout the country. The ultimate aim of all types of economies is to achieve full employment of labour and resources. Therefore, the Government has to adopt appropriate measures for a coordinated, integrated, progressive, and balanced development of the nation, for which it must mobilize and utilize all its resources properly.

Social and Institutional Framework: The socio-cultural attitude of the people of underdeveloped countries is generally not favourable for modern economic development. The people are generally orthodox and lack the spirit of competition and enterprise. But the speed of industrialization depends upon the quality of human factor. To bring about changes in attitudes of the people, the Government is required to make institutional and organizational changes in the social set-up and structure. The people must be educated and motivated to develop positive attitude towards work, thrift and problems related to development.

Simultaneously, measures should be adopted to develop harmonious relationship between *labour* and *capital*. For achieving this objective, legislations can be passed and enforced to reduce the loss of production by way of curbing strikes and lock-outs.

Direct Participation in Economic Sectors: To exercise political and economic powers over national resources and to achieve rapid transformation in economies, the Government's intervention is considered essential, particularly in developing countries. Nationalization of some of the productive and distributive units and some essential services is one such measure which a Government can easily adopt. However, this involves several complications like acquisition of assets, payment of compensation and operational controls, etc. There may be several merits and demerits involved in each case. But in certain important and key sectors, the role of the Government must be regulatory as well as participative in the form of public sector units.

Organizational Modifications: This includes expansion of the size of the market and labour organizations. These modifications can be accomplished only by the Government. To expand the market, there should be proper facilities of transport and communication. Moreover, financial institutions are very essential for expanding the markets. The development of agriculture and industry can be accelerated with the assistance from financial institutions like cooperative banks, land mortgage banks, industrial development banks, investment corporations, etc. All such financial institutions can be established only by the State, because of huge capital involved in form of money.

Public Distribution: The public distribution system is operated by the State to help the weaker sections of the society, so that equitable distribution of essential goods can be made. This activity of Government has social and moral aspects.

The other importance of Government in economic development is to frame various monetary and fiscal policies and also in the proper implementation of the said policies; as discussed below :

Monetary Policy: Too much or too less supply of money in the market is not good for the economic progress of the nation. There should be an equilibrium between the demand and supply of money. The surplus supply of money causes inflation and less supply causes deflation. So, the Government has to formulate a balanced monetary policy according to the needs of the country.

Fiscal Policy: The fiscal policy has very significant and long-lasting effects on the socio-economic condition of the country. The fiscal policy includes direct taxation and it is also framed very carefully and implemented properly by the Government for achieving socio-economic objectives.

Tariff Policy: This is a taxation policy related to foreign trade. The state makes some rules and regulations in respect of imports and exports. Duty and tariff policy has a very important effect on revenue, especially foreign exchange.

Price Policy: In the absence of a price policy, the private businessmen and entrepreneurs have a tendency to exploit common masses and to earn more profits. To control such tendencies, the Government prepares and implements price policy. However, while framing the price policy, the Government has to safeguard the interests of common masses as well as that of the producer, *i.e.*, the policy should be fair.

The economic policies should be framed to encourage and promote economic development. Fiscal and monetary measures should be enforced in such a way that they prevent fluctuations in business activities and a sustained growth is maintained. The commercial and foreign policies should be conducive to economic growth. As a result, there should be a higher level of capital formation and an accelerated speed of economic progress should be achieved.

In India, the Government has adopted several direct and indirect measures to achieve various socio-economic objectives for the economic development of the country. The concept of *Progress* for India revolves around achieving *Socialistic Pattern of Society* and the concept of *Welfare State*.

(IV) HOUSEHOLD–MEANING AND ITS ROLES

The households play a dual role in an economy:
- They purchase different consumer goods for their own consumption and pay prices for these consumer goods. For example, the households purchase various consumer items such as clothes, food items, furniture, home appliances, etc.
- They are also the owners of different factors of production (*e.g.*, capital, labour, etc.) and sell these factors to the firms. They earn factor incomes by supplying these factors. For example, the households earn wage income for supplying labour power to the firms.

Thus, the households create demand for various products on the one hand, and they also arrange supply of different factors of production on the other.

IMPORTANCE OF HOUSEHOLD

Household as Provider of Factors of Production: The primary function of a household is to provide factors of production, *i.e.*, land, labour, capital and entrepreneurs to the firms. By providing these factor services, the households earn their incomes which they spend on the commodities produced by the firms.

Household as a Small or Cottage Producer: They produce goods and services for sale in the market to earn profit but they produce at a very small-scale. Sometimes these enterprises are owned and controlled by the family members. The organisation of these enterprises is entirely different from those of corporate and quasi-corporate enterprises.

Household as a Consumer: Household is also a consumer of goods produced and services rendered. Producers produce those goods that consumers demand. If any type of goods are not in fashion, producers do not like to produce them. Thus, in this role, households' choice becomes the basis of determination of production and the households, as consumers, move the wheel of production in an economy.

Household as a Taxpayer: Household is also a taxpayer. He pays tax to the Government on his income and other taxes like sales tax on the commodities he purchased and wealth tax on his wealth. Thus, he contributes to the sources of revenue to the Government. This revenue is utilized for welfare of masses and development of economy.

Household and Savings: Savings are the basis of capital formation. Household also contributes in capital formation in the form of whatever he saves from his income. Small savings of households when pooled, make a huge contribution in the process of capital formation.

Household as a Professional: Professional services are the demand of the day and realised in every field of economy. Thus, household as professionals, *i.e.*, a doctor, engineer, lawyer, scientist, etc., contribute through their services in different activities of economy.

LESSON AT A GLANCE

Economy: A total system comprising farms, factories, mines, shops, roads, railways, offices, schools, colleges, hospitals, etc., are all looked upon as growing institutions which provide various types of goods and services to the people, is called an economy.

Basic Economic Entities: The consumers, producers, government and households, are regarded as basic economic entities because they perform the basic economic activities of production and consumption in an economy.

Consumers: Consumers are the persons who purchase goods or services for the purpose of consumption.

Importance of the Consumers: (i) Create demand for various goods; (ii) Encourage product diversification; (iii) Expand the market for consumer goods; (iv) Expands the demand for various service items.

Producers: Producer is a person who produces different goods.

Role of the Producers: (i) Organizing business activities; (ii) Supply of various goods and services; (iii) Efficient utilization of different factors of production; (iv) Expand the demand for various factors of production; (v) Help in creating employment and income opportunities; (vi) Help in raising the export income of a country; (vii) Determines level of investment.

Government: Government is the regulatory authority that looks after administration and law and order situation of the economy.

Role of Government:

Direct Role of Government: (i) Regulating the functioning of economy; (ii) Social and economic overheads; (iii) Agricultural development; (iv) Industrial development; (v) Removal of socio-economic inequalities; (vi) Allocation of resources and creation of full employment; (vii) Social and institutional framework; (viii) Direct participation in economic sectors; (ix) Organizational modifications; (x) Public distribution.

Indirect Role of Government: (i) Monetary policy; (ii) Fiscal policy; (iii) Tariff policy; (iv) Price policy.

Households: Household or family is a unit which takes decisions regarding purchases. They are also the owner of the different factors of production.

Role of Household: (i) Household as provider of factors of production; (ii) Household as a small or cottage producer; (iii) Household as a consumer; (iv) Household as a taxpayer; (v) Household and savings; (vi) Household as a professional.

QUESTIONS

A. Short Answer Questions
1. What do you mean by economic entities?
2. Define economy.
3. Who are consumers?
4. What is meant by producers?
5. Why are consumers important in the economy?
6. Give the importance of producers in the economy.
7. Write the meaning of government.
8. How is government indirectly involved in the economy?
9. Give the meaning of household.
10. What are the dual roles played by Households?
11. How does government regulates the functioning of an economy?
12. Explain the role of producers as the organiser and employer of various factors of production.
13. Distinguish between household and a consumer.

B. Long Answer Questions
1. What do you mean by economy? Give a brief classification of economic entities.
2. Who are consumers? Discuss the importance and role of consumers.
3. Describe the role of government in the economy.
4. What do you mean by producers? Discuss the importance or role of producers.
5. Give the meaning and importance and role of household in any economy.

03 Basic Problems of an Economy

ECONOMIC PROBLEMS

Human wants and the means available to satisfy them are two fundamental facts of life which give rise to various economic problems. Human wants are unlimited and they vary in intensity and importance. The available resources or means to satisfy them are not only limited but have alternate uses. In other words, it simply means that a number of human wants can be satisfied by any given resource or means. These two basic facts of life either for an *'individual or society or nation'* give rise to all economic problems. Since no individual can satisfy all of his wants because of limited means and also due to the time at his disposal, he has to *'choose'* the want that he would like to satisfy first. In other words, he will have to evolve a *'preferential scale'* to measure the intensity of his wants and decide on their priority aspect. Again, the scarce resources at his command can be put to various uses. As such he also has to decide as to which resource he would like to put on priority. Thus, he is faced with a set of alternatives in respect of his wants and also in respect of the use of resources. *"He is to choose and decide on any one of the alternatives."* **Prof. Lionel Robbins** defined Economics as, *"A science which studies human behaviour as a relationship between ends and scarce means which have alternative uses."*

Like an individual, the society or the nation also has to make a choice among various alternatives. Economic problem is the problem regarding allocation of limited resources for the production of alternative goods and services. In other words, economic problem is basically a problem of choice, whether it is exercised by an individual or the society or the nation. The economic problems of individual entities fall within the domain of micro-economics, whereas the same problems of social groups, society or the nation are studied under macro-economics.

OVERVIEW

The fundamental aim of all types of economies is the 'well-being' of its people through 'socio-economic' progress. But in achieving this objective there emerges several types of problems due to unlimited human wants and limited availability of resources. These problems are common to all economies whether they are rich or poor, capitalistic or socialistic, agricultural or industrial, underdeveloped or developed.

The basic problems of an economy are: (a) what to produce, (b) how to produce, and (c) for whom to produce. All these aim at maximizing welfare of human beings. The efficient exploitation of available resources and achieving sustained economic growth are problems of modern-day economies.

The economic development refers to structural changes by which an economy is transformed from low per capita income to sufficiently self-sustaining economy and it is related to under-developed countries.

The economic growth does not require any special or deliberative efforts and it is related to already developed economies.

It must be remembered that the root cause of all economic problems is the *'scarcity of resources'*. Had the resources been unlimited like sunshine and air, there would have been no economic problem whatsoever. In the words of **Donald Dewey,** *"Any Economic System—Capitalist, Socialist, or Mixed—must be content with the brutal fact of scarcity".* It must decide the following:

- Which types of wants are to be fulfilled and it must set the *'goals of production'*.
- How scarce resources are to be allocated so as to achieve these production goals to the maximum limits.
- How the results of production (goods and services) are to be distributed among the population.
- What provision (if any) is to be made for economic progress, *i.e.*, the system must allocate some resources for the creation of additional capital goods and also for research and development.

These four tasks are common to any economic system and would not be eliminated. *"As long as human beings retain their capacity to be envious, ambitious for themselves or their children, or otherwise discontented, the economic system will have to face up to scarcity."*

BASIC/CENTRAL/FUNDAMENTAL PROBLEMS OF AN ECONOMY

The economy has to decide how to use the scarce resources so that maximum possible satisfaction can be given to the members of the society. And for achieving this target, it becomes essential to solve the fundamental or basic problems of an economy. It is worth mentioning that economists do not have unanimity in respect of fundamental problems. **Prof. Samuelson** emphasizes *three problems*, **Stigler** favours *four*, whereas **F.H. Knight, MC Connel** and **Leftwich** described *five* basic problems. **Prof. Halm** has mentioned as many as seven basic problems. But, all agree on the three problems of any economy, whether it is capitalistic or socialistic, developed or undeveloped. These problems are:

- What to produce?
- How to produce?
- For whom to produce?

Economic problems can be depicted through the following chart:

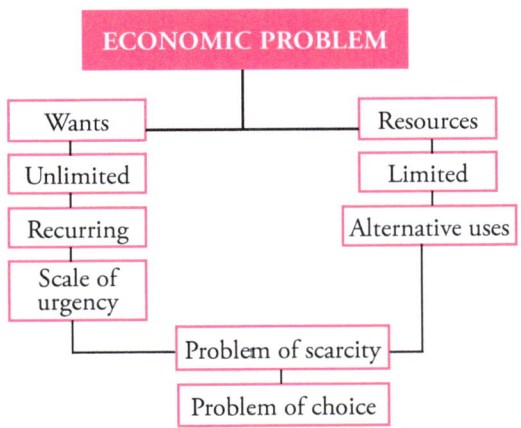

WHAT TO PRODUCE?

In a traditional economy, much effort is spent in producing items to meet every day needs, such as water, warmth, food, clothing and shelter. In modern economies, huge amount of human efforts are expanded on providing for the same needs but there comes the problem of paucity of resources which gives the birth to the question "*What to Produce*" with the given resources. Whatever the economic system is, what is to be produced is of great importance.

The function *'what to produce' has two parts. The first part deals with, what is to be produced or to say what is not to be produced,* under any given circumstances. The second part is related to the *quantities of goods to be produced.*

Therefore, the fundamental function of an economy is to determine the composition of output, *i.e.,* what are the commodities or goods to be produced.

On the other hand, an economy has to decide the quantities of resources which should be allocated for capital goods and also for consumer goods respectively. Since the means and resources are limited, this allocation becomes very important, keeping in view the present and future requirements. Under these conditions, a decision to increase the production of one commodity is likely to affect the production of another commodity. Thus, an increase in defence production would possibly be achieved only at the cost of other goods which may be necessary like steel for domestic use or an irrigation project.

In a free society or a capitalistic economy, the decision for '*What to Produce*' is affected by two considerations, i.e.,

- Input-output co-efficient for various factors of production, and
- The taste and preferences of consumers for a particular product. The first consideration determines the cost factor whereas the second consideration fixes the relative prices of various products.

Under socialist system, the economic planning authority has to decide as to how much quantity of a particular commodity needs to be produced to fulfill the requirements of people during a certain time-period.

So, depending upon the type of economy adopted by the nation, the problem of '*What to Produce*' can be solved in different ways. In a capitalistic economy, this problem gets solved through price mechanism, as it reflects the consumer's taste and preference whereas in a socialistic economy, the *Central Planning Authority* decides about the goods to be produced.

HOW TO PRODUCE ?

Once the function of deciding the production targets of various commodities is over, the problem of *'How to Produce'* arises. This function is taken up by industries or business units.

This function is related to the selection of the technique of production. This problem arises because there are various alternative methods or techniques available to produce a commodity. Most of the goods can be produced by different methods as there is a wide spectrum of methods having varying combination of capital and labour factors. Also there are wide varieties of machines for different purposes.

Thus, an economy determines a particular method of production for particular goods. Countries which are highly populated, would prefer a method involving less capital and more labour. On the contrary, the industrialized nations would prefer capital-intensive industries. Moreover, technique to be used also depends on the type and quantities of goods to be produced. For instance, in order to produce capital goods, complicated and expensive machines and techniques are required. On the other hand, for simple consumer goods, smaller and less expensive machines are required.

In modern economies, commodities and services can be produced with different factor combinations and techniques and there is sufficient scope for choice from the alternatives. Such choice is generally guided by consideration of assuring the least possible cost per unit of the commodity and overall increase in productivity in the economy.

In capitalistic countries, this issue is decided by the entrepreneur, in view of the prevailing price mechanism in the country. The entrepreneurs will adopt those techniques of production which provide the least cost factor. In socialist economies, the decision regarding "*How to Produce*" is taken by government which considers social factors as well for deciding about the technique of production. Minimum cost is not the only dominant consideration in socialist countries.

It is now clear that the problems of '*What to Produce*' and '*How to Produce*' are inter-related to each other. The output of goods or commodities which a country produces, depends on the nature and amount of resources available and the mode or manner in which various resources are combined together to achieve the least cost factor.

FOR WHOM TO PRODUCE?

This aspect actually relates to the '*Distribution of National Product*' among the members of the community. The function of distributing the national product involves two aspects:
- To determine the relative size of the shares which each individual has to receive, and
- To exactly ascertain in respect of kinds and quantities of various goods and commodities which constitute the share of an individual. Moreover, the producer or the resource owner is also a consumer in one way or the other. A careful consideration for deciding his share has to be made while determining the shares for each individual or household. Thus, it becomes highly important that decisions about production and distribution of goods must be consistent with each other.

It is true that the sharing of national product is directly influenced by the income of an individual. The people with higher income definitely possess higher purchasing capacities. Therefore, for proper and equitable distribution, there should be a fair equality of income of people. At this juncture, a normal problem arises as to how equality of income can be achieved. **Karl Marx**, for this purpose, suggested, "*From each according to his ability, to each according to his needs.*" In other words, the principle in this regard is that distribution of national income should be according to the contributions made, by each individual, to the total production. Thus, a person should get income exactly equal to what he produces.

The problem of distribution of national product or income is associated with another serious complication. If an approach is adopted to achieve perfect equality, then the initiatives and creativities of the producers will be affected adversely. This may result in a decrease in total national output which may be available for sharing and under extreme cases, it may become so small that even the standard of living will slip down considerably. Thus, we see that the problem of distribution of *national product* is very complex and it becomes more serious in a *capitalistic economy*. In fact, the distribution function, in a free economy, is accomplished according to the principle of productivity. In such systems, every factor is remunerated according to its contribution to productive process, even though there is a general complaint that the workers are not fairly paid in capitalistic economies.

Thus, we see that every economic system has to attend to the above mentioned basic problems. Some economists have mentioned about other problems also, but subsequently when detailed studies were carried out, it became clear that all those problems have their origin, in one way or the other, basically from the above three economic aspects. However, to understand the scope of economics more clearly, we shall make an attempt to discuss some additional important problems.

ADDITIONAL PROBLEMS OF AN ECONOMY

Efficient Use of Resources (Welfare Maximization)

Having decided '*what*' and '*how*' the goods are to be '*produced*' and '*distributed*', an important question arises, *"Is the production and distribution efficient?"* In other words, this involves an efficient utilization of resources for both '*production*' and '*distribution*' purposes.

In the economic sense, the production is considered to be efficient when the resources are utilized in such a way that any kind of re-allocation of resources is impossible for increasing the production of goods without reducing the production of other goods. Similarly, the distribution of national product would be called efficient, if it is impossible to make re-distribution of goods which can make any person better off without making at least one person worse off. Resources are efficiently utilised if their allocation is such that they are able to produce the maximum output avoiding wastage of resources.

It should, however, be very clearly noted that certain degrees of inefficiencies always exist in all types of economies. It is because of this reason only that constant efforts are always made so as to overcome those inefficiencies and to improve the status of people.

ECONOMIC GROWTH

The problem of economic growth is the problem of expansion of economy's capacity to produce goods and services which is largely determined by the amount of resources and efficiency of resources. This expansion is very much necessary to fulfill the ever increasing needs of the increasing population. So every economy wants to increase its national income and per capita income.

Economic growth has been defined by **Arthur Lewis** as *"the growth of output per head of population"*.

In other words, economic growth refers to an increase in per capita national income. It may be noted that the subject matter is growth not distribution. For example, during the Industrial Revolution in the U.K., there was economic growth. But there was no improvement in the standard of living of the working classes because they were exploited and made to work for long hours at low wages.

CHARACTERISTICS OF ECONOMIC GROWTH

Increase in Per Capita Real Income: Economic growth is closely associated with the increase in national and per capita income. If population of a country increases in a greater proportion than the national income, the per capita income is bound to decline. Per capita income will increase only when the following conditions are satisfied:

$$RI > RP$$

where, RI = Rate of growth of the national income, and
RP = Rate of growth of population.

Suppose that the national income of a country in 2003 is ₹ 10,000 crores and population is one crore. The per capita income of this country will be ₹ 10,000. Now, suppose that the national income in 2004 becomes ₹ 10,500 crores (*i.e.*, growth rate of 5 per cent, $\frac{500}{10,000} \times 100 = 5\%$) and the population goes up to 1·02 crores (an increase of 2 per cent in population). The per capita income will increase to ₹ 10,294. The increase in per capita income is on account of larger proportionate increase in the national income as compared to increase in population.

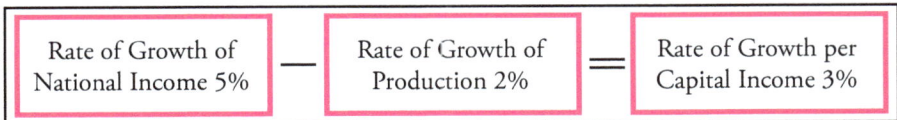

Economic Growth is a Long and Continuous Process: Economic growth of a country would be possible only when the per capita income continues to grow in the long run. Irregular or cyclical increases in per capita income will not constitute economic growth.

In brief, the primary aim of economic growth is to attain sustained increase in per capita income. Along with this objective some other objectives like equitable distribution of wealth and income, fixation of the national minimum needs, public welfare, etc., must also be added.

FACTORS DETERMINING ECONOMIC GROWTH

The slow rate of growth of the national income can be attributed to a number of factors which can be grouped as follows:
- Economic factors,
- Non-economic factors.

ECONOMIC FACTORS

The important economic factors for retarding the rate of growth of the Indian economy are as follows:

Lack of Capital: First, the major bottleneck in the Indian economy is the lack of capital. The deficiency of capital holds up the productive potential of the economy restricting investment and thereby reducing the employment opportunities in the economy.

Not only the available capital is much less, also the rate of capital formation (*i.e.*, addition to the available capital) is also slow. It hardly compensates for the depreciation of the existing capital stock, leaving the available capital stock almost unchanged.

Technological Backwardness: Secondly, technological backwardness has resulted in the employment of primitive and backward techniques in almost all the sectors of economy, which, in turn, have restricted the productivity.

Lack of Dynamic Entrepreneurship: Thirdly, dynamic entrepreneurship has been lacking in India owing to the absence of favourable economic and socio-cultural climate.

Absence of Skilled Labour: Fourthly, the absence of skilled labour is another factor hindering economic development.

Lower Productivity of Capital: Fifthly, the productivity of capital in India has been very low. The low productivity of capital is reflected in the high Incremental Capital Output Ratio (ICOR), i.e., the number of units of capital required to produce a unit of additional output.

Absence of Essential Financial Institutions: Finally, the absence of well developed financial institutions has prevented India from becoming an advanced country. It was very difficult for securing credit for different needs of the entrepreneurs. Similarly, the mobilisation of savings is also very difficult due to lack of sufficient expansion of financial institutions.

Non-economic Factors

Non-economic factors are equally important in hampering economic growth. In these we include various social, religious and political institutions like the caste system, joint family system, etc., as well as health standards, educational standards, social outlook towards technology, participation of women in workforce, etc., that have been hindering economic growth.

For rapid economic development, concerted efforts of both economic and non-economic factors are required.

On the economic front, the basic need is to raise the rate of capital formation in the economy.

ECONOMIC DEVELOPMENT

In the past, economic growth and economic development were used more or less with the same meaning. For example, various economists used rate of growth of income per capita or per capita GNP as index of economic development. This rate of growth of per capita income was required to be greater than the rate of growth of population. We have to note one more thing. The well-being of population depends on the rate of growth of 'real' per capita GNP. Real per capita GNP refers to the monetary growth of GNP per capita minus the rate of inflation.

But economic development is a broader concept and it is deliberative and multidimensional. Economic growth may be expressed in terms of growth in real per capita income but when there is decline in poverty, unemployment, and inequality, there is economic development in the country. Otherwise, even if per capita income is doubled, we cannot say there is economic development. So, when we say there is development, there must be improvement in the quality of life. That means, people must have higher incomes, better education, better health care and nutrition, less poverty and more equality of opportunity. So, according to **Michael P. Todaro** and **Stephen C. Smith**, *"Development must be conceived of as a multidimensional process involving major changes in social structures,* *popular attitudes and national institutions, as well as the acceleration of economic growth, the reduction of inequality and the eradication of poverty".*

Growth and Development: A Contrast in Concepts

As has been said earlier, economists often tend to use the two terms economic development and economic growth interchangeably, as they appear to be synonymous with each other. Although they are similar in meaning, they have some essential differences.

Economic development is not purely an economic phenomenon but rather a multi-dimensional process involving re-organization and re-orientation of the entire economic and social system. It is a process of improving the quality of all human lives with three equally important aspects. These are:

- Raising people's living levels *i.e.,* incomes and consumption, levels of food, medical services, education through relevant growth processes.
- Creating conditions conducive to the growth of people's self esteem through the establishment of social, political and economic systems and institutions which promote human dignity and respect.
- Increasing people's freedom to choose by enlarging the range of their choice variables.

Thus, economic development is a sustainable boost in the standards of living of the people of a country, and aimed at the overall well-being and development of the citizens of a country. It implies that individuals of a country take into account, changes in economic and social structures that will reduce or eliminate poverty.

Economic growth, on the other hand, is a narrower concept than economic development. It is defined as an increase in a country's ability to produce goods and services. It merely refers to an increase in the real Gross Domestic Product, or GDP per capita over a period of time. So, it is natural to be misled by the idea that economic growth is the key to economic development and perhaps a condition of development itself, but development is more than simply increasing economic output *i.e.,* GDP per capita. It is a wider concept than economic growth. A country's economy may experience real growth of GDP with no economic development taking place.

Distinction between Economic Growth and Economic Development

Economic Growth	Economic Development
1. It refers to increase in country's real per capita income.	1. It refers to progressive changes in country's socio economic structure.
2. It is a *quantitative* improvement in the scale of the economy in terms of investment, output, consumption and income.	2. It is a *qualitative* improvement, which entails improvement in the structure of the economy, including innovations in institutions, behaviour and technology.
3. The objective of economic growth can be easily realised by mobilising larger resources and raising their productivity.	3. The objective of economic development cannot be realised so easily. Apart from a rise in output, it involves changes in the composition of output as well as a shift in the allocation of productive resources.

4. Economic growth does not include economic development.	4. Economic development includes the factors of economic growth.
5. Economic growth does not require much of Government intervention.	5. Economic development demands active involvement of the Government
6. Economic growth is defined strictly in terms of economic indicator *i.e.*, income.	6. Economic development involves not only economic indicators but also non-economic indicators like literacy, health services, etc.

LESSON AT A GLANCE

Economic Problems: Economic problems are concerned with the use of scarce resources among alternative human wants and using these resources towards the ends of satisfying wants as fully as possible.

Basic Problems of an Economy: The economy faces the following three basic problems : (i) What to produce ? (ii) How to produce ? (iii) For whom to produce ?

Additional Problems of an Economy: (i) Efficient use of resources; (ii) Economic growth and Economic development.

Economic Growth: Economic growth has been defined by Arthur Lewis as *"the growth of output per head of population"*.

Factors Determining Economic Growth

Economic Factors: (i) *Lack of Capital* (ii) *Technological bvackwardness* (iii) *Lack of dynamic entrepreneurship;* (iv) *Absence of skilled labour;* (v) *Lower productivity of capital;* (vi) *Absence of essential financial institutions.*

Non-economic Factors: Various social, religious and political institutions like the caste system, joint family system, etc.

Economic Development: According to **Michael P. Todaro** and **Stephen C. Smith**, "Development must be conceived of as a multidimensional process involving major changes in social structures, popular attitudes and national institutions, as well as the acceleration of economic growth, the reduction of inequality and the eradication of poverty".

QUESTIONS

A. Short Answer Questions
1. Mention any three problems of an economy.
2. Mention the causes of economic problem.
3. What are the three 'basic problems' of any economic system?

4. With which aspect is the problem, 'how to produce', related?
5. Describe briefly the problem of 'what to produce'.
6. How does an economy solve the problems of distribution?
7. Define economic growth.
8. Define economic development.
9. Why is economic development regarded as qualitative term?
10. What is the problem of choice?
11. Explain the problem of 'for whom to produce'.
12. What do you mean by 'welfare maximization'?

B. Long Answer Questions
1. What are the basic problems of economy? Describe any three in detail.
2. The problem, 'how to produce', is an important basic problem of an economy. Explain how it is solved in free economy. On what factors does the solution of this problem depend?
3. Why the question 'What to Produce' is answered differently in different economies?
4. What do you understand by economic growth and economic development? Differentiate clearly.
5. Explain the problem of efficient utilisation of resources.
6. Discuss 'welfare maximization' and 'economic growth' in the context of Indian economy.

04
Type of Economies

Economy is "*A total system comprises of farms, factories, mines, shops, roads, railways, offices, banking institutions, health institutions, educational institutions, economic institutions, etc., and are all looked upon as growing institutions which provide various types of goods and services to the people*".

- "*Economy is a system which provides people with goods and services which directly or indirectly satisfy their wants.*"

—**Prof. A. J. Brown**

In present world, every modern society comes across certain fundamental economic problems such as:

- What goods and services are to be produced and in what quantity?
- How and where production should be organised so as to produce the required goods and services?
- How can the resultant output be distributed?

All the above problems center around the emergence of human wants. Human efforts aimed at the production of goods and services and are capable of providing satisfaction to their wants in any particular society, result in economic activities and these economic activities take place in the framework of an economic system, which is defined as "the legal and institutional framework within which economic activity takes place" *i.e.,* an economy.

OVERVIEW

The basic objective of an economy is to improve the overall 'well-being' of its people. Thus, an economic system consists of 'production', 'distribution', 'exchange' and 'consumption' of various goods and services in a proper way so that every individual is equitably benefited.

The economic system may be either simple or complex. It may adopt either a 'capitalistic' or 'socialistic' system or may be a 'mixed' one (as is in our country). The economy itself may be predominantly agricultural or industrial.

The 'Economy' of any country may be either 'under-developed' or 'developing' or 'developed', depending upon the economic progress achieved through proper application of technology and industrialization. The under-developed economies have priorities to alleviate poverty and to achieve industrialization. In contrast to this, the developed nations have objectives of maintaining the higher standards of living and providing the more and more comfortable living to its people.

An economy is greatly influenced by the social framework of the society, the political structure of the country and the level of economic growth. An economy may, therefore, be classified either on the basis of ownership of factors of production or on the basis of the level of growth.

CLASSIFICATION/TYPES OF ECONOMY

Keeping above facts in mind, economy can be classified as shown below:

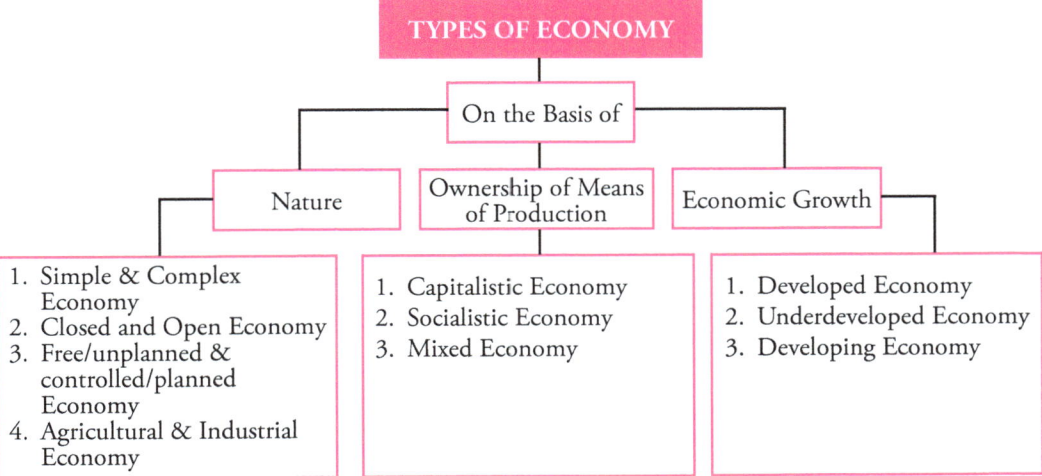

(A) CLASSIFICATION ON THE BASIS OF NATURE

Simple and Complex Economy

This classification is based upon the working nature of the system.

Simple Economy: Simple Economy refers to a system in which people produce simple goods in limited numbers or quantities for the satisfaction of their wants. These goods are exchanged with other goods, *i.e.,* through barter system. In general, the people have very limited wants as they live an isolated life and are self-sufficient. Here goods are produced for self consumption and no market surplus generated.

Complex Economy: Complex Economy is that in which several kinds of goods are produced in large quantities. The technique of production is complicated and mechanized. The goods produced in such an economy are not only for self-use but are also supplied and sold to distant markets. The infrastructures like transport, communication, modern banking and monetary system facilitate the internal and external trade. Economic progress and growth are accelerated. Most of the economic systems of modern period belong to complex economies.

Distinction between Simple Economy and Complex Economy

Simple Economy	Complex Economy
1. In this economy, simple goods are produced in limited quantities.	1. In this economy, several kinds of goods are produced in large quantities.
2. Technique of production is simple.	2. Technique of production is complicated and mechanized.
3. The goods are exchanged with other goods, *i.e.,* through barter system.	3. The goods are supplied and sold to distant markets.
4. It refers to isolated and self-sufficient economy.	4. It refers to growth and economic progress.

CLOSED AND OPEN ECONOMY

This classification is based on trade relations with other countries.

Closed Economy: Closed Economy refers to an economy in which there is no trade relation with other countries. In a closed economy, a country tries to remain self-sufficient and self-reliant and does not either import or export goods. For example, erstwhile USSR had almost a closed economy.

Open Economy: Open Economy refers to an economy in which a country has trade relations with other countries and believes interdependence on each other. The goods produced in the country are exported and in turn several commodities are imported from other countries. These days almost all the countries of the world have an open economy.

Distinction between Closed Economy and Open Economy

Closed Economy	Open Economy
1. In this economy, there are no trade relations with the other countries.	1. It is an economy which believes interdependence on each other.
2. Price fluctuations in the international market do not have any impact on closed economy.	2. Price fluctuations in the international market have impact on open economy.
3. It refers to an economy where Gross National Product equals to Gross Domestic Product (GNP = GDP), net factor income from abroad remains zero.	3. It refers to an economy where GNP may be greater or lesser than GDP, net factor income from abroad may remain positive or negative.
4. This type of economy does not exist in the modern world.	4. Most of countries of the present world indicate such economy.

FREE (UNPLANNED) AND CONTROLLED (PLANNED) ECONOMY

This classification is based on whether the market forces of demand and supply are allowed to take their own course or these factors are determined by the State or the Central Authority, so as to bring social welfare to the people.

Free Economy: Free Economy is one in which the economic activities and problems of production, distribution and prices are determined and influenced automatically by the free play of the market forces of demand and supply. The State does not interfere in this system and every individual is free to take up the profession or business as per his own liking. USA, UK, Japan are the good examples of free economy.

Controlled Economy: Controlled (Planned) Economy is a system in which the State (Central Authority) has full control on all the economic matters and activities. The Government decides and determines the matters pertaining to issue of capital, prices of goods and commodities, distribution and rationing, etc. Indian economy is a good example of planned economy.

Distinction between Free (Unplanned) Economy and Controlled (Planned) Economy

Free (Unplanned) Economy	Controlled (Planned) Economy
1. The State (Central Authority) does not interfere in this system of economy.	1. The State (Central Authority) has full control on all the economic matters and activities.
2. Problems of production, distribution and prices are determined automatically by the market forces of demand and supply.	2. Government decides the matters pertaining to issue of capital, prices of goods, distribution and rationing, etc.

Agricultural and Industrial Economy

This categorization is based on the condition whether the economy is predominantly agricultural or industrial and majority of people belong to which sector of the economy.

Agricultural Economy: Agricultural Economy is one in which the main occupation of the people is agriculture and handicrafts. The system of transport, communication, banking, trade, etc., is underdeveloped. The people in such countries are usually illiterate and orthodox and follow traditional methods.

Industrial Economy: Industrial Economy employs most of the people in industry and trade and very few people have agriculture as their main profession. The production is carried on large-scale by scientific method under the system of complex specialization. Extensive use of mechanization is done. The infrastructure facilities like transport, communication, banking, etc., are well-developed and the production of goods is done mainly for commercial purposes.

Distinction between Agricultural Economy and Industrial Economy

Agricultural Economy	Industrial Economy
1. It mainly produces agricultural goods.	1. It mainly depends on industries.e.
2. Most of the people are employed in agriculture and handicrafts.	2. Most of the people are employed in industries and trade.
3. Infrastructure facilities like transport, communication and banking, etc., are under developed.	3. Infrastructure facilities are well developed.
4. People are usually illiterate and orthodox.	4. People are well educated and modern in thoughts.
5. Primitive techniques of cultivation are used.	5. Extensive use of mechanization is done.

(B) CLASSIFICATION ON THE BASIS OF OWNERSHIP OF MEANS OF PRODUCTION

Capitalistic Economy

The *Capitalistic economy* is defined as, *"One in which economic decisions, regarding production in different sectors (i.e., in farms, factories, mines, workshops, etc.), the distribution of products and fixation of prices are taken by private entrepreneurs for the purpose of profit alongwith no control or pressure of the Government."* In simple words, it is that system wherein, means of production are owned by private individuals, called capitalists, profit is the sole motive and there is no interference by the Government in the economic activities of the economy. Some of the most advanced countries of the world *e.g.,* the United States of America, Germany, France, Canada, the Great Britain, etc., have been capitalist from the beginning of modern times or even before. It has been generally observed that people of capitalistic economies have higher standards of living as they have better opportunities to earn and a better capacity to spend on various goods.

Main Features of Capitalistic Economy

Free Enterprise: All economic activities and businesses are conducted by private individuals, bodies and institutions. Thus, a capitalist economy is a free enterprise economy. Private sector is the sole sector under pure capitalism.

Private Property: In a capitalist economy, all means of production are privately owned, i.e., they belong to private individuals, institutions and companies. The private property implies that the owner of property can use it in any way he likes.

Consumers' Sovereignty: Under capitalism, a consumer is supposed to be supreme and is compared to a king. The entire productive machinery follows the dictates of the consumers. The quality and quantity of production depends upon the demands of the consumer.

Role of Self-interest: Each economic unit attempts to do what is best for it. The consumers want to maximise their utilities while the motive of self-interest gives directions and consistency to producers to work hard and to earn maximum income by satisfying the consumers.

Economic Freedom: The capitalist system is based on a number of economic freedoms. Individuals and households are free to consume whatever they like. Free choice of consumption determines the nature and volume of goods and services which should be produced. Similarly, business units are free to produce any product or service of their choice.

Competition: Freedom of choice provides the basis for competition or economic rivalry. Competition in economics implies the presence of a large number of buyers and sellers who are free to buy and sell and also free to enter or leave any particular market.

Markets and Price: The capitalist economy functions through 'price-mechanism'. The medium through which economic problems are solved, is the operation of prices in the market. There are two types of prices. One is the price of goods and services or product. The other is the price of the factor of production.

Freedom of Contract: Under capitalism, people are free to make contract and settle transaction. Every person is free to sell his goods and services to anyone according to his own choice. The state does not interfere in any way unless the transactions become illegal.

Merits of Capitalistic Economy

Profit-Motive: In a capitalistic economy, production decisions involving high risks are taken by the entrepreneur only to earn large profits. The lure of earning profit compels the entrepreneur to take risks and enter new fields of production. Hence, profit-motive is the basic force that drives the capitalist economy.

Cheap and Standard Commodities: In a capitalistic economy, producers have the freedom to decide '*what to produce?*' Similarly, consumers have the freedom to buy any thing they want. This leads to high competition in the market and commodities are available at comparatively low prices and of standard quality.

Limited Resources Put to Maximum Use: In a capitalist society, resources are put to maximum use through the price-profit mechanism. The persons who use the resources in the best possible manner, get rewards while persons responsible for waste and duplication of resources, receive punishment in the form of losses or bankruptcy.

Higher Standard of Living: Since a capitalistic economy is a free trade economy, any individual has the freedom to buy and sell any number of goods and services and to choose any occupation. Thus, a variety of quality goods and services are available at minimum rates that make it easy for them to be within the reach of poor and weaker section of society. This in turn leads to increase in savings and investment, and results in rise in their standard of living.

Less Expenditure on Centralised Planning: It is also agreed that in capitalistic economic system, there is less expenditure on centralised planning as all the decisions regarding production and pricing are taken by private entrepreneurs.

Rewards According to Merits: An entrepreneur who takes the initiative and shows extraordinary resourcefulness is amply rewarded while the inefficient is eliminated from the field.

Technological Improvement: Competition is the essence of capitalism. This drives the producers to innovate something new to boost the sales and thereby bring about progress.

Free and Automatic Operation: A free enterprise economy operates freely without any restriction under the guidance of market forces. The consumers get what they want while the seller sells and earns enough profit, leading to the maximum satisfaction all around.

Minimal role of Government: As most of the basic economic problems are expected to be solved by market forces, the Government has minimal role in the economy. There is no conflict between the individual interest and the society. The economic institutions function automatically preventing the interference of the government.

Demerits of Capitalistic Economy

Too Much Emphasis on Materialism: A capitalist economy is carried on in terms of wealth, price, cost and profit. These have no relationship to human welfare. Production of wines and cigarettes is an example.

Inequality of Income and Opportunities: This system leads to inequality of income and wealth; leading ultimately to inequality in economic and political power. This inequality increases with the passage of time.

Leads to Monopoly and its Abuses: In such an economy, competition can be wasteful. In a cut-throat competition, a lot of money is spent on advertisements and salesmanship. Often competitors combine themselves into monopolies and exploit the consumers.

Trade-cycles of Booms and Depression: Saving, investment and production being unplanned and uncoordinated at national level, lead to over-production or under-production of commodities and distortions in money supply and vice-versa. This over-production may lead to depression while under-production may lead to scarcity of goods and hence inflation.

Perpetuates Class Struggle: Capitalist economy is generally divided into two groups—capitalists and labourers. They generally have hostile relation with each other.

Misallocation and Wastage of Resources: Under capitalistic economy, the resources are often misallocated and wasted. Since goods are produced with profit motive, the resources are diverted to the production of luxury goods in place of necessities of life.

Leads to Imperialism: Capitalism leads to imperialism. The capitalist countries try to find new markets to sell their goods. The stronger nation often exploits the weaker ones (as was done during 17th & 18th centuries by Britain).

Socialistic Economy

In this type of economy, the State or the government has total control on all economic matters. It is defined as, *"An economic system where the sources of production (farms, factories, mines, offices, etc.) are owned and operated by the community as a whole and the achievements are utilized for the welfare of the society according to pre-planned programmes."* In such an economy, the entire economic development is carried out in accordance with a Central Plan. The Central Planning Authority takes important decisions as *"What to produce ?", "How to produce ?" and "For whom to produce ?"* In simple words, it is an economy where economic institutions engaged in production and distribution are owned and controlled by the State; so as to ensure welfare and equality of opportunity to the people in a society. It was first adopted by the USSR in 1971. However, the socialistic economic system continues to exist today in very few countries like Cuba and Venezuela, etc.

The State, thus, exercises almost full control over all economic aspects.

Main Features of Socialistic Economy

Collective Ownership: The social or collective ownership of all the means of production is one of the essential characteristic of socialism. All property belongs to the society as a whole.

Clear Social and Economic Objectives: A socialist economy is not a blind, purposeless and irrational system but has clear objectives such as maximization of national income, achieving self-sufficiency and fixed targets for realization. It attains these objectives through conscious efforts.

Central Economic Planning: A socialist economy is a centrally planned economy. In such an economy, profit motive and the automatic pricing processes are eliminated.

Economic Freedoms: According to socialist thinkers, a socialist economy allows free choice of consumption as well as free choice of occupation. Free choice of consumption implies : (a) that the goods produced are available to consumers without any restriction, and (b) that production in general is governed by the choice of consumers.

The Price Mechanism: In a socialist economy, the pricing process is only of secondary importance. Since the socialist economy is a planned economy, production and allocation of productive resources will be used according to a pre-determined plan.

Maximum Social Welfare: The maximum social welfare is the sole objective of socialism. The State assumes the role of an employer and there is no exploitation of workers.

Absence of the Right to Property: The right to property is an important aspect of the free enterprise system. This is absent in socialist economy. Personal property is rarely seen in the socialist system, except in the articles of daily consumption and personal belongings.

Lack of Competition: Unlike capitalistic economy, there is no cut throat competition. It means lack of competition as State is the sole entrepreneur.

Merits of Socialistic Economy

Social Security and Welfare: Social security in terms of food, health and education to everybody is guaranteed under socialistic society. The cost of social security is borne by the administration.

Maximum Utilization of Economic Resources: Under this system, the allocation of economic resources is done by the Central Planning Authority and as such they are put to the best use. Wastage and duplication is avoided.

Absence of Competition: In socialist economy, the Government has virtually the monopoly in almost every sector. But individual enterprise may work with competitive spirit only to reach planned target.

Secures Equality of Income and Opportunities: A socialist economy is a classless society. In this economy, private property and profit motive are abolished. Thus, there are no rich and no poor people. Equal opportunities for work, etc., are provided to all.

Prevents Cyclic Fluctuations: In a socialistic economy, cyclical fluctuations are eliminated and smooth working of the economy is secured. Since a socialist economy is essentially a planned economy, there is neither surplus nor any shortfall.

Better Solution of Central Problems: A socialist economy has a better solution to the problem of what goods should be produced and in what quantities. It discards profit motive and self interest of private individuals and hence, this economic system is free to use materials and means of production now owned by the public authorities, more efficiently.

Demerits of Socialistic Economy

Less Democratic: Socialist economy is always less democratic as it possesses no element of freedom. The freedom of choice regarding products and occupation is absent.

Loss of Initiative and Enterprise: In a socialist economy, the entire economic activity of the country is controlled by the Central Planning Authority. In this system, the people are simply made to work according to the dictates of the central authority.

Inefficient Use of Economic Resources: It is argued that in a socialist economy, there is no basis of cost calculation as this system does not work with profit motive and social welfare is the primary motive. So, the economy cannot function efficiently.

Rigid Economy: Socialistic economy is a rigid economy and is not susceptible to changes according to the need.

Bureaucratic Control: It is argued, that the officials of the government do not work efficiently, because they have no personal interest in their work. Hence, a socialist economy cannot be an efficient economy.

Concentration of Economic and Political Powers: In a socialist economy, both political and economic powers are concentrated with the government. Thus, the liberties of people are curtailed in a drastic way.

Mixed Economy

Mixed economy is a term used to describe an economic system, where production of strategic and some important items is undertaken by the State directly or through its nationalized industries and some is left for private enterprise. It can be defined as *"An economy containing the characteristic of both capitalism and socialism, that is, a combination of private and public ownership of the means of production, with some measure of control by the Central Government."* In other words, it is an economy in which resources are allocated and exploited partly through the decision of private individuals and firms on the basis of market direction and partly through the Government and state-owned enterprises as per the central direction. It is a type of economy in which private and public sectors co-exist and try to retain the advantages of capitalism and socialism, while trying to eliminate the evils of both the systems. The examples are India and China.

Main Features of Mixed Economy

Co-existence of Public and Private Sector: In a mixed economy, co-existence of public and private sector is the main feature. In public sector, industries of national importance are set-up such as defence industries, basic industries, power generation, etc., while in private sector, consumer good industries, agriculture, small-scale industries are developed. The sole objective behind the promotion of both sectors is to reap the benefits of both and to help each other.

Individual Freedom: Under mixed economy, there is full freedom of choice of occupation, production of goods and consumption in the private sector. But at the same time, Government is able to regulate the prices and these choices in public interest.

Economic Planning: In a mixed economy, Government endeavours to promote economic development of the country. For this purpose, economic planning is adopted. Thus, economic planning is essential for a mixed economy.

Economic Equality: In a mixed economy, citizens enjoy economic equality at large. Some concessions are allowed on consumption, production and choice of occupation. But, Government can also impose certain restrictions.

Profit Motive and Social Welfare: In a mixed economy, there is a profit motive like capitalistic economy and social welfare as in socialist economy.

Role of the Government: In a mixed economy, there is a positive role of the Government by way of some controls and regulations, to regulate private sector so as to promote the larger welfare interest of the entire economy even though non-intervention policy (*Laissez-faire*) is followed.

Merits of Mixed Economy

In recent times, mixed economy enjoys many advantages of capitalism and socialism. However, its chief merits are summarized below:

Encouragement of Private Sector: The most important advantage of a mixed economy is that it provides encouragement to private sector and gives it a proper opportunity to grow. It leads to higher capital formation.

Efficient Use of Resources: As freedom is found in mixed economy, both public and private sectors work for the efficient use of natural resources. Public sector works for the social benefits while private sector makes optimum use of these resources for the maximization of profit.

Advantages of Economic Planning: Under mixed economy, there are all the advantages of economic planning. The Government takes measures to control business fluctuations and to meet other economic evils.

Lesser Economic Inequalities: Capitalism leads to economic inequalities but under mixed economy, inequalities can easily be controlled to significant extent by the efforts of the Government.

Competition and Efficient Production: Due to competition in private sector, the level of efficiency remains high. All factors of production work efficiently with the objectives of better profit. Similarly, there is competition between private and public sector companies which compel the government companies to be more efficient.

Useful to Under–developed Countries: Mixed economy has proved useful for less developed countries as well as developing countries; as both sectors work simultaneously and these economies get the benefits of both the sectors.

Demerits of Mixed Economy

Unstable Economy: It has been alleged by some economists that a mixed economy is the most unstable. The public sector is over emphasized and private sector is unduly controlled or nationalized.

Inefficient Planning: Generally, mixed economy lacks comprehensive planning. As a result, a large sector of the economy remains outside the control of the Government.

Delay in Economic Decision: In a mixed economy, there is always a delay in making certain decisions specially in case of public sector. Delay always leads to a great hindrance in the path of smooth functioning of the economy.

Fear of Nationalization: Under mixed economy, another problem is also found which is the constant fear of nationalization of private sector. For this reason, private sector does not put into use their resources for the common benefits.

Ineffective Control on Private Sector: In a mixed economy, private sector is not effectively or efficiently controlled to the full extent.

More Burden on Government: In modern times, democratic Governments are heavily burdened with social welfare activities. Thus, the adding of more functions to public sector is the extra burden on a mixed economy.

Distinction between Capitalistic, Socialistic and Mixed Economies

Basis of Distinction	Capitalistic Economy	Socialistic Economy	Mixed Economy
1. Ownership of the means of production	Private ownership.	State ownership.	Both private and state ownerships.
2. Solution of the central problems	Price mechanism.	Economic planning.	Price mechanism and economic planning.

3. Objective of production	Profit maximisation.	Maximisation of social welfare.	Maximisation of profit as well as social welfare.
4. Distribution of income	Unequal.	Equal	Not highly unequal.
5. Competition	High degree of competition.	Lack of competition.	Low degree of competition
6. Consumer's sovereignty	Complete sovereignty.	No sovereignty	Limited sovereignty.
7. Class conflict	High degree of class conflict.	No class conflict.	Low degree of class conflict.
8. Flexibility	High degree of flexibility.	Lack of flexibility.	High degree of flexibility in the private sector and low degree of flexibility in the public sector.
9. Inducement to work	Very high.	Does not exist.	Relatively low.

(C) CLASSIFICATION ON THE BASIS OF ECONOMIC GROWTH

Developed Economy

The economy of a country which has acquired a very high stage of development and where per capita income and standard of living is high, is termed as developed economy.

In these economies, inspite of having achieved substantial economic development, the development programmes continue even further so that people of the country can have more and more of material welfare. USA, UK and Germany are the examples of developed economies.

Features of a Developed Economy

The main features of a developed economy are as follows:

High National Income: National product or national income in developed economies is very high. High national income implies a greater flow of goods and services in the economy. This leads to the prosperity of the people.

High Real Per Capita Income: Not only total income, but also per capita real income is very high in these economies. Per capita real income is obtained as the ratio between national income at real price and total population. According to one report, per capita real income in USA is more than $ 52000 in 2016.

High Standard of Living: High per capita real income results in high standard of living of the people. People enjoy good health besides being highly educated. They also enjoy all luxuries and comforts of life.

Full Utilization of Resources: Natural resources are fully utilized in developed economies because of the availability of modern technology as well as skilled labour.

Industrialization: Developed economies are industrialized economies. All important industries are found in these economies. Contribution of industrial sector to the gross national product is fairly high in these economies. The contribution of secondary sector and tertiary sector in national income is more than 95 per cent in USA and UK.

Advanced Technology: There is a high degree of technical development in these economies. Lot of expenditure is incurred on research and development. As a result, new and economical techniques are always available.

More Employment: There is hardly any serious problem of unemployment in developed economies. If at all, unemployment occurs, it is only cyclical in nature; it does not stay for long.

High Ratio of Urban Population: Generally, we find high ratio of urban population in the developed countries. Besides this, in these countries, birth-rate and death-rate are also low. It reduces the rate of population growth and enhances the average life expectancy. As a result of all this, the population has no pressure on the economy and creates no hurdle in the way of development.

Under-developed Economy

In an underdeveloped economy, the indicators are just opposite to those of developed countries. The level of real income and per capita income is usually very low. Consequently, the condition of living is very poor. The reasons for the poor condition are multifaceted such as the lack of scientific and technological application in productive processes, the shortage of capital, social and cultural backwardness, high gender discrimination, etc. Most of the countries of Asia, Africa and Latin America belong to this category.

Features of an Under-developed Economy

The principal features of under-developed economies are as follows:

Low Per Capita Real Income: Per capita real income is very low in these economies as the majority of the population in these countries are poor. According to the World Bank Report, per capita real income in under-developed economies is just about $350, compared to much higher per capita real incomes in developed economies. As a result, people in under-developed economies, enjoy a very low standard of living. It is very difficult for them to get even the basic necessities of life, *viz.*, food, clothing and shelter.

Backward Agriculture: Agriculture continues to be in a backward state in these economies as productivity per hectare as well as per worker is very low.

Under-utilization of Natural Resources: Natural resources remain under utilized because of the lack of skilled personnel and technical know-how.

Backward Industrial Structure: Industrial structure of the under-developed economies is highly backward. A very small per centage of the working population is engaged in the industrial sector. Contribution of the industrial sector in gross national product is very low. Industrial productivity is also very low.

High Growth Rate of Population: In most under-developed countries, size of the population is very large compared to the available resources. Also, population has the tendency to rise at a very high rate. As a result, the bulk of production is consumed and very little is saved for further investment and so the rate of growth is slow. People generally do not enjoy good health and are therefore, less efficient.

Outdated Technology: Under-developed economies depend largely on the use of outdated technology. Because of the lack of capital resources, these countries can't afford the use of modern technology. As a result, productivity suffers and rate of economic growth continues to be low.

Unemployment: Under-developed economies are inflicted with large-scale unemployment. Disguised unemployment in the rural sector is a distinct feature of such economies.

Developing Economy

The countries of such an economy are neither very advanced nor very backward. Such countries are at present engaged in making maximum possible use of their resources of raw material, capital and manpower, so as to accomplish rapid economic development. A good example of *Developing Economy* is our country. Other countries that can be mentioned are Indonesia, Iran, etc., which are very close to take-off stage.

Features of a Developing Economy

The main features of a developing economy are as follows:

Low Per Capita Income and Widespread Poverty: All developing countries are faced with the problem of mass poverty. This poverty is reflected in their low per capita income. When compared with the developed countries of the world, their per capita income is very low. For example, the per capita income of India is nearly 1/20th of the per capita income of various developed economies. Actually speaking, the per capita income in these countries is so low, that even the basic needs of food, cloth and shelter of a large section of population are not fulfilled. In a report, the poverty in India was estimated to be approx. 22 per cent which equals to approx. 30 crore people which is more than the population of very large number of countries.

Economic Inequalities: There are wide inequalities in the economic field of all the developing countries. We can find inequalities both in the rural and urban sectors of these countries. In the rural sector, a major chunk of land-holdings is owned by big landlords. On the other hand, there is a very big number of marginal and small farmers and landless tillers. As a result of this inequality in land-holdings, landlords exploit the tillers of the soil. It further adds fuel to the inequalities of income and wealth in the agricultural sector. Similarly, in urban sector also we find the monopoly of big industrial houses over the industries and other assets. In this situation, if there is any increase in national income, it is grabbed by these rich people. This further increases the poverty and inequality in the country. It is estimated that in India, top one per cent family have the 58 per cent share in the country's total wealth. This inequality in the economic field leads to inequality of opportunities and social inequalities.

Rudimentary State of Infrastructure: Infrastructure facilities such as banking, transport, communication, irrigation, energy, education, health, housing, etc., are in rudimentary stage in developing countries. A very small portion of total agricultural land is under irrigation facilities in India.

Backward Technology: Developing economies use backward and low level technology in their production sector both industrial as well as agriculture.

Predominance of Agricultural and Rural Sector and its Backwardness: One of the striking features of developing countries is that agricultural and rural sector predominates in their economies and side by side it is in a very backward state.

Rapid Increase in Population: Population is also increasing at a very rapid rate in these developing countries. It is one of the important reasons that their development efforts are not bearing fruits. For instance, during post-independence period, the death rate in India has declined more rapidly than its birth rate. As a result, the country is facing the problem of population explosion.

Unemployment: It is also one of the important features of a developing economy that all people do not get employment. It leads to wastage of human power on the one hand and creates pressures on the limited resources of the country on the other. India is also continuously facing the problem of unemployment since a very long time.

Others: Besides these, some other features are also found in these countries. They are—under-utilization of human and natural resources due to lack of capital, slow growth of industrial sector, foreign dependence, market imperfections, lack of banking, insurance, transport and communication facilities, loose and corrupt administration, etc.

But, inspite of these features of backwardness, these developing countries are moving forward, though slowly, on the path of development. So, in a sense, a developing economy can be understood as an under-developed economy making efforts to become a developed economy. India has chosen the path of development through five-year plans after its independence. Our national and per capita incomes are steadily increasing. We have started to adopt modern scientific techniques in the agricultural sector and it has resulted in Green Revolution. In the industrial sector also, many basic and key industries have been established and now we are producing many commodities indigenously. Transport and communication facilities have been expanded. In view of all these facts, it will be appropriate to term our economy as developing economy.

Distinction between Developed and Developing Economies

Developed Economy	Developing Economy
1. High per capita income.	Low per capita income.
2. High rate of capital formation.	Low rate of capital formation.
3. Predominance of industrial and service sectors.	Predominance of primary or agricultural sector.
4. Use of advanced technology.	Use of backward and low level technology.
5. Highly developed infrastructure.	Rudimentary state of infrastructure.
6. High level of efficiency and productivity.	Low level of efficiency and productivity.
7. Low rate of population growth.	High rate of population growth.
8. Low incidence of poverty and unemployment.	High incidence of poverty and unemployment.
9. Full utilization of human and natural resources.	Under utilization of human and natural resources.

10. High ratio of urban population.	Low ratio of urban population.
11. Exports of largely industrial products and services.	Predominance of primary exports.
12. Less inequalities.	Relatively large inequalities.

LESSON AT A GLANCE

Economy: The legal and institutional framework within which economic activity takes place.

Classification of Economy:

Classification on the Basis of Nature: (i) Simple and Complex economy; (ii) Closed and Open economy; (iii) Free/Unplanned and Controlled/Planned economy, and (iv) Agricultural and Industrial economy.

Classification on the Basis of Ownership of Means of Production: (i) Capitalistic economy; (ii) Socialistic economy and (iii) Mixed economy.

Classification on the Basis of Economic Growth: (i) Developed economy; (ii) Under-developed economy; and (iii) Developing economy.

PROJECT WORK

Survey a nearby Industrial Estate located in rural area. Prepare a list of some industries, businesses and trading establishments, engaged in various types of economic activities.

Classify all these industries and business organizations according to various economic systems.

Case 1 : Prepare a final list in respect of each unit, mentioning exactly, as to which type of Economy it belongs to; giving suitable reasons for your conclusion.

For example, let us suppose an Industry named 'XY & Co.' Its final category may be:

"Complex, Industrial unit adopting a capitalistic pattern of Economy."

Case 2 : On the basis of information collected in respect of various units, draw conclusion whether the economy of the region or area under study is Under-developed or Developing one. Give reasons for your conclusion.

QUESTIONS

A. Short Answer Questions

1. What is an economic system?
2. Mention three fundamental economic problems faced by a society.
3. In how many categories is the economic system categorized? Name them.
4. What is a capitalistic economy?

5. What is a socialistic economy?
6. What do you understand by a mixed economy?
7. What do you understand by developing economy?
8. Differentiate between the following:
    (a) Simple and Complex economy.
    (b) Closed and Open economy.
    (c) Free and Controlled economy.
    (d) Agricultural and Industrial economy.
    (e) Developed and Under-developed economy.
    (f) Developed and Developing economy.

B. Long Answer Questions
1. Describe the main features of various types of economies.
2. Define capitalistic economy. Mention its merits and demerits.
3. Define a socialistic economy. What is the role of Central Planning Authority in a socialistic economy?
4. What are the merits and demerits of a socialistic economy?
5. Explain in detail the main features of mixed economy.
6. What is a mixed economy? Why has India adopted mixed economy?
7. How does a socialist economy differs from capitalist economy?
8. Point out the main merits and demerits of mixed economy.
9. Differentiate between capitalist, socialist and mixed economies.
10. What is meant by developed and developing economies ? What is the basis of their classification?
11. What is a developed economy? Give its main features.
12. Explain economy. What are the various types of economies?
13. "Mixed economy is the blending of capitalistic and socialistic economy." Justify the statement.
14. Distinguish between under-developed economy and developed economy.

05
An Overview of Indian Economy

INDIAN ECONOMY ON THE EVE OF INDEPENDENCE

At the time of Independence in 1947, the nationalist Government in India was faced with the huge task of undoing the damage caused by British rule. Agriculture was the primary occupation of the economy, employing about 72 per cent of the workforce. Basic industries were few and continued to act as catalyst for their parent companies in Britain. The secondary sector contributed only 16.6 per cent of the GDP in 1950–51. The per capita income was very low which meant that a major portion of earnings had to be spent on food. Birth and death rates were very high and health conditions were highly deplorable. Lack of advanced scientific and technical know-how had led to low productivity levels in all the sectors. For most of the Indians, the satisfactory fulfillment of their basic necessities of life was a distant dream.

Now Indian economy is on a developing stage and the *primary, secondary* and *tertiary* sectors are not yet fully developed. Hence, it is desirable and important, in order to understand the basic structure of Indian economy, to make a brief review of all the sectors of economy in reference to structure, transformation and its development, etc. Especially Agriculture, being the oldest economic sector and perhaps the most dominant one, needs a special study.

OVERVIEW

The Indian economy predominantly depends upon agricultural and major portion of the population gets its livelihood from this sector. But even after the implementation of Twelve Five Year Plans since Independence and a substantial increase in agricultural production, the productivity of this sector is quite low as compared to other advanced countries of the world.

There have been significant developments in Industrial sector. The Government of India has also ventured in basic and capital-intensive industries and infrastructure network. The tertiary sector has also registered a phenomenal progress. As a matter of fact, almost all types of consumer and capital goods are being produced in our country. But when we look at other end we find that the per capita income is increasing very slowly because of rapidly increasing population.

To achieve faster economic growth, the policy of 'liberalization' has been adopted recently in the field of advanced technology. The foreign collaborations are also being encouraged in selected areas.

FEATURES OF INDIAN ECONOMY—AT PRESENT JUNCTURE

Unexploited Natural Resources: India possesses huge natural resources but most of the resources are under-utilised. The judicious exploitation and proper utilization of natural resources is the basic foundation of economic development. The natural resources need to be discovered, conserved and developed scientifically, systematically and judiciously for achieving maximum advantages. But, we find that many of the natural resources like minerals, forests, water bodies, etc., have not been properly exploited in several parts of the country. This is why, it is stated that *'Poor people live in Rich India'*. If it is possible to make judicious use of resources, the growth potentials can be easily exploited.

Heavy Population Pressure: Heavy population pressure or population explosion, along with a high growth rate of population is one of the most alarming feature of Indian economy. The population of the country as per Census 2011 was 1.21 billion and the annual population growth rate was 1.64 per cent. The reasons responsible for it are high birth-rate, falling death rate, high immigration from adjoining countries. The growing population imposes a huge economic burden upon the society because of the growing requirements of food, clothing, shelter and other necessities which are to be met by the Government. All economic progress gets neutralised against heavy population pressure. Economists believe that if the growth rate of population becomes more than that of the gross domestic product, the per capita income would remain at a very low level.

Dependence on Agriculture: In our country, a large part of population depends on agriculture which itself is a major economic sector of our economy. In developed nations, a small sector of population depends on agriculture, for example, only 1·9% in USA, and 1·3 % in UK, etc. In our country, more than 58 per cent as per FY 2020 of the population depends upon agriculture for their livelihood, whereas the contribution of agriculture to National Income is only about 17 per cent to the GDP.

Uneven Distribution of Wealth: Although the national income of India has been increasing during the plan periods, it is not distributed properly among different sections of the people. Only some of the people are very rich whereas most of the people are poor. In a study it was found that the top one per cent people of High Class own 58.4 per cent of National Wealth while 99 per cent people own only 41.6 per cent of the National Wealth. The richest 10% of Indians own 80.7 per cent of wealth.

Low Agricultural Productivity: In India, most of the farmers are uneducated and orthodox. They have adopted outdated methods and techniques in agricultural activities. The use of good quality seeds and improved fertilizers is not so popular. Most of the farmers do not use modern tools and machines for production. The irrigation facilities have not covered large area of agricultural land. All these factors result in low agricultural productivity. The low productivity leads to backward nature of agriculture and scarcity of food. In addition to this, a large section of population is dependent on agriculture, which ultimately lowers the per capita income and results in the lowering of the standard of living.

Inadequate Capital and Outdated Technology: The availability of capital is inadequate and several schemes of development suffer for want of capital. Besides, the technology adopted is of low level. Due to the lack of capital and shortage of highly skilled technocrats, the technological productivity is very low. All these factors result into inefficient production and low per capita income.

Unemployment: Because of the rapid growth in population, inadequate job opportunities in the secondary and tertiary sectors, insufficient capital and improper utilization of resources, the problem of unemployment and under-employment exists continuously in rural as well as in urban areas. The occupational structure of the economy failed to provide employment to the additional population in the economy. Due to the rise in population, the supply of labour exceeds the demand for labour. The data available from the 969 employment exchanges in the country indicates that in 2010, the number of jobseekers registered with the employment exchanges (all of whom are not necessarily unemployed), was of the order of 3·88 crore out of which, approximately 70 per cent are educated (10th standard and above).

Lack of Entrepreneurship Talent: The position of entrepreneurship is also highly unsatisfactory in our country. Our education system does not promote entrepreneurial acumen among our students. Only a limited number of persons possess top-class entrepreneurial and managerial skills in our country. This has caused a great setback to the efficient working of productive units and has retarded the economic progress of the nation.

Poor Living Standard of an Average Indian: Low level of per capita income results in poor purchasing power of the average people and hence, leads to a poor standard of living. An average Indian does not get a balanced diet, proper housing, adequate medical aid and proper education. The average condition of common people in rural areas is the worst. This low standard of living has adverse effect on health of people which finally results in low efficiency of working people. **Prof. Amartya Sen** has also expressed about the need for further development in health, education and nutritional facilities in India, for a sustainable development.

Dual Economic Structure: India possess dual economic structure. Certain sectors, sections or areas are fully developed like Punjab, Haryana, etc., using advanced techniques and on the other hand, other areas, sectors, or sections are undeveloped like Rajasthan, Bihar, Orissa, etc. On one hand, we see the advanced technology and on the other side, the traditional technology. The traditional structure coincides with the modern structure in Indian economy.

Under-developed Infrastructure: The economic growth of any country is reflected by the growth in infrastructure. Infrastructural facilities consist of transport and communication facilities, energy, banking and insurance, science and technology and social overheads. At the time of Independence, these facilities were very poor in India. There has been a substantial progress in infrastructural facilities during the plan periods, but when compared with other developed countries, we find ourselves far behind these countries.

Other Non-economic Factors: The prevailing customs and orthodox outlook of the people have created an indifferent attitude towards materialistic progress. The general religious thinking advocates renunciation of material life. The laws of inheritance, attitude towards women, low education among women, caste system and several social traditions have been highly unfavourable to the industrial development.

Apart from the above factors, *favoritism, nepotism,* and *corruption* have penetrated every sphere of life and causing a setback to efficient and dedicated working of the entire production and distribution system. The natural outcome of all these factors is retardation of economic progress.

NATURE OF THE INDIAN ECONOMY

An economy is called under-developed when its per capita income is very low and the primary sector has the maximum share in GDP. While a developing economy has features of an under-developed economy but there are indicators of progress in all the sectors of the economy.

Indian Economy is both under-developed and developing. There are certain features of Indian Economy—low per capita income, predominance of primary sector, heavy population pressure, prevalence of chronic unemployment and under-employment, low rate of capital formation, mal-distribution of wealth/ assets, poor quality of human capital, prevalence of low level of technology, low living standard, poor economic organisation, etc., that place the country in the under-developed category. But such an assertion is only partially valid, because certain improvements have taken place in the economy since independence in 1947, which are permanent and structural in nature. These improvements have the potential of sustaining economic life at a higher level than before. An uptrend in output, increase in productive capacity, improvement in human capital, some modernization and institutional improvements are some of the important changes that are progressive, and are pointers of the developing character of Indian economy. Hence, it would be more appropriate to call the Indian economy a developing one.

India as an Under-developed Economy

Several typical features of an under-developed economy can be found in India:

Typical of an under-developed economy is its reliance on the agricultural sector. In India, more than 50 per cent of the population is dependent on agriculture—the dependence having declined only marginally since independence. The predominance of agriculture is also indicated by the fact that the agricultural sector's contribution to the GDP is about 15·87 per cent at present, though it was more than 50 per cent in 1950-51.

In India 21·8 per cent of population still lives below the poverty line. Amazingly nearly 50 per cent of those who are absolutely poor in the world are living in India. The problem of mass poverty is aggravating the problem of income inequalities.

Scarce availability of capital owing to many reasons such as smaller savings, smallness in size of the capitalist sector has been a severe setback to the country's development plans.

In India, the techniques of production are not advanced even in the agricultural sector that sustains about half of the population. Though the industries have been pervaded by modern techniques of production, yet they are less advanced than those in use in developed economies.

India has witnessed a rapid growth in population. The growth has been at the annual rate of 1·64 per cent over the decades till recently. The transfer of population from one sector to another has also been restricted. As a result of increasing population pressure on cultivable land, disguised unemployment has been on the rise. The dependency ratio is high because only 39·2 per cent of population was in the working age (15–62 years).

Chronic unemployment resulting from structural defects in the employment has been a serious restricting factor of development activities.

Private enterprises in India has failed to play a prominent role in development, *i.e.,* employment generation and providing basic industrial and infrastructural facilities, right from the time of the British rule. This is one of the major reasons behind the Indian economy's under-developed status.

India as Developing Economy

India's development process can be assessed in terms of quantitative and structural aspects.

Quantitative Aspect: Studying the national income trends over the past years, it is noted that the country's net national product at factor cost as per the 2019-20 prices was

₹ 135.40 lakh crore as compared to ₹ 129·07 lakh crore in 2018-19. Though national income has not been rising at a steady pace, its rate of increase has been higher than the rate of population growth. So per capita consumption has seen some improvement and capital accumulation has been possible to a certain extent. Per capita income has also shown a growing trend—it grew from ₹ 1,26,406 in 2018-19 to ₹ 1,35,050 in 2019-20.

Structural Aspect: Since independence, India's economy has been subjected to structural changes, but the process of development has been slow in bringing the expected transformation. So in a sense it is very difficult to be certain that the change has affected each and every sector of the economy. Nevertheless the following points regarding development are worth bearing in mind:

- The share of agriculture and allied sectors in India's economy has come down over the years. The share of industrial sector (including mining, manufacturing, electricity supply and construction) in the GDP has witnessed a rise since the 1950-51. Its share was 26·13 per cent in 2018. The service sector (including trade, hotels, transport, communication, finance, real estate and community, social and personal services) contributed about 49·88 per cent to the GDP in 2019-20.
- A developing economy is necessarily characterized by changes in the occupational structure of population moving away from the primary sector. In India's economy, however, this feature does not exist. This could be because India's economic planning has been indicative in character and this feature has failed to gain desired growth in the secondary and tertiary sectors.
- Land relations in India have assumed a new form since India's independence, owing to the abolishment of the *zamindari* system and distribution of agricultural land among the tenants and agricultural labourers after independence, but still much more needs to be done in this regard.
- Since independence, there has been a growth of basic industries yielding important raw materials and capital equipments despite the fact that at the time of independence, the contribution of such industries was only one-fourth of the industrial production. Today, mineral-related industries, heavy engineering, locomotives, machine tools and heavy electrical equipment industries have a substantial share in industrial production.
- Development in social overhead capital that brings under its purview transport, educational and irrigation systems, health and energy production facilities, etc., has given rise to growth and better living.
- Progress in the financial sector has been in terms of better money organisation, capital markets and establishment of specialised industrial set-up related to finance. The banking sector has witnessed growth in banking services mainly through commercial banks and cooperative credit societies.
- As far as human development is concerned, the education level of people has improved since 1950-51. The literacy rate grew from 18.33 per cent in 1951, to 74.04 per cent in 2011. Similarly life expectancy has also increased to 68·7 years from 49.7 years in 1970-75.

In short, Indian economy is showing a perceptible growth. Indian economy is consistently moving forward to higher and higher level of productions, consumption, per capita income standard of living, etc.

LESSON AT A GLANCE

Indian Economy on the Eve of Independence: At the time of Independence in 1947 the nationalist Government in India was faced with the huge task of undoing the damage caused by British Rule.

Features of Indian Economy—At Present Juncture: (i) Unexploited natural resources; (ii) Heavy population pressure; (iii) Dependence on agriculture; (iv) Uneven distribution of wealth; (v) Low agricultural productivity; (vi) Inadequate capital and outdated technology; (vii) Unemployment; (viii) Lack of entrepreneurship talent; (ix) Poor living standard of an average Indian; (x) Dual economic structure; (xi) Under-developed infrastructure; (xii) Other non-economic factors.

Nature of the Indian Economy: (i) India as an under-developed economy; (ii) India as developing economy.

PROJECT WORK

Collect statistical data on per capita income, capital formation, population growth, infrastructure, etc., of some of the less developed countries of Africa, Asia and Latin America (from the World Development Report published by the World Bank) and identify the common features of these countries including India.

QUESTIONS

A. Short Answer Questions

1. Write any five features of Indian Economy.
2. Discuss the nature of Indian economy.
3. Mention two basic characteristics of the Indian economy as an under-developed economy.
4. What do you mean by economic under-development?
5. What do you mean by economic development?
6. Give two features of Indian economy which characterise it as developing economy.
7. Enlist any four reasons behind slow economic development of a country.

B. Long Answer Questions

1. What do you mean by features of an economy? Explain main features of Indian economy.
2. Describe four important features of Indian economy.
3. Explain the nature of Indian economy.
4. What do you understand by under-developed economy? Briefly explain how Indian economy is an under-developed economy?
5. Explain how Indian economy is a developing economy.

06 Sectors in Indian Economy

MAIN SECTORS OR REGIONS OF THE INDIAN ECONOMY

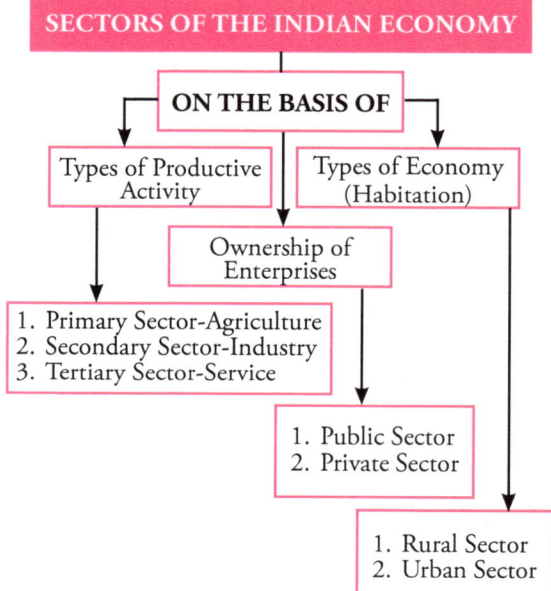

OVERVIEW

Every economy consists of the three sectors, though in varied proportions depending on the level of development in the economy.

The three sectors of the economy, i.e., primary, secondary and tertiary sectors are dependent on each other and modern economic development of India cannot be imagined without adequate coordination of each sector; particularly that of agricultural sector.

In India, the economic life and activities of people revolve around agricultural sector. Agriculture is a traditional way of life apart from being an occupation. Agriculture has shaped the entire social and cultural structure of our nation.

On the eve of Independence our economy was highly underdeveloped. It was generally felt that the Government should frame an industrial policy which may bring about rapid industrial development in the country.

Role of service sector in Indian economy is very wide and significant as both primary and secondary sectors need it for their development.

There is a very stark difference in pace of development of rural and urban sectors. Population in India is migrating to cities. Unless there is not a balanced development, Indian economy cannot grow.

The main sectors or regions of the Indian economy can be divided as follows:

- One way of dividing the economy into sectors may be in terms of the *main types of productive activities*. The sectors are: (a) Primary sector which mainly consists of agriculture and allied activities like forestry, animal husbandry, etc., (b) Secondary sector which comprises of the manufacturing of goods like cloth, car, electricity, housing, etc. and (c) the Tertiary sector which includes of all the services like transportation, banking, insurance, medical services, etc.
- It is sometimes useful to describe a developing economy by dividing it into two broad sectors according to *habitation* in towns and villages, *i.e.*, the urban and rural sectors.

- Another way is suggested by the definition of the mixed economy itself; the division into the public and the private sectors. This division is on the basis of ownership of the *enterprises.*

SECTORS ACCORDING TO PRODUCTIVE ACTIVITY
PRIMARY SECTOR–AGRICULTURE

Agriculture occupies a very important place in the economic life of our country as India is primarily an agricultural country. Agriculture is the backbone of our economic system and the major source of livelihood in the Indian economy. The fortunes of the economy are, even now, dependent on the course of agricultural production.

At the time of Independence in 1947, agricultural condition was deplorable. Our farmers worked under unfavourable circumstances and were exploited by the land owners and money lenders. They lived in extreme poverty. Agricultural production was at a very low level. No investment worth the name had taken place in agriculture towards its modernization and improvement. The Government of India recognized the dismal situation and decided to initiate required measures to improve the situation substantially.

Agriculture in our country used to be the source of livelihood of 70 per cent of the country's population at the time of independence. Still approximately 50 per cent of the Indian workforce is dependent on it for their livelihood.

It is a large sector of the economic activity and has crucial role to play in the country's economic development by providing food and raw materials, employment to a very large proportion of population, capital for its own development and surpluses for national economic development.

Nature of Indian Agriculture

Though the agricultural production has increased manifold after independence, certain features of Indian agriculture indicate unbalanced growth and slow development.

Agriculture still exhibits feudal relations of production mainly because the land reforms envisaged have not been properly enforced. Despite the introduction of rural banking and credit societies, the small and marginal farmers still go to money lenders and become victims of usurious capital. The excessive pressure of population on land has resulted in low wages for agricultural labour. The agricultural labour on its part is unable to opt out in favour of something else due to lack of opportunity, ignorance or low skills. The cheapness of labour leads to adoption of labour intensive methods of production instead of mechanization. Low wages and lower per capita income is also related to low productivity.

A majority of our farmers continue to use obsolete techniques and are occupied in what is known as subsistence farming. Financial constraints prevent the small and marginal farmers from adopting techniques for better productivity and production.

Indian agriculture even now is dependent to a large extent on the monsoons. Nearly 60 per cent of net sown areas continues to depend on rainfall rather than irrigation. Poor marketing and inadequate storing facilities add to further problems, characterizing Indian agriculture.

Role of Primary Sector—Agriculture in the Development of an Economy

The role of agriculture in the Indian economy is explained below:
1. **Contribution to National Income:** Agriculture is the main source of national income. Though, its share in national income has been decreasing steadily. The share

of agriculture and allied activities was 57 per cent in national GDP growth rate during beginning of the plans. Now, it has become 15 per cent at present.

2. **Employment:** Agriculture provides employment and work to an overwhelming majority of the Indian masses. According to the recent Economic Surveys, nearly 50 per cent of India's population is still engaged in agricultural activities. Besides, a large number of people earn their living by working in occupations dependent on agriculture, like storage, processing, and trade and transport of agricultural products.

3. **Food and Fodder:** In India, agriculture meets almost the entire food requirements of the people. Here a large proportion of income is spent on food. Agriculture sector provides fodder to about 38 crores of animals.

4. **Foreign Trade:** Agriculture occupies an important place in the foreign trade of India. We export tea, coffee, cashew kernels, raw cotton, rice, tobacco, spices, jute, marine products, meat and meat products, etc., which are agricultural and allied products. The total value of exports of agricultural products has risen, however, in per centage terms it has declined. Agricultural products have approximately 10 per cent share in the total exports of the country.

5. **Industrial Development:** In India, agriculture plays an important role in industrial development. Agriculture provides raw material to the industries. Cotton and jute textile industries, sugar, vanaspati and plantations depend on agriculture.

6. **International Ranking:** At the international level, Indian agriculture has a fairly high ranking in certain commodities. In the case of groundnuts, India occupies the top position in the world.

7. **Role in National Economy:** Agriculture set a pace for the economic growth rate of the country. Fluctuations in agricultural output levels play a key role in the state of the national economy and influence the growth rate.

8. **Contribution to Domestic Trade:** It is borne out by the fact that huge expenditure in India is incurred on purchase of farm products.

9. **Fulcrum of Transport Industry:** Agriculture serves as an economic fulcrum of transport industry in India. Both Railways and Roadways are the major carriers of agricultural produce in India.

Rural consumption of industrial goods is nearly three times that of urban consumption. According to a recent **NCAER** survey, for several consumer durables the rural market is growing much faster than the urban market. As a matter of fact, the current spurt in rural consumption of durable goods has led to a redefinition of consumer demographics itself. Obviously, there is a direct relationship between agricultural production and income and demand for industrial goods. These are known as demand linkages among the two sectors.

Similarly, performance in agriculture also influences total demand via Government savings and public investment. For example, a rise in agricultural production results in increased Government savings both as a result of the buoyancy of Government revenues and reduction in expenditures like drought relief which might otherwise become necessary.

Primary Source of Saving in the Economy: Since agriculture is an important source of national income, this sector also is a significant source of savings, and hence capital formation for the economy. These are known as savings and investment linkages. The pace of development is largely conditioned by the rate of capital formation in the economy.

Agricultural Productivity

Productivity of agriculture depends on:
- Land productivity; and
- Labour productivity

Land productivity depends on the types of soil, climatic conditions of a region, and irrigation facilities etc. On the other hand, labour productivity depends on the literacy rate, technical skills of cultivators, agriculture implements, average income of cultivators and fulfillment of basic amenities of life.

Even though the production of almost all the important crops has increased, yet the agricultural productivity (yield per hectare in quintals) is very low in our country as compared to what has been achieved in other countries.

Trend in Agricultural Production

Table 6.1 shows the production of different crops since 1970-71, which reveals that the total production of each crop has been increasing but the rate of productivity growth is different for different crops. The rate of productivity growth is more in respect of foodgrain crops as compared to non-food crops.

Table 6.1 : Production of Principal Crops in India (Million Tonnes)

Crops	1970-71	1990-91	2000-01	2006-07	2008-09	2009-10	2010-11	2019-20
Rice	42.2	74.3	85.0	90.0	99.0	89.1	95.3	117.94
Wheat	23.8	55.1	69.7	72.5	81.0	80.8	85.9	107.14
Pulses	11.8	14.3	11.1	14.5	15.0	14.7	18.1	23.01
Coarse cereals	30.6	32.7	31.1	32.0	44.0	33.5	42.3	47.54
Total Foodgrains	**108.4**	**176.4**	**196.9**	**209.0**	**235.0**	**218.1**	**241.6**	**295.67**
Oilseeds	9.6	18.6	18.4	23.6	28.0	24.9	31.1	35.50
Sugarcane	126.4	241.0	296.0	315.5	274.0	292.3	339.2	358.14
Cotton	4.8	9.8	9.5	21.0	23.0	24.0	33.4	36.05
Jute & Mesta	6.2	9.2	10.6	11.4	10.0	11.8	10.6	9.92

* Third Advance Estimate Source : Ministry of Agriculture and farmers welfare.

The above table depicts that the yields of rice and wheat have increased much faster than the coarse foodgrains but the production of pulses has increased comparatively at a much slower rate. However, the output of commercial crops like cotton, sugarcane, oilseeds, etc, has increased much faster than that of foodgrains, but this is due to increased cultivated area for these crops.

Reasons of Low Productivity

Uncertain Rainfall: In India, the monsoon rains are uncertain. Sometimes, they are insufficient or unevenly distributed and at times, may cause either famine or floods. The uncertainties of rainfall seriously handicap the farmers in increasing the production of agricultural crops, since majority of the farmers depend upon rainfall for their agricultural activities.

Inadequate Irrigation Facilities: Most of the farmers do not have adequate irrigation facilities. Only a few farmers could avail the facilities of irrigation from various sources such as canals, tubewells, etc. Despite the development of many minor and major irrigation systems since independence, only 40 per cent of agricultural sector in our country has irrigation facilities. Another aspect is that the irrigation facilities even though available, are not being utilized fully by the farmers. The result is that the product is of poor quality and productivity is low.

Natural Inclemencies: Besides uncertain rainfall and inadequate irrigation facilities, there are natural inclemencies like hailstorms, frost or attack by pests and insects, which handicap the farmers in stepping up the production.

Old Methods and Techniques: The majority of Indian farmers use old methods and techniques of production. Also, they are usually orthodox and conservative and belong to poor classes. They have not adopted new techniques and modern methods (which are adopted by advanced countries). However, a very small per centage of farmers have started adopting modern methods and started using improved implements.

Improper Use of Inputs: Indian agriculture is suffering from improper use of inputs like chemical fertilizers, urea, pesticides, etc., as they are proving harmful for good production. These practices of indiscriminate use of improper pesticides and fertilizers also reduce the fertility of land and result in its low productivity.

Uneconomic Agricultural Holdings: The agricultural holdings in our country are not only small, but they are fragmented too. The average area of agricultural holdings is usually less than 2 hectares or so and because of this reason, scientific cultivation with improved implements and tools is not possible. The small holdings, on the other hand, cause wastage of time, labour and animal power and pose difficulties in proper utilization of the irrigation facilities.

Conservative and Superstitious Nature of Farmers: The Indian farmers are generally illiterate, superstitious and conservative who usually follow outdated customs and believe in fate. Therefore, they remain contented and satisfied with their primitive system of agriculture. Because of illiteracy, ignorance, superstitions and conservative nature, they do not get motivated by the considerations of modern economic progress. So, in this way, in spite of all facilities, which can possibly be arranged, the desire is lacking amongst farmers which ultimately results in low agricultural productivity.

Lack of Financial Facilities: Most of the farmers in a village depend upon the village money lenders for their credit requirements—whether productive or consumable and pay a high rate of interest on the borrowed money. Usually, the farmer is not in a position to clear the debt and in turn loses his land.

In recent years, credit facilities have expanded through credit cooperatives, commercial banks and the Government, yet the availability of adequate finance is not satisfactory.

Unsatisfactory Tenancy Legislations: The land legislations and the *Zamindari* system prevailing in the country had adversely affected agricultural development. Consequent to abolition of *Zamindari* system and enactment of new tenancy legislation, there is some improvement but the condition of tenants is far from satisfactory. Many of the cultivators do not have their own land and have to pay high rents on the land which they cultivate. Moreover, they are not certain about their rights on the land. All these factors usually demotivate the cultivators and there is no serious effort to increase the productivity of agriculture.

Excessive Population: There is a large-scale sub-division and fragmentation of land because of large population depending upon agriculture. This reduces the area of land available to each cultivator and also leads to high per centage of disguised unemployment. It is worth mentioning that despite the increase in total agricultural land, the area of cultivated land has declined.

Unsatisfactory Storage and Marketing Facilities: Due to improper storage and marketing facilities in the village, the farmers have to depend upon the middlemen, the wholesaler and the commission agents in the mandi or town, where all these people pay a very low price and the farmers lose inducement to increase the production. However, the Government is fixing the support price every year, yet the effect is not significant.

Inadequate Agricultural Research: The agricultural researchs have neither been properly organized nor due importance is given to them. Whatever achievements have been made in agricultural researchs to improve the overall productivity, these are not transformed into actual utility because of poor coordination between research institutes and the productive farms.

Secondary Sector—Industry

Industrialization refers to the establishment and development of manufacturing industries. However, the process of industrialization is not confined to the establishment of a manufacturing industry but involves a change in the whole economic structure of the country concerned with bringing and accelerating economic development.

According to **Prof. A.H. Hansen**, *"It is the deepening process as one where more capital is used for per unit of output, the sidening process means that less capital is used for per unit output, while the widening process means that capital formation grows pari-passu with the increase in the output of final goods."* Therefore, it is equally true to say:

- That high productivity promotes industrialization, and
- That industrialization promotes high productivity.

To be more specific, industrialization implies:
- Utilization of power, machinery and modern techniques of production.
- Capital investment on a large-scale.
- Division of labour.
- Exchange and distribution of goods with the help of developed monetary system.
- Transformation of the whole economy.
- Industrialization of agriculture through intensive use of inputs.

Thus, it is a part of the broader process of economic development especially which involves the operation of a modern economic infrastructure, *i.e.*, growth of railway, communication, factories, mills, mines, power plants, dams and so on.

Role of Secondary Sector—Industry in the Development of an Economy

The need for and role of industrial sector have been fully recognized by the development thinkers all over the world. Industrial sector through its forward and backward linkages with other sectors plays a very important role in achieving rapid growth and development. Most modern and rich countries have well developed industrial sector through their early industrial revolution.

Almost all the economists agree that industrialization is essential for the economic development of any country. Some of the countries have achieved a very advanced stage of industrialization, and are called developed economies.

India, at present, is in a developing stage and still faster industrialization is very essential to absorb large population in secondary and tertiary sectors, because the primary sector is already heavily loaded with large population. Main points in favour of rapid and large-scale industrialization are discussed below:

Balanced and Rapid Development: Industrialization is essential for balanced and rapid development of the economies. Total dependency on agriculture alone is not desirable, because agriculture is subject to vagaries of nature. By total dependence upon agriculture, the economic stability cannot be ensured. Simultaneous industrialization and development of agriculture duly supported by infrastructure is a pre-requisite of real economic progress for a nation, like India. Industry and agriculture will then mutually supply the various items and support each other. This is the rationale of the balanced economy and the cumulative interactions of industry and agriculture that increases the national output and help to raise the living standard of the people.

Increase in National and Per Capita Incomes: Industrialization leads to increased national and per capita income. On the other hand, in an agricultural economy, the domestic production is mainly from agriculture which is subject to diminishing returns. This results in lower per capita and aggregate incomes in an agricultural country as compared to industrialized nations. This fact is evident from the gap between the rich and the poor nations which seems to be directly related to the degree of industrialization.

Exploitation of Natural Resources: Rapid industrialization would help in proper exploitation of our natural resources. The full utilization of mineral resources, water resources, forest resources, etc., of our country can be done through establishment and expansion of various industries which use these natural resources as their inputs.

Increase in Export Earnings: To diversify export items and to make them cost competitive, rapid industrialization is needed. Most of the traditional export items of India are primary products. Their values are relatively lower than our import items of industrial goods. Even the industrial products which are exported are of low value. Thus, if India can produce industrial goods of higher value and export these products, then this will increase India's export earnings as well as create favourable terms of trade.

Industrialization and Agricultural Development: Apart from the fact that agricultural and industrial developments depend upon each other, it is also a fact that many agricultural inputs are possible only with industrial progress. In modern times, the extensive use of machines, chemical fertilizers, irrigation by pump sets and tubewells (all products from industries) can achieve better agricultural productivity. Thus, we can conclude that subsequent agricultural development itself depends upon the degree of industrialization.

Employment for Surplus Labour: Indian economy faces a setback due to surplus labour and growing population. The *man-land ratio* is deteriorating in agricultural sector and thus the only source of possible employment for additional hands remains in the industrial sector. Only industrialization can generate more employment opportunities at accelerated pace. Also, it will draw away surplus labour from agricultural sector and thereby help in increasing the marginal productivity of agricultural labour and the capital income from land.

Security Considerations: Any country can opt for the development and production of primary products and can depend upon other countries for the manufactured goods and may totally avoid industrialization. But, in practice this is neither desirable nor feasible for the Independence and self-reliance of the nation. For security reasons, a country cannot take risks of dependency particularly in the case of defence equipments and the capital goods. Therefore, industrialization is a must; it may be to the limited extent or otherwise—from the security point of view.

Change in Outlook: The people attached to agriculture stay in rural areas and normally their outlook is parochial and narrow. Most of the agricultural people are superstitious and conservative. Industrialization leads to liberal outlook. It promotes urbanization under social contacts between persons belonging to different classes and professions when they work together at one place. The greatest advantage is that it also promotes a breakdown of psychological barriers and generates a feeling of togetherness and oneness in the society.

Modernisation: Industrial development has generated elements of modernisation in the form of technological progress, emergence of scientific outlook, promoting industrial cult, etc., which are ingredients of economic progress.

Rate of Industrial Growth in India

The trends in growth rates of overall Index of Industrial Production (IIP) and its sectoral components *viz.,* basic goods, capital goods, intermediate goods and consumer goods, are given in *Table 6·2.* From a peak level of 5·0 in 2000-01, the index of industrial growth increased to 8·2 in 2010-11. The improvements are particularly noticeable in manufacturing. As per use-based classification, consumer goods, intermediate goods, capital goods and basic goods are having higher growth rates than the previous year.

Table 6·2 : Growth Rates of Industrial Production by Use-based Classification (Base 1993-94 = 100) (Per cent)

Sector	Weight	2000-01	01-02	02-03	03-04	08-09	09-10	10-11
Basic Goods	45·7	3·7	2·6	4·9	5·4	1·7	4·7	6·0
Capital Goods	8·8	1·8	− 3·4	10·5	13·6	11·3	1·0	14·8
Intermediate Goods	15·7	4·7	1·5	3·9	6·4	0·0	6·0	7·4
Infrastructure/construction goods.	29·8	8·0	6·0	7·1	7·1	0·9	7·7	8·6
Durables	8·5	14·5	11·5	− 6·3	11·6	11·1	17·0	14·2
Non-Durables	21·3	5·8	4·1	12·0	5·8	− 5·0	1·4	4·3
IIP (Index of Industrial Production)	100	5·0	2·7	5·7	7·0	2·5	5·3	8·2

Source : Central Statistical Organisation

During 2010-11 growth accelerated in all the sectors of economy except Durables.

Industrial production has shown a distinct improvement in the recent years. The industrial growth increased to 8·8 per cent in 2015-16 and declined to 5·6 per cent in 2016-17.

Causes of Unbalanced Industrialization and Regional Disparities

The following are the some important factors which are responsible for unbalanced industrialization among different regions of the country :

Historical Factors: It has been assumed by economists and scholars that regional imbalances started occurring since the advent of British. The port cities like Mumbai, Kolkata and Chennai, where the Britishers settled first were deliberately developed very fast. Similarly, Maharashtra, West Bengal and Tamil Nadu, which already possessed potential for manufacturing and trading activities, received generous attention from British industrialists and businessmen and made progress in these fields.

Natural Factors: Some regions have the advantage of richness of productive resources like fertile soil, good deposits of minerals and ores and abundance of fossil fuels and petroleum. The demand of such resources activates and accelerates the process of development. Gradually, these areas attract more and more industries, particularly when the raw material components have an important role in determining the location of the industry. Thus, natural availability of important components also becomes a strong reason for unbalanced growth of the industries.

Planning Process: In spite of Government's policy of bringing out balanced regional development throughout the country, the process itself is such that it has tended to increase the regional imbalance. The planning mechanism of our country had shown a strong bias in favour of industrially advanced States in the allocation of plan outlay.

Statutory Regulations and Controls: The industrial licensing policy, labour laws and other rules and regulations of the Government influence the regional distribution of industries. The regulations and controls exercised in industrial licensing system also worked in favour of already developed regions and the backward regions remained undeveloped.

Common Development Pattern: The planner of industrial policy adopted a common pattern for the industrial development for the entire country, irrespective of giving any careful consideration to different potentialities of the particular region. Different regions have different growth potentials depending upon the availability of raw materials, manpower, infrastructure facilities, export potential, etc. To bring out reasonable and appropriate industrial development, the pattern has got to be modified which escaped the preview of the planners.

Urbanization: It is another important indicator of economic development. Per centage of urban population was higher in States like Maharashtra, Tamil Nadu, Gujarat, etc., but lower in States like Orissa, Himachal Pradesh, etc. Industrialisation is rapid where urbanisation is higher and urbanisation is rapid where industrialisation is higher. So both supplement each other.

Favourable Climatic and Natural Conditions: In many cases, the climatic conditions, local topography and the supply of other natural resources of any region, determine the location of various types of industries. For example, the humid climate of any region provides it with an additional advantage to attract the cotton textile industries.

Availability of Transport Facilities: Transportation facilitates industrialisation. The better are the transport facilities, the better is industrialisation. The regional distribution of transport facilities is also determined by cheap transport facilities (*e.g.,* road transport, air transport, etc.). Again one of the most important reasons for industrial backwardness is inadequate availability of these facilities in the North-Eastern region of our country.

Availability of Cheap Labour: Availability of cheap and skilled labour in any particular region also influences the regional distribution of industries. For example, the reason for the initial concentration of textile mills in interior Mumbai region was the availability of cheap and skilled labour.

Importance of Industrial Productivity

Productivity is defined as *the ratio of output to input, both measured in real terms.* Fundamentally, productivity refers to a comparison between the production of goods and services produced and the quantity of resources utilized to produce these goods and services. For example, if a factory produces 120 units per day (keeping all other conditions unchanged) instead of 100 units, the productivity will be said to have increased by 20%.

The industrial productivity is a measure of production per man-hour and the increase in productivity refers to *'production becoming more efficient'* or *'the same commodity or thing or service stands less costly.'* Thus, the concept of productivity reflects the maximum economic utilization of available resources of manpower, machinery, material, utilities (electricity, water and fuels), land, etc., in order to achieve the maximum possible production at a lower cost.

The output of production depends upon several factors of inputs, *e.g.,* raw materials, machines, power, labour, time, etc. Hence, it is generally considered appropriate to have only one factor as a basis for calculating the productivity which is present in all production activities. The man-hour or working time is the most common factor present in all productivity studies. It is also called *Labour Productivity.*

Labour productivity has been defined by *International Labour Organization* as follows:

"The ratio between the volume of output as measured by production indices and the corresponding volume of labour input as measured by employment indices." This definition is widely accepted because of the following reasons:

- That labour-time is more readily measurable than other input factors and it is a universal element common to all industries, processes and productive activities.
- That this definition possesses a deep-rooted interest in labour savings, because such savings can have significant impact on costs, prices, profits and can even raise the standard of living of the common people.

Determinants of Productivity

As pointed out earlier, there are several factors, which are sometimes not accounted for at the time of calculating productivity index and as such in present day methods of production, making use of manpower and machines, it cannot be precisely pinpointed as to which factor has affected the productivity. Therefore, we shall try to discuss certain important factors, which directly affect productivity.

Technological Factors: The economic sectors based on capital goods industries have comparatively better productivity on account of technological progress. In such industries, long-term gains are achieved mainly due to proper and effective application of scientific and technical progress. In this regard, the most important factors are application of mechanical power, innovations and improvements in equipments, better and efficient integration of plant, machinery and process, greater degree of specialization of work and output, and more effective and efficient co-ordination and integration of productive process and operations.

Organizational Factors: It is a very important fact that efficient organizations have significantly contributed towards recent improvements in industrial productivity. With the increasing complexity of the productive system, the organizational factors have a very dominating effect. For increasing productivity, the management must possess a high degree of organizational capacity, capability, imagination, far-sightedness, judgment and willingness to bear the risks.

Financial Factors: It is a well-established fact that with abundance of capital and easy borrowing facilities, the industry has better opportunities to adopt modern technological improvements and innovations as compared to those units which face financial problems. The modernization has definitely helped in increasing the overall productivity. The move for modernization has made the greatest progress where capital is comparatively abundant and easily available.

Efficiency of Labour: A worker, being the only active factor (input) of production, plays the most important role in the production and distribution of goods and services and thus significantly contributes in raising industrial productivity. Further, productivity of labour is related directly to the ability of worker, willingness of worker and the environment in which he has to work.

The above factors are further influenced by worker's inherent and acquired skill, general training, experience, aptitude, capacity, intelligence and outlook.

Natural Factors: The geographical, climatic and physical factors have a considerable influence on industrial productivity. However, the relative importance of natural factors varies according to the nature and character of the industry and the type of output also depends upon the extent to which above natural factors can be controlled or modified.

Sociological Factors: The social values and the general attitude of the community as a whole, accepted for a particular job or industry serve as a guide to the habits, behaviour, reaction and approach of the people and significantly affect their productivity. For example, the caste system in India is highly unsuitable in modern industrial era. These social institutions in our country have affected the industries in an adverse way as well as economic productivity.

Government Policies: The Government has a special responsibility of creating and maintaining favourable atmosphere for rapid industrialization and improved productivity. As a matter of fact, the higher rates of taxation on industries tend to discourage the entrepreneurs and in turn adversely affect industrial productivity. Therefore, a favourable industrial policy of Government acts as a catalyst to improve the industrial productivity.

TERTIARY SECTOR—SERVICE

The service industry forms the backbone of social and economic development of a region. It has emerged as the largest and fastest-growing sectors in the world economy, making higher contributions to the global output and employment. Its growth rate has been higher than that of agriculture and manufacturing sectors. It is a large and most dynamic part of the Indian economy both in terms of employment potential and contribution to national income. It covers a wide range of activities, such as trading, storage, insurance, transportation, communication, financial, real estate and business services, other services (consisting various types of professional services such as services of lawyers, teachers, etc.) as well as community, social and personal services. In India, services sector, in 2019, contributed as much as 54.40 per cent in the national income.

Services hold immense potential to accelerate the growth of an economy and promote general well-being of the people. They offer innumerable business opportunities to the investors. They have the capacity to generate substantial employment opportunities in the economy as well as increase its per capita income. Without them, Indian economy would not have acquired a strong and dominating place on the world platform. Thus, service sector is considered to be an integral part of the economy and includes various sub-sectors spread all across the country.

Services can be divided into two parts:
- Productive Services
- Consumer Services

Productive Services: Productive services include all those services and operations through which productivity of producing sectors in terms of flow of final goods and services increases in the economy. The transport of the raw materials during production, the transport of the finished product to the market and finally the advertisement of the product to push its sales, can be called '*productive services*'. So services can be called '*productive*', when they help in the process of production and distribution and thereby add to the value of goods.

Consumer Services: Consumer services are those services which directly satisfy human wants and once consumed, their utility is over. These are the services like transport of passengers as well as health services or education that we buy or consume directly just like we consume a product.

Services can also be categorised into:
- Social services which include education, health, sanitation and other community services, etc.
- Economic services which include trade, transport, communication, banking, insurance, etc.

Without services, we cannot even dream of the existence of a modern civilized world. The standard of living among people is high only when they enjoy all such personal and public services. Service sector has become a synonym for developed countries. Such services are rarely available among backward countries.

Role of Tertiary Sector—Service in the Development of an Economy

Supplement to Primary/Agriculture Sector : Agriculture is the backbone of Indian economy and despite concerted industrialization in last few decades, agriculture occupies a place of pride. Service sector plays a significant role in the growth and development of agriculture sector as it provides good transportation system for the supply of agricultural produce to different parts of the country. Indian agriculture largely depends on monsoon for irrigation that is not sufficient and certain. Development of additional irrigation facilities are required for increasing the productivity of agriculture. Provision of irrigation facilities, warehouses, banks, agricultural insurance is also a part of service sector.

Supplement to Secondary/Industrial Sector: Development of industrial sector is highly dependent on the availability of various services that constitute transportation and communication system, energy and power, banking and insurance facilities, marketing facilities, skilled manpower, management, etc. Without the proper arrangement of these facilities, full industrial development of the economy cannot be imagined.

Improvement in Efficiency of Workforce: Human factor is an important aspect in any economy. Involvement of human factor in the productive process construct the workforce. Efficient workforce is encouraged in any productive process. There are some factors that can improve the efficiency of workforce, *i.e.,* education, health and environment. It is the responsibility of state to provide these services to its masses. Thus, service sector contributes in the development of efficiency of workforce and indirectly in the development of the economy by providing high standard of living to the people through well developed social infrastructure.

Support to Foreign Trade: A developing economy like India is required, for its development, to encourage its foreign trade. Transportation and communication services are the inseparable part of the foreign trade. A well developed transport and communication system is required for improving the position of foreign trade. Services like business consultancy, tourism, transportation, medicare, etc., also act as direct foreign exchange earners for the country.

Advancement of Rural Areas: An economy like ours cannot progress by ignoring the status of rural economy. India is a country of villages and it is very unfortunate to say that our villages, except a few, are in a backward state due to lack of facilities like transport, communication, electrification, education, water, sanitation, etc. Advancement of rural areas can be possible only by providing a good system of transport and communication, electrification in gloomy areas, spread of education among people, facilities of water and sanitation in such areas.

Importance of Service Sector

Natinal Income: The service sector in India has emerged as an important sector in terms of its contribution to the national income. According to the Economic Survey, the share of the service sector in India's GDP increased from 33.3 per cent in 1950-01 to 54.3 percent of the Indian GDP in 2018-19. Currently, this sector is the backbone of the Indian economy. The service sector has become the largest contributor to India's GDP because:

- The development of basic services such as educational institutions, hospitals, communication services, etc.
- The development of primary and secondary sectors have resulted in the rise of several services which are required for the smooth functioning of these sectors such as banking, transportation and insurance.
- Services such as software and telecom were big ticket items which gave India a brand image in services.

Employment: Service sector is growing at a rapid rate. In 2018, 43.86 per cent of the workforce in India was employed in agriculture sector, while the other half was almost evenly distributed among the two other sectors, industry and services. While the share of Indians working in agriculture is declining, it is still the main sector of employment. In 2018, 31.45 per cent of India's employed population is working in the services sector.

Regional Development: Balanced growth is necessary for the harmonious development of a federal state such as India. India, however presents a picture of extreme regional variations. The factors in the way of rapid development of a region are: the geographical isolation, lack of facilities like transport, labour, technology, etc. Thus, a step for promoting the availability of these services in any undeveloped region, is highly needed for the balanced regional growth.

Inter-relationship of Primary, Secondary and Tertiary Sectors

Primary, secondary and tertiary sectors also depend upon each other. Primary sector supplies raw materials to secondary sector and on the other hand receives tools and equipments from it. Tertiary sector also depends on primary sectors for the food supplies. In turn, it supplies its services to both the sectors.

The following *Table 6.3* shows sector-wise composition of India's national income.

Table 6.3 : Composition of National Income (*At Current Prices*) In per cent

Sector	1950-51	1960-61	1970-71	1980-81	1990-91	2000-01	2010-11	2016-17	2018-19
Primary	53.1	48.7	42.3	36.1	29.6	22.3	14.5	15.2	17
Secondary	16.6	20.5	24.0	25.9	27.7	27.3	27.8	31.2	29.6
Tertiary	30.3	30.8	33.8	38.0	42.7	50.4	57.7	53.6	54.3

It shows the size and magnitude of our enlarging economy.

The balanced growth of the economy needs that all the sectors of the economy should have proper and balanced development. The development of primary sector provides sound base for the development of secondary and tertiary sectors. In the same way, the development of secondary sector provides necessary machines, tools and equipments for improving the productivity of primary sector. Tertiary sector grows automatically with the development of primary and secondary sectors.

All these sectors contribute to the economic development. Initially, the contribution of primary sector was more than the contribution of secondary and tertiary sectors. This is the case of underdeveloped economies. Later on, with the advancement of the economy, the share of secondary and tertiary sector grows. It enlarges the economy and increases its magnitude.

INTER-RELATION BETWEEN SECTORS–PRIMARY, SECONDARY AND TERTIARY

Contribution of Agriculture to Industry

The industry has to depend upon agriculture in the following respects:

Provide Raw Materials: Agriculture provides basic raw materials to some of the important agro-based industries like cotton, jute, sugarcane, oilseeds, etc. Inadequate supply of raw materials would mean stunted growth of these industries.

Supplies Food: Agriculture plays the most important role of supplying food for the industrial workers too.

Provider of Savings and Foreign Exchange: In the initial stages of industrialization, the capital (national or foreign) for investment comes only from agricultural sector (primary sector) of the economy in the form of savings. It may also be earned through export of agricultural produce and may be utilized for importing machinery, spare parts and raw materials.

Provides Market: Agricultural sector provides a good market for industrial goods—both consumable and capital. It is termed as market contribution of agriculture.

Source of Labour : Another important factor-contribution of Indian agriculture towards industrialization is the supply of labour force. Agriculture is a source of labour (manpower) for the industries, because when agricultural productivity increases, the people attached to agriculture are released without disrupting the food supplies.

Contribution of Industry to Agriculture

Improves Agricultural Productivity: Industry helps to improve agricultural productivity by way of providing many inputs like chemical fertilizers, pump sets, tractors, electric power and other implements. For example, agricultural output (particularly the wheat crop) increased to a large extent after the adoption of improved methods of cultivation during 1960s. This phase is called as the Green Revolution in Indian agriculture.

It is estimated that for every one per cent hike in agricultural growth, industrial growth increases by about a third of one per cent that year as well as the next.

Over the last six decades, these linkages have got further strengthened with agriculture's dependence on industry increasing at a faster rate than the dependence of industry on agriculture, reflecting the fast-moving modernization of the agricultural sector.

Creation of Infrastructure: The infrastructure created for agriculture in the form of irrigation projects, connecting roads, transportation vehicles, etc., would not have been possible, if the industrial sector would not have produced cement, motor trucks, etc. It induces the agricultural sector to produce more for the market and thus, marketable surplus of food crops may increase. Distant markets become easily accessible.

Opens New and Additional Avenues of Employment: Industry opens up new and additional avenues of employment, in which most of the surplus people from agricultural sector get absorbed and their overall personal economies improve. Expansion of various small, medium and large-scale industries, cottage industries, etc., create enough employment and income opportunities among the rural people of India.

Rise in the Income of People: When agricultural productivity improves with the help of industrialization, the level of income of the people attached to agriculture also rises. These people tend to spend on various items other than food. All these items for the agricultural people are provided by industry only.

Demand Linkages: There are strong demand linkages between the two sectors. The impact of urban income and industrialization on the demand for food and agricultural raw materials is generally recognised.

Equally significant is the impact of rural income on industrial consumption goods, *i.e.*, clothing, footwear, sugar, edible oils, TV sets, washing machines, refrigerators, motor-bikes, etc. A recent study concludes: "*Rural bazaar outbuys urban market.*"

Thus, we find that agricultural sector provides a foundation for the industries and subsequently the industries help in improving the productivity and economy of the agricultural sector. Therefore, it is evident that the progress of industry and agriculture is possible only when these two sectors grow simultaneously, because they supplement each other's needs.

Contribution of Service to Industry

Industries and Services have acted as twin engines propelling overall growth in an economy. They are attracting large inflow of capital and foreign investments into the country from all over the world. They play a vital role in accelerating socio-economic development of a nation, thereby providing several categories of goods and services (both tangible and intangible) and catering to the diverse needs of the masses. These sectors are the largest generator of employment opportunities in the country and a facilitator of trade and commerce with other countries.

Service sector has always been an attractive investment option for the corporate world. It has facilitated the creation of several infrastructural facilities in the country as well as enhanced the productivity of various industries through providing various services like business consultancy, transportation, banking services, insurance and other utility services, etc.

Contribution of Service to Agriculture

India is a country of villages and about 50 per cent of the villages have very poor socio-economic conditions. Since the dawn of independence, concerted efforts have been made to ameliorate the living standard of rural masses and improving agricultural productivity in the rural areas.

The era of economic liberalisation has ushered in a rapid change in the service industry. As a result, over the years, India has been witnessing a transition from agriculture-based economy to a knowledge-based economy. The knowledge-based economy creates, disseminates, and uses knowledge to enhance its growth and development.

Services, being one of the largest industry in terms of gross revenue and foreign exchange earnings, stimulates growth and expansion in other economic sectors like agriculture, horticulture, poultry, handicrafts, etc., as well as gives momentum to growth of service exports. It is a major contributor to the national integration process of the country as well as preserver of natural and cultural environments.

So, services as an integrated concept of growth and poverty elimination contributes to socio-economic development through providing basic facilities in the rural areas *e.g.,* education, health facilities, agriculture extension services, etc. It also contributes by providing banking and other financial services and internal trade facilities for agricultural sector.

Contribution of Service to Society

Service not only helps in economic upliftment of the society, but also promote political and social well-being among the masses. The service industry comprising of information technology (IT), education, health, media, tourism, etc., helps to shape the people's opinion about various national and international issues as well as increase their awareness by giving them participative role in formulation of plans. In other words, a country cannot achieve a higher growth rate without a larger proportion of services in Gross Domestic Product (GDP). Accordingly, the concerned authorities have been making all efforts to strengthen the pace of development of the sector in a sustainable manner.

SECTORS ACCORDING TO TYPES OF ECONOMY (HABITATION)

Rural and Urban Sectors

We have already seen that the Indian economy has a large rural sector and a relatively small urban sector accounting just 31·2 per cent approx imately of total population. One important characteristic of a developing economy is that the rural sector gradually becomes smaller as the urban sector grows over time. The rural sector today includes about 68·8 per cent of the entire population of India.

The rural sector plays a vital role because it provides the basic raw materials to the main industries. Apart from food, the rural sector provides the economy with a large quantity of non-foodgrain agricultural output. For example, Cotton, Jute, Oil seeds, etc. These are the basic raw materials for some of our big Industries. On a second note, one of the biggest contributions of rural sector is that, it provides other economic supports like food supplies and demand support to urban sector without which the urban sector might be in a stagnant state.

Agriculture in India is still based on traditional methods of production in most of the areas. The systems of land tenure are also oppressive in the most parts of the country. Land reforms and modernization of methods of production alone can mitigate the gross inequality and social injustice that hampers production in the rural sector, and thereby slows down India's economic development.

Main features of the rural sector

Dependence on Agricultural Activities: More than 50 per cent of the rural people are engaged in agricultural activities. So, most of the rural people are farmers or agricultural labourers.

Greater Dependence on Other Primary Activities: The primary activities imply the activities relating to agriculture, forestry, and fisheries. In the rural sector, most of the people earn their livelihood by doing those primary activities.

Greater Portion of Rural Land Areas are Used for Agricultural Activities : In the rural sector, maximum portion of the available land areas is used for cultivation works, pisciculture, horticulture, sericulture, etc.

Low Density of Population: The number of people living per square kilometer of any region is called the density of population of that region. The population density of the rural sector remains below the urban sector.

Dominance of Agricultural Income in Total Income: In the rural sector, some people are also engaged in small business, cottage industries, money-lending activities, etc. But the share of agricultural income becomes maximum in the total rural income (arising out of all such activities).

Existence of Seasonal Unemployment: In the absence of proper irrigational facilities and subsidiary employment opportunities in rural areas, multiple cropping (*i.e.*, production of more than one crop on any farm during any year) is not possible in most of the rural areas of India. Thus, a large number of cultivators or agricultural workers remain idle for about 4 to 6 months in any year. This feature is known as seasonal unemployment.

Existence of Disguised Unemployment: The agricultural workers or the members of any farmer's family, whose contributions towards agricultural output are almost nil, are called disguisedly unemployed. Thus, even if these people are removed from cultivation work, total agricultural output would remain unchanged. This feature is observed because of excessive pressure of population in rural areas. At present, 68.8 per cent of the Indian population live in rural areas.

Under-developed Infrastructure Facilities: The economic infrastructure of any sector consists of transport and communications, electricity, irrigational facilities, etc. On the other hand, the social infrastructure of any sector consists of primary health and educational facilities, supply of safe drinking water, sanitation facilities, etc. However, such social and economic infrastructure are under-developed in most of the rural areas of India.

Main Features of the Urban sector

Greater Dependence on Non-agricultural Activities: The maximum portion of the urban population live by doing non-agricultural activities. In fact most of the urban people are engaged in industrial and service activities. Hence, we find greater number of industrial workers, managers, teachers, doctors, lawyers, businessmen and traders in the urban areas of India.

Greater Dependence on Secondary and Tertiary Activities: The secondary activities consist of manufacturing activities (in the small, medium and large-scale industries), construction works such as the construction of roads, bridges, house buildings, factory sheds, etc. On the other hand, the tertiary activities consist of different service activities like, banking and insurance service, medical service, education service, hotel and tourism service, trading and commercial service, etc. Most of the urban people earn their livelihood from such service activities.

Contribution of Non-agricultural Income to Total Income: Since most of the urban population are engaged in non-agricultural activities, so the share of non-agricultural income to total urban income becomes maximum.

Urban Land Areas are Used for Industrial and Service Activities: As opposed to the rural sector, maximum portion of urban land areas are used for building factory sheds, housing complex, super markets, educational institutions, hospitals, police stations, banks, etc.

Higher Density of Population: The density of urban population remains higher than the rural areas. For example, the population density of Delhi was 11,297 people per square kilometer in 2011. It is important to note that maximum portion of the population of Delhi live in urban areas. On the other hand, the population density of Arunachal Pradesh (where maximum portion of population live in rural areas) was only 17 people per square kilometer.

Greater Availability of Social and Economic Infrastructural Facilities: The transport and communication network, electricity, education and health facilities, drinking water and sanitation facilities, etc., are available more in the urban areas compared to those in rural areas of India. So, rural people often come to the urban areas for having better health and educational facilities.

Higher Incidence of Environmental Pollution: Industrial emissions, emissions from motor vehicles, etc., cause air and water pollution in the urban areas. Various types of industrial wastes and improperly treated sewage cause water pollution in the urban areas. Various forms of pollutants raise the level of carbon monoxide, sulphur dioxide, hydrocarbons and nitrogen compounds in the air. Such air pollution poses serious health hazards in the urban areas.

Existence of Educated and Industrial Unemployment: In urban areas due to inadequate job opportunities and slow growth of industries, the problem of educated and industrial unemployment is constantly increasing.

LESSON AT A GLANCE

Main Sectors or Regions of the Indian Economy:

Sectors According to Productive Activity: (i) Agriculture or primary sector; (ii) Industry or secondary sector; (iii) Service or tertiary sector.

Sectors According to Types of Economy: (i) Rural sector; (ii) Urban sector.

Sectors According to Ownership of Enterprises: (i) Public sector; (ii) Private sector.

Primary Sector—Agriculture: It is the main source of livelihood of approximately 50 per cent of the country's population.

Role of Primary Sector—Agriculture in the Development of an Economy:

(i) Contribution to national income; (ii) Employment; (iii) Food and fodder; (iv) Foreign trade; (v) Industrial development; (vi) International ranking; (vii) Role in national economy; (viii) Contribution to domestic trade; (ix) Fulcrum of transport industry.

Reasons of Low Productivity in Agriculture: *(i) Uncertain rainfall; (ii) Inadequate irrigation facilities; (iii) Natural inclemencies; (iv) Old methods and techniques; (v) Improper use of inputs; (vi) Uneconomic agricultural holdings; (vii) Conservative and superstitious nature of farmers; (viii) Lack of financial facilities; (ix) Unsatisfactory tenancy legislations; (x) Excessive Population; (xi) Unsatisfactory storage and marketing facilities; (xii) Inadequate agricultural research*

Secondary Sector–Industry: It is the main source of growth in modern economic infrastructure.

Role of Secondary Sector—Industry in the Development of an Economy: *(i) Balanced and rapid development; (ii) Increase in national and per capita Incomes; (iii) Exploitation of natural resources; (iv) Increase in export earnings; (v) Industrialization and agricultural development; (vi) Employment for surplus labour; (vii) Security considerations; (viii) Change in outlook; (ix) Modernisation.*

Causes of Unbalanced Industrialization and Regional Disparities

(i) Historical factors; (ii) Natural factors; (iii) Planning process; (iv) Statutory regulations and controls; (v) common development pattern; (vi) Urbanization; (vii) Favourable climatic and natural conditions; (viii) Availability of transport facilities; (ix) Availability of cheap labour.

Determinants of Productivity: (i) Technological factors; (ii) Organizational factors; (iii).Financial factors; (iv) Efficiency of labour; (v) Natural factors; (vi) Sociological factors; (vii) Government policies.

Tertiary Sector Service: It can be divided into two parts: (i) Productive services; (ii) Consumer services.

It can also be divided into: (i) Social services ; (ii) Economic services.

Role of Tertiary Sector—Service in the Development of an Economy:
(i) Supplement to primary/agriculture sector; (ii) Supplement to secondary/ industrial sector; (iii) Improvement in efficiency of workforce; (iv) Support to foreign Trade; (v) Balanced regional growth; (vi) Advancement of rural area.

Contribution of Agriculture to Industry: (i) Provide raw materials; (ii) Supplies food; (iii) Provider of savings and foreign exchange; (iv) Provides market; (v) Source of labour.

Contribution of Industry to Agriculture: (i) Improves agricultural productivity; (ii) Creation of infrastructure; (iii) Opens new and additional avenues of employment; (iv) Rise in the income of people; (v) Demand linkages.

Rural and Urban Sectors: The rural sector today includes about 68.8 per cent of entire population. however, the size of urban sector is increasing. The rural sector plays a vital role because it provides the basic raw materials to the main industries.

Main Features of the Rural Sector: (i) Dependence on agricultural activities; (ii) Greater dependence on other primary activities; (iii) Greater portion of rural land areas are used for agricultural activities; (iv) Low density of population; (v) Dominance of agricultural income in total income; (vi) Existence of seasonal unemployment; (vii) Existence of disguised unemployment; (viii) Under-developed infrastructure facilities.

Main Features of the Urban Sector: (i) Greater dependence on non-agricultural activities; (ii) Greater dependence on secondary and tertiary activities; (iii) Contribution of non-agricultural income to total income; (iv) Urban land areas are used for industrial and service activities; (v) Higher density of population; (vi) Greater availability of social and economic infrastructural facilities ; (vii) Higher incidence of environmental pollution; (viii) Existence of educated and Industrial unemployment.

PROJECT WORK

Take a table of food grain production in India from any other secondary source such as internet. Interpret the changes in the production over a given period of time.
  (i) Make a deep study of the Table no. 6·1 given in this book showing food production in India during last few years (Particularly in respect of important food grains like wheat and rice).
  (ii) Note whether the production is increasing or decreasing or changing.
  (iii) Find out the causes for variations in the production.
  (iv) Analyse the effects of changes in productivity on the Indian Economy.
  (v) Suggest the measures which can be taken either by the individuals responsible for it or by modifying policies of the Government for improving the productivity in coming years.

QUESTIONS

A. Short Answer Questions
1. Classify the sectors of Indian economy according to ownership.
2. Classify the sectors of Indian economy according to type of economy.

3. What do you mean by industrialization?
4. Why is the development of Secondary and Tertiary sectors important for India?
5. How is agriculture and industries complementary to each other?
6. Briefly mention the importance of agriculture in the Indian economy.
7. What do you mean by service sector?
8. How the different sectors of our economy are complementary to each other?
9. Differentiate between 'primary', 'secondary' and 'tertiary' sectors of the economy.
10. Mention the long-term trend in the shares of secondary and tertiary sectors in domestic product and the working population of India.
11. What do you think are the main causes behind low industrial productivity?

B. Long Answer Questions

1. Explain the importance of agriculture in Indian economy.
2. Discuss the important features of agriculture in India.
3. Describe the three sectors of the Indian economy.
4. Discuss the inter-relationship of three sectors of an Indian economy.
5. Discuss briefly:
   (i) Contribution of agriculture to industry.
   (ii) Contribution of industry to agriculture.
6. Discuss the inter-relationship of primary, secondary and tertiary sector.
7. Give a brief classification of economic sector according to type of activities.
8. Discuss the relative significance of rural and urban sectors in the economic development of Indian Economy.

07 Public and Private Sectors in Indian Economy

SECTORS ACCORDING TO OWNERSHIP OF ENTERPRISES

Indian Economy is a mixed economy. Public sector and private sector both have co-existence in Indian economy. Indian economy divides productive enterprises into public and private sector institutions on the basis of their ownership. The public sector however, worked as the leading sector and has achieved much in the key areas of the economy.

At the time of independence, the activities of public sector were confined to irrigation, power, railways, ports, communication, etc. Since independence, the activities of public sector expanded in a considerable way. But simultaneously, it was assured by Industrial Policy Resolution of 1948 and 1956 that private sector will also be allowed to grow and therefore, the industries were divided into different categories and their fields were also specified. Some of the fields were reserved for public sector and some for private sector and remaining ones were left for both the sectors.

OVERVIEW

In a country having a mixed economy, like that of ours, private sector, public sector and the joint sector each play a specific and significant role.

The public sector units are generally in priority sectors like basic industries and infrastructures. Both of these are essential for bringing about further industrialization and socio-economic developments. Moreover, the public sector units also help to maintain the price stability in the market and also exercise a check on concentration of economic powers.

In our country, the entire agriculture, retail trade and the consumer sector belong to private sector, inspite of these being in either large-scale, small-scale or cottage industry sector. The private sector introduces new commodities, new equipments, new techniques and new innovations. In fact, the private sector is the main moving force behind further industrialization of a nation.

PUBLIC SECTOR ENTERPRISES

Public sector enterprises are called by variety of names such as 'Public sector undertaking', 'Nationalized industries', 'Sector enterprises', 'Government concerns', etc. For Public enterprises, the annual report regarding the working of public enterprises, published by the Bureau of Public Enterprises, uses the term 'Industrial and Commercial Undertaking of the Central Government'.

PUBLIC SECTOR IN INDIA

Public sector includes all those economic organizations which are engaged in production and distribution of goods or services, and are entirely State or government owned and controlled either wholly or substantially. According to Industrial Policy Resolution, 1956, the following industries were under the category of public sector.

1. Arms and ammunition, 2. Atomic energy, 3. Iron and steel, 4. Heavy casting, 5. Heavy plant and machinery, 6. Heavy electrical industries, 7. Coal and Lignite, 8. Mineral oils, 9. Mining of iron ore, manganese ore, chrome, gypsum, sulphur, gold and diamond, 10. Mining and processing of copper, lead, zinc and tin, 11. Aircraft, 12. Air transport, 13. Rail transport, 14. Ship building, 15. Telephones and telephone cables, 16. Telegraph and wireless apparatus, and 17. Generation and distribution of electricity.

Now the public enterprises with exclusive monopoly in economic areas have been severely curtailed and have been restricted to very few areas like railway, atomic energy and minerals and metals, etc.

Role of the Public Sector in India

The public sector in India has been playing an important role in shaping the basic structure of the economy. The following are some of the positive roles played by this sector during the plan periods in our economy:

Public Sector and Income: The share of public sector in Gross Domestic Product (GDP) at current prices has increased from 7.2 per cent in 2019–20 to 24 per cent in 1991. This is largely due to a rapid expansion in the public sector. In 2005-06, the share of the public sector in Gross Domestic Product (GDP) was about 1 to 2 per cent.

Public Sector and Capital Formation: Public sector investments in establishing large-scale and medium-scale industries, building roads, power projects, dams, railway tracks, etc., lead to capital formation. The share of the public sector in gross domestic capital formation (expressed as a per cent of GDP) has also increased from 3.5 per cent during the First Plan (1951–56) to about 11 per cent during Sixth Plan (1980–85). During Tenth Plan this share was 22.2 per cent.

Public Sector and Employment: Public sector employment in India are of two categories:

- Public sector employment in Government administration, defence and other Government services.
- Employment in public sector enterprises run by the Union Government, State Governments and local bodies.

PEs have provided direct employment to about 15.35 million people as on 31st March, 2009. The maximum extent of employment has been generated in the transport, storage and communication sectors. However, the Economic Survey (2011–12) report of the Government of India shows that public sector employment increased by 0.25 per cent in 2010 over 2009. As per economic survey (2019-20), the share of regular wage salaried employees has increased by 5 percentage points from 1870 in 2011-12 to 23 percentage in 2017-18.

Public Sector and Infrastructure: Public sector investment in the infrastructure sector like power, transport and communication, heavy industries, irrigation, education and technical training, etc., has paved the way for agricultural and industrial development of the country. Private sector investments also depend upon such infrastructural facilities developed by the public sector of the country.

Strong Industrial Base: The growth of the public sector in the fields of iron and steel, coal, heavy engineering, heavy electrical machinery, petroleum and natural gas, fertilizers, etc., has also created a strong industrial base for further industrialization.

Export Promotion: PEs also contributed a great deal towards foreign exchange earnings of the country through export promotion. Some PSUs have also shown creditable records in achieving import substitution and thereby saved the precious foreign exchange of the country.

Contribution to the Central Exchequer: The PEs have also been contributing a good amount of resources to the central exchequer in the form of dividends, excise duty, customs duty, corporate taxes, etc. The share of public sector was ₹ 3.5 trillion in 2017-18.

Checking Concentration of Income and Wealth: Expansion of PEs in India has successfully helped in checking the concentration of economic power into the hands of a few persons and it has also been able to redress the problem of income inequalities to some extent by checking monopolistic and restrictive trade practices which might be adopted by private entrepreneurs.

Removal of Regional Disparities: From the very beginning, industrial development in India has been relatively higher in certain big port-cities like Mumbai, Kolkata and Chennai. Now, in order to remove regional disparities, the public sector has tried to disperse the industrial units towards the backward regions of India. Hence, at present, we observe the Orissa, formerly an industrially backward region, has developed in respect of industrial growth.

Inspite of the important role played by the PEs in India, their performance is not noteworthy. Different economists have pointed out several loopholes in their performance pattern.

Reasons for Poor Performance of the Public Sector

Low Return on Capital: The performance of some public enterprises can be represented with the notion of profitability (defined as net profit after tax as a per centage of total capital employed). Though this profitability increased gradually during the 1980s, yet if the petroleum and power sectors are excluded, this becomes negative for most of the other central sector public enterprises.

In India, 70 PSU's were in loss on 31st March 2019 with their total stress amounting to over ₹ 31,000 crores collectively.

Cost Over-run: Non-completion of many public sector projects within the stipulated time period led to an unnecessary increase in the cost of construction. Improper project planning seems to be responsible for such delay and cost over-run. Thus, it puts an additional burden on the scarce resources of our country.

High Capital-output Ratio: The amount of capital invested per unit of value added is relatively higher in public sector enterprises. This type of over-capitalization happened due to unnecessary expenditure during construction work, surplus machine capacity, tied-up aid resulting in compulsion to purchase imported machinery and equipment, expensive turn-key contracts, etc.

Improper Price-Policy: Most of the public sector enterprises do not follow a rational price-policy. In most of these enterprises, prices of their products or services are kept at a low level, keeping in mind the needs and purchasing power of the general people. However, the quality of some of these public utility goods supplied by the public sector, seems to be very poor. The prices charged for supplying such products or services also do not cover the average cost of production which results in the loss on sales.

Excessive Man-power: Most of the public sector enterprises are also burdened with excessive man-power. The number of employees remains far above their actual requirements. Hence, a huge sum of money is required for the payment of their wages and salaries.

Under-utilization of Capacity: Some public sector enterprises also do not utilize the full capacity of their plants and machinery. Such under-utilization of capacity leads to an increase in the average cost of production in these enterprises. As the prices of products and services, in most cases, do not cover the rising average cost of production, these units become sick after some time.

Absence of Proper Work Culture: Indiscipline and lack of responsibility among the workers, frequent labour unrest and bad relationships between the management and the workers also paralyze many public sector enterprises.

Improper Management: Efficient management, alongwith proper delegation of authority from the top level of management to the lower levels, are supposed to be the precondition for smooth functioning of an enterprise. Unfortunately, political interference, lack of sufficient autonomy to the management and bureaucratic entanglements degrade the managerial efficiency in public sector enterprises.

Lack of Functional Autonomy: Most of the public sector enterprises are subject to excessive control, exercised by the Ministry of Finance and the Ministry-in-charge over these public sector enterprises. Thus, development plans of such public sector enterprises are constrained by these rigid control mechanisms. So, the poor performance of public sector enterprises is often ascribed to lack of functional autonomy to the management.

Inappropriate Technique of Production: Inappropriate techniques of production are also an important explanation for inefficient operations in many public sector enterprises. For example, in the case of the steel industry, our blast furnace productivity is only around 45 per cent of that of Japan. Our public sector enterprises could not develop such blast furnaces which could function well even with the quality of coal (*i.e.,* high ash content), available in India.

Consequences of Poor Performance

In view of this declining popularity of public sector enterprises, we can point out some of its negative consequences:

Inefficient Industrial Structure: The poor performance of many public sector enterprises have led to a growing number of sick units. Again, poor performance of these units, particularly in the core sector, implies industrial retrogression because bad performance in this sector (*e.g.,* iron and steel, coal, heavy engineering, etc.) would mean lesser availability of capital goods for the growth of other industries. Thus, as a whole, our industrial structure has become inefficient.

Growing Burden on Government Exchequer: Huge subsidies or state support was given to most of the economically unviable public sector units just to keep them alive. This led to a growing burden on the Government exchequer in the form of fiscal deficit.

Poor Competitive Strength: In most of the public sector enterprises, the quality of output was very poor and hence these units could not gain sufficient competitive strength, both in the domestic and in the international markets. Hence, they fell into loss due to insufficient demand for their products.

Conclusion

Thus, the role of public sector in promoting economic development cannot be neglected. The Prime Minister Late. Mrs. Indira Gandhi advocated the public sector: to gain control of the commanding heights of the economy; and to provide commercial surpluses with which to finance further economic development.

PRIVATE SECTOR ENTERPRISES

Private sector includes agriculture and all those institutions which are engaged in the production and distribution of goods or services and are entirely in private hands. These enterprises are run in private interest, but are subject to social control through Government regulations and directions under different provisions of law. It is an important sector of Indian economy. It includes individual owners, *i.e.,* cultivators and rich farmers employing hired labour; firms of all types and sizes, *i.e.,* proprietorships, partnerships, joint-stock companies; cooperative enterprises; small-scale industries, medium sized industries and big industries, etc.

Private sector plays very significant role in the Indian economy. Its contribution is more than 60 per cent of the Gross National Product at factor cost. Private sector works under the control and direction of the Government.

Private Sector In India

Private sector or private enterprise refers to all types of individual or corporate enterprises, both domestic and foreign, engaged in different fields of productive activity. Private sector enterprises are characterized by ownership and management in private hands, personal initiative and profit motive.

In India, the distinction between the private sector and the public sector gained its importance particularly after the passing of Industrial Policy Resolutions in 1948 and 1956, making India a mixed economy. These industrial policy resolutions reserved certain industrial areas for public sector; and allowed certain existing industries both in the public and private sector but future development would be in the public sector alone and finally, reserved certain other areas exclusively for the private sector.

Role of the Private Sector in India

India, in her 'mixed economic' set-up, intended to combine the advantages of both the capitalistic and socialistic pattern of economic development. So, in the Industrial policy Statement of 1948 and 1956, emphasis was given to the development of both public and private sectors in India. Though the productive activities in the private sector are guided by profit motives, the Government of India has allocated a specific role to the private sector in agricultural and industrial development in India. In fact, the risk-taking and innovative capabilities of private entrepreneurs have been appreciated by the Government. The role of this sector in the economic development of India can be well understood, if we consider the following points :

Agricultural Development: Agriculture forms the principal economic activity in India because more than 60 per cent of the working population was engaged in this sector for their livelihood till some time ago. It not only consists of cultivation but also some allied activities like dairy, poultry and piggery development. The production decisions in this sector are undertaken by individuals (*viz.,* farmers) and private bodies. This sector not only supplies essential food grains to millions of the Indian people, but also produces some exportable surplus.

Industrial Development: The economic history of India shows that several industries like cotton and jute textiles, sugar, paper, iron and steel, etc., expanded in our country under the initiative of private entrepreneurs. For example, the credit for the production of steel in India goes to the pioneering spirit, enterprise and foresight of the late Shri

Jamshedji Tata. His dream took shape in 1907, when the Tata Iron & Steel Company (TISCO) was founded in Bihar.

After independence and during the plan periods, several private sector enterprises, producing a variety of industrial products, have come up.

Growth in Business and Trading Activities: Private businessmen also played an important role in fostering business and trading activities (both in the case of internal and external trade) in India. Economic progress of a country greatly depends on the expansion of such business and trading activities. For example, some traders may purchase food grains and create stocks of such food grains at the time of a bumper crop, and gradually release supplies from this stock during the year. They create '*time utility*' through such activities, because consumers get an uninterrupted supply of food grains both during the busy and lean seasons. Again, these traders create '*place utility*' when they collect goods from the production point and carry them to distant places for sale.

Growth in National Output, Saving and Capital Formation: The importance of the private sector in India can also be assessed in terms of its contribution to Gross Domestic Product (GDP), Gross Domestic Savings (GDS) and Gross Domestic Capital Formation (GDCF). The National Accounts Statistics, provided by the Central Statistical Organization (CSO), indicated that in 2005-06, the shares of the private sector in GDP, GDS and GDCF was about 76 per cent, 93 per cent and 70 per cent respectively.

Market Expansion: The consumption expenditure of the private sector on final goods (e.g., ready-made garments, tea, coffee, bread, bicycles, motor cars, etc.), also contributes to the expansion of markets for all such products within the economy. For example, the final consumption expenditure in India was ₹ 1,72,500 crores in 2005-06 and the share of the private sector in this expenditure was about 90 per cent.

Growth in Small-Scale and Cottage Industries: Different types of small-scale and cottage industries are run by private entrepreneurs in India. These units have also contributed substantially in terms of production of consumer goods, creation of employment opportunities, creation of exportable surplus, etc.

Employment: The private sector includes both organized and unorganized segments. The organized segment of the private sector comprises medium and large-scale industries, financial houses, etc. (these may be private limited companies). The unorganized segment of the private sector comprises small trading and business activities, agricultural activities, etc. Although the contribution of the private sector towards employment generation in the organized sector employment is less than that of the public sector, it becomes enormous when we consider the unorganized segment of the private sector. In fact, about 80 per cent of the working population of India are engaged in the private sector (in both the organized and unorganized segments) for their livelihood.

Other Contributions: Regional balanced development, helping mobilisation and optimum utilisation of available resources, development of entrepreneurial skills, etc. are other contributions of private sector.

CAUSES OF INDUSTRIAL SICKNESS IN THE PRIVATE SECTOR

The causes of industrial sickness can be divided into two broad categories; external or exogenous causes and internal or endogenous causes.

Exogenous Causes

Exogenous causes are those which are beyond the control of any industrial unit. Some of these exogenous causes resulting in industrial sickness are as follows:

Inelastic Supply of Raw Materials: Different industrial units often face the problem of inelastic supply of different raw materials. Hence, growth in industrial output is constrained by this supply condition. Further, if these raw materials are to be imported from abroad, problems may arise due to higher import and transport cost and other policy-induced restrictions.

Power Crisis: The energy crisis and inadequate supply of electric power also stand in the way of smooth operations of the industrial units.

Economic Depression: Indian industries also suffered from economic depression, particularly during 1965-75 and 1996-2009. This implies that demand for industrial products declined during the said period. Again, one of the most important sources of demand for industrial products is Indian agriculture. Hence, during the period of any crop failure (say, during droughts, floods, etc.), the agricultural sector is not able to create sufficient demand for industrial products (like tractors, power tillers, pump sets, etc.). Moreover during 1996-2009, the demand for industrial products also declined in the world market.

Government Policies: Different policies of the Government are also held responsible for creating industrial sickness in India. The tax policy, industrial licensing policy, export-import policy, etc., could not create sufficient competitive strength and efficiency among Indian industries. For example, some economists believe that the restrictive nature of industrial licensing policy, alongwith some bureaucratic tangles was one of the important factors inhibiting industrial growth.

Unfavourable Political Forces: Major changes in the political environment also creates a substantial impact upon the inflow of foreign capital or investment in the industrial sector. Lack of political will or unfavourable political attitudes also hindered the inflow of foreign capital to Indian industries.

Competition from public sector enterprises and global enterprises is another factor responsible for sickness of private sector industries.

Apart from these external forces, some internal or endogenous factors were also responsible for industrial retardation in India.

Endogenous causes

The internal or endogenous causes of industrial sickness mainly arise out of the weak organizational structure of industrial units. However, the major endogenous causes are as follow:

Weak Management: Lack of proper management in industrial units is one of the most important causes for industrial sickness. Again, improper co-ordination among different departments of the industrial unit, improper work culture, lack of motivation, etc., lead to poor organizational structure in any such industrial unit. Different incidents of industrial disputes (in the form of strikes and lock-outs) also arise because of the poor relationship between the workers and the management. Thus, such industrial disputes cause huge losses in man-days in industrial units (1 man-day = 8 working hours).

Financial Constraints: Under-utilization of production capacity in many industrial units also leads to higher average cost of production and a decline in profitability. Again, an improper fund management policy and inadequate credit facilities may also lead to such industrial sickness.

Lower Quality Products: Most of the Indian companies did not produce quality products. When such companies faced better competitive products, the demand for their products fell drastically leading to their loss.

Faulty Planning: Faulty planning with respect to the preparation of different industrial projects also leads to cost over-run and industrial sickness in many cases.

Performance of the Public and Private sectors: A Comparison

The organized sector in India consists of 293·77 thousand industrial establishments. Out of these, 172·34 thousand are public sector enterprises while 121·43 thousand are in private sector. Since 2004, an increase of 1·4 per cent has been recorded in the number of establishments in the organized sector. As on 31st March, 2010 the total employment in the organized sector was estimated to be 287·08 lakh while in 2009, it was 281.72 lakh. This means there has been an increase of 1·9per cent in employment. The public sector employs about 178·62 lakh persons in 2010 while in 2009 it was 177·95 lakh. The private sector employs 107·87 lakh persons in 2010 while in 2009 it was 102·91 lakh. The positive growth of employment was recorded in public sector and private sector showed an increasing trend.

Difference between Public and Private Sectors

From our previous discussion, we can now identify some basic differences between the private and public sectors in India. These are given ahead:

Difference between the Public and Private Sectors

Basis	Public Sector	Private sector
1. Ownership and management	Public sector enterprises are owned, controlled and managed by the Central or State Government authorities.	Private sector enterprises are owned, controlled and managed by the private persons/bodies.
2. Constituent parts	Public sector undertakings consist of: (a) Departmental Enterprises like Indian Railways, Posts & Telegraphs, etc. (b) Statutory Corporations like DVC, LIC, etc (c) Government companies such as BSNL, VSNL, SAIL, etc.	Private sector enterprises consist of: (a) Sole proprietorship business, (b) Partnership business, (c) Joint stock companies.

3. Goods and services supplied	(a) Goods and services required for social benefit such as primary health service, defence service, etc. (b) Goods and services required for building economic infrastructure such as railway transport, telecommunications, electricity generation and distribution, etc	(a) Different consumer goods such as bread, butter, cotton and non-cotton clothes, bicycles, TV, radio, etc. (b) Different capital items such as machines and machine tools. (c) Different services such as hotel and tourism, banking and insurance, etc.
4. Motive	Maximize social welfare.	Maximize private profits.
5. Economic decisions	Decisions regarding the production and allocation of factors of production in different product-lines are taken by the Government authorities	Decisions regarding the production and allocation of factors of production in different product-lines are taken by the private enterprises on the basis of price-movements.

LESSON AT A GLANCE

Public Sector: Public Sector refers to all those enterprises which are owned, controlled and managed, by various government authorities.

Role of the Public Sector in India: (i) Public sector and income; (ii) Public sector and capital formation; (iii) Public sector and employment; (iv) Public sector and infrastructure; (v) Strong industrial base; (vi) Export promotion; (vii) Contribution to the central exchequer; (viii) Checking concentration of income and wealth; and (ix) Removal of regional disparities.

Reasons for Poor Performance of the Public sector: (i) Low return on capital; (ii) Cost over-run; (iii) High capital-output ratio; (iv) Improper price-policy; (v) Excessive man-power; (vi) Under-utilization of capacity; (vii) Absence of proper work culture; (viii) Improper management; (ix) Lack of functional autonomy; and (x) Inappropriate technique of production.

Consequences of Poor Performance: (i) Inefficient industrial structure; (ii) Growing burden on government exchequer; and (iii) Poor competitive strength.

Private Sector: The Private Sector refers to all those enterprises which are owned, controlled and managed by the private bodies.

Role of the Private Sector in India: (i) Agricultural development; (ii) Industrial development; (iii) Growth in business and trading activities; (iv) Growth in national output, saving and capital formation; (v) Market expansion; (vi) Growth in small scale and cottage industries; and (vii) Employment.

Causes of Industrial Sickness in the Private Sector:

Exogenous causes: (i) Inelastic supply of raw materials; (ii) Power crisis; (iii) Economic depression; (iv) Government policies; and (v) Unfavourable political forces.

Endogenous causes: (i) Weak management; (ii) Financial constraints; (iii) Lower Quality Products; (iv) Faulty planning.

PROJECT WORK

Conduct a survey of a nearby industry in your region (*i.e.*, public sector undertaking or private sector or joint sector). Prepare a detailed note on its nature, production, number of employees, financial report of one year. On the basis of available data, classify which category it belongs to. Find out whether it is a risk unit and Government is planning for its disinvestment or decentralization or to operate under joint sector. Explain the reasons clearly for the same with justification whether new structure of the surveyed industrial unit will earn profit and improve the overall economy of the region or not.

Note: This project may be allotted to a group of students and the concerned teacher is requested to guide them from time to time in collection of data to avoid complication in preparing final results.

QUESTIONS

A. Short Answer Questions
1. Classify the sectors of Indian economy according to ownership.
2. Define public sector enterprises.
3. What are the reasons of poor performance of the public sector? Mention any two.
4. What are the causes of industrial sickness in the private sector? State any three.
5. State any three differences between the private and public sectors.
6. Name any three public sector enterprises in India.
7. How does public sector enterprises promote balanced regional development?
8. Name the different forms of organisations in which public and private sector enterprises exist.

B. Long Answer Questions
1. Discuss the role of public sector in India.
2. Discuss the performance of public sector in India. What are the reasons for poor performance of the public sector?
3. Differentiate between public sector and private sector in India.
4. Discuss the role of private sector in India.
5. Is there industrial sickness in private sector? What are the causes of industrial sickness?

08 Environment and Agriculture

ECOSYSTEM

The term ecosystem was proposed by **Tensely** (1953). An ecosystem is an ecological unit consisting of both biotic (living) and the abiotic (non-living) factors existing in the environment. These elements and the environment are inseparably inter-related and are interactive in their nature.

Odum has defined ecosystem as the basic fundamental unit of ecology which includes both the organisms and the non-living elements in an environment each influencing the properties of the other and each is necessary for the maintenance of life. **S. Mathavan** (1974) defined ecosystem as the sum total of living organisms, the environment and the process of interaction between various components of the system.

An ecosystem is any spatial or organizational unit which includes living organisms and non-living substances interacting to produce and exchange of materials between the living and non-living elements. The term ecosystem is more inclusive than the terms population and community and is somewhat more similar in scope to the terms environment and habitat. The ecosystem refers to the dynamic interaction of all the parts of the environment.

OVERVIEW

In India, the economic life and activities of majority of people revolve around agriculture sector. Agriculture is a traditional way of life apart from being an occupation. Agriculture has shaped the entire social and cultural structure of nation.

It is of great importance for us to be aware of its indispensability and the need for its proper management in the most sustained manner.

Due to the reckless exploitation of natural resources, the physical environment of the country has been totally degraded leading to an ecological imbalance. This ecological imbalance has resulted from land degradation and soil erosion, deforestation, desertification, faulty utilization of water, etc.

Environmental economics is primarily concerned with the impact of the economy on the environment, the implication of the environment to the economy, and the appropriate way of regulating economic activity, so that balance is achieved among environmental and other social goods.

The concept of ecosystem provides the central theoretical framework for ecology. Newer studies are quantifying different components of the ecosystem structure and function, so that independent relationships are more precisely understood. It is increasingly important for us to comprehend the dynamics of ecosystems, and their patterns of development, diversity and stability.

ECOLOGICAL IMBALANCE IN INDIA

For attaining economic development at a faster rate, India launched a number of economic plans since the adoption of new development strategy. These economic plans have resulted in substantial expansion of agricultural and industrial sector along with the expansion of other infrastructural facilities.

It is sad to point out that due to poor planning and mismanagement of the economy along with the reckless exploitation of natural resources, the physical environment of the country has been totally degraded leading to an ecological imbalance. Thus, ecological imbalance refers to total destabilisation of soil, water, climate biotic factors and abiotic factors. This ecological imbalance has resulted from land degradation and soil erosion, deforestation, faulty utilization of water and mineral resources, and infrastructural, industrial, domestic and atmospheric pollution. Let us now explain these factors in detail.

Degradation of Land and Soil Erosion: Ministry of Agriculture, Government of India has reported about the serious problem of land degradation and soil erosion in the form of following heads as shown in **Table 8.1** given below:

Table 8·1: Problem of Soil Erosion and Land Degradation

Heads/Particulars	Area (in million hectares)
1. Total geographical area	329
2. Area subject to water and wind problems (soil erosion)	150
3. Area degraded through special problems (ravines, salinity, water logging, etc.)	26
4. Annual average rate of encroachment of table lands by ravines (hectares)	8000
5. Average area annually subject to damages through shifting cultivation	1
6. Annual average area affected by floods	9
7. Annual average cropped area affected by floods	4
8. Total drought prone area	260

Source : Indian Agriculture in Brief.

It reveals from Table 8·1 that about 176 million hectares (*i.e.,* 53 per cent of the total land area) of land in India is facing the serious problem of land degradation. 150 million hectares is subjected to soil erosion through water and wind and the remaining 26 million hectares is subjected to other problem. Moreover, heavy population pressure has led to conversion of forest and permanent pastures into crop lands leading to indiscriminate grazing.

Deforestation: Large scale deforestation has been continuing since independence due to over-exploitation of forest resources. During the first two decades of planning India has lost about 2.4 million hectares of forest land out of which about 70 per cent of that area was lost to river valley projects, roads and communications and industries. Deforestation is still continuing at a rapid scale and the problem has reached to such a proportion that it has totally disturbed the ecological balance of the country.

Faulty Utilization of Water Resources: Being one of the wettest country in the world, India is still suffering from flood and droughts due to defective utilization of resources. Since independence, too much importance was laid on the development of big dams. But these have displaced crores of tribal people, drowned million hectares of rich forest areas to prevent and control floods and often create destructive flash flood to the downstream valley. Besides, these huge dams multi-purpose projects have created environment impact in the form of degradation of soil in the command areas due to continuous waterlogging and increasing soil salinity.

Environmental Problems from Faulty Practices: In India, large scale extraction of minerals have been creating another serious environmental problems, ruining the country's land, water, forest and air. Large scale mining has resulted in conversion of agricultural and forest land into stock yards and townships, roads, railway lines, etc., and removed vegetation and top soil. The disposal of mining waste, mineral dust from mines are constantly polluting air and also reducing agricultural productivity. Underground mines are often creating subsidence of land due to its over exploitation. Mining activity is also polluting water resources as the rain waters passing through mineral wastes are flowing into rivers and streams. Mining operation has also resulted in large scale deforestation, soil erosion and is also responsible for various health hazards to human beings in the form of respiratory problems and other illness.

Industrial and Atmospheric Pollution: In India, unplanned and uncontrolled growth of industries and ill-maintained automobiles are creating huge atmospheric pollution problems. They include carbon dioxide, carbon monoxide, oxides of nitrogen, sulphur dioxide, hydrocarbons and metallic traces. Again some specific pollutants are also being mixed with atmosphere which include lead from automobiles, nuclear power stations, etc. Moreover, industrial wastes coming out of fertilizer factories, paper mills, leather factories, etc., are constantly being discharged in rivers, lakes and seas, creating huge health hazards for the population of the country.

Infrastructural and Domestic Pollution: Equally important is the infrastructural and domestic pollution. The poor handling of materials used in infrastructure like roads, bridges, dams, buildings, etc., create pollution in the atmosphere. Similarly, domestic waste material like dust, vegetable leftovers, polybags etc., also create pollution in the atmosphere.

In short, environmental problems are being added up in increasing proportion in our country. Thus, it is high time that planners and policy makers should take necessary steps to reduce the degree of environmental pollution in the country and should preserve proper environment at any cost.

IMPACT OF AGRICULTURAL PRACTICES ON THE ECOSYSTEM

CONSTRUCTION OF DAMS—LOSS OF HABITAT SPECIES

Rivers possess a delicate ecology that depends on a regular cycle of disturbance within certain tolerance limits. The plant and animal communities that inhabit the river and river margins have evolved to adapt to their river's own peculiar pattern of flood and drought, slow and fast current. Dams disrupt this ecology.

Dams are huge and giant structures which are constructed across a river to obstruct its natural flow and enormously large artificial lake is created to store water. The construction of a dam/river valley project encompasses a large area of land.

Dams built on rivers serve as artificial (man-made) lake that store a huge amount of rainwater which is advantageous for different purposes, it is problematic too in many respects.

The reservoir or lake created by a dam may encroach many thousands of acres of forest that once served as habitat, for wild animals and plants. It has contributed to the extinction of many species. For example Sardar Sarovar Dam in Gujarat, Narmada Sagar in Gujarat, Idukki in Kerela, Tehri in Uttarakhand are causing a serious problem to ecosystem in India.

The construction of dam and the flooding of valleys for power generation, the use of pesticides, toxic contamination of soils have all been associated with unintended species extinction.

The first effect of a dam is to alter the pattern of disturbances that the plants and animals of a river have evolved for. Many aquatic animals coordinate their reproductive cycles with annual flood seasons. As an example, a fish on a certain river may only reproduce during April of every year so that its offspring will have abundant food and places to hide. If the flood never comes because a dam holds the river back, the offspring may be produced during a time when they cannot possibly survive.

The effects of dams vary depending on their size and ecological and environmental setting.

Construction of dams has also affected water resources in the form of fertilizers, insecticides, etc., used in agricultural fields which get lost in running water ultimately find their destination in various water bodies, thus posing a threat to the existing flora and fauna.

Over growing needs and construction of dams causes deforestation which decreases the rainfall and the temperature of atmosphere increases and the wildlife is becoming extinct.

Every flood is valuable as it takes nutrients from the land and deposits them in the river, providing food for the stream's residents. If the dam is allowed to release water from its reservoir, it will often do so only once in a while, rather than in frequent, small floods as are seen in nature. This leads to *scouring* and *armoring* of the riverbed. The higher energy of the sudden floods picks up and removes smaller sediments like silt, sand and gravel, as well as aquatic plants and animals, leafy debris and large woody debris. The life of organisms (including fish) downstream depends on the constant feeding of the river with debris. This debris includes leaves, twigs, branches and whole trees, as well as the organic remains of dead animals. Debris not only provides food, it provides hiding places for all size of animals. Without flooding and without a healthy riparian zone, this debris will be scarce, the food web is removed. All in all, the loss of sediment and debris means the loss of both nutrients and habitat for most animals.

Temperature is another problem. Rivers tend to be fairly homogenous in temperature. Reservoirs, on the other hand, are layered. They are warm at the top and cold at the bottom. If water is released downstream, it is usually released from the bottom of the dam, which means the water in the river is now colder than it should be. Many macro invertebrates depend on a regular cycle of temperatures throughout the year. When this heated water comes from industries and power plant and runs into lakes and rivers, it increases the temperature which harms the animals and plant species. When we change that, we compromise their survival.

Migratory birds from the sub-polar regions that settle in wetland areas during the winter will suffer from disturbance in their migratory pattern and breeding habits, if wetlands disappear. Building of dams along rivers inundates adjacent lands, destroying forests and killing all life forms in it.

These species being lost today contain unknown food, medical values and industrial uses. Thus, the present and future generation will have to pay a heavy price for the loss of species, genetic diversity and degradation of habitats.

Loss of Top Soil

The top most layer of soil is the most fertile zone of soil profile. It contains rich organic matter, good amount of mineral nutrients, soil air and micro-organisms which facilitate crop production and high yield. Agriculture is a practice by which crops are produced on a large scale by farmers. This is a primary occupation of people in our country and governs the economy to a great extent but unfortunately certain natural factors and agricultural practices are disturbing the top most layer of soil and makes the fields infertile. This is also called as *soil erosion* and *degradation*.

Soil erosion

Soil erosion is the greatest single menace to the country's prosperity. It means the cutting away of the valuable top soil *i.e.*, plant food nutrients by natural agencies like rain, wind currents, etc. It may also be due to the coming up of injurious salts or sand through water-logging or desert spreading. Consequently, it results in a gradual decline in crop yields, affects pastures for cattle and makes unfit a very large area of land for cultivation. In India, the soil erosion was estimated to be 6 billion tonnes in 1972 which amounted to be the loss of ₹ 700 crores. According to **Mr. Kellong**, *"Soil erosion is an important symptom of bad relationship between people and soil just as headache is often a symptom of some more fundamental illness."*

According to **Dr. H.H. Bannet**, *"The vastly accelerated process of soil removal brought about by human interference, with the normal disequilibrium between "soil building" and "soil removed" is designated as soil erosion."* To quote **Dr. R.H. Gone**, soil erosion can be defined, as, *"the theft of the soil by the natural elements and its the removal of soil particles either singly or in mass."* Similarly, the Indian Council of Agricultural Research defined it as, *"Soil erosion is the wearing away of land surface by action of such natural agencies as water and wind."*

Components of soil needed by plants remain in the top soil. This top soil is gradually eroded as a result of natural weathering as well as man's lack of foresight.

(i) **Natural weathering:** Soil erosion takes place by flow of river, stream of air, rainfall, storm and gale, inundation, etc.

(ii) **Man-made causes:** Indiscriminate cutting of trees, unplanned tilling of land, uncontrolled grazing, Jhoom farming, terrace farming, etc., lead to soil erosion.

Causes of Soil Erosion

Various agricultural practices that lead to soil erosion or its depletion are:

Intensive Irrigation: An important feature of farming is making the provision to irrigate the land. Modern agricultural practices demand intensive irrigation. canals and reservoirs are made for constant supply of water or devices like tubewells are used to irrigate the land. Heavy watering of fields cause water logging resulting in salinisation of soil as the irrigation water is rich in salt content. Salinisation of soil refers to a process by which the salt content of the soil move upward and accumulate on the top layer of the ground surface. This accumulation of the salt turns a fertile land into a waste land.

Jhoom Farming: It is a type of shifting cultivation practiced on hilly slopes of Assam and other north eastern states in India and on global level it is commonly practised in Malaysia, Indonesia and Sri Lanka too. Here a part of forest is cleared and trees are burnt. This land is cultivated for a few years and when the fertility of the soil is exhausted the farmer moves and clears another part of the forest for cultivation. Jhoom farming is also called '*slash and burn*' farming and is very dangerous for ecosystem as it results in soil erosion and loss of species too.

Nature of Crops: The crop grown is also responsible to soil erosion. For example, barley and wheat have low unit of index of soil loss while crops like corn, cotton, soyabean have higher units of index. Therefore, it has been noticed that areas where crops like tobacco, potato and cotton are grown, there is heavy loss of soil at the time of heavy showers. On the contrary, where rice, jute and sugarcane are grown, there are little chances of loss of soil.

Faulty Land Use Practices: These include indiscriminate use of the soil for generations without putting back into the elements of fertility and cultivation on unstable and hill slopes. On the steeper slopes, when land is ploughed; and is exposed to rain, the most fertile particles are carried down the rivers and deposited uselessly in the sea. According to the First Plan : "*Failure to practice such measures as ploughing along the contour on sloping lands, proper crop rotations and in particular, growing of cover crops are causes of erosion over large areas. Much damage originates also in fallows, grazing lands or unculturable waste land which are generally neglected.*"

Indiscriminate Cutting of Trees: Deliberate deforestation and removal of vegetation for the supply of timber, fuel and other purposes cause an increased run-off of rain water and thereby causes soil erosion. In fact, forests and vegetation act as a protection against forces of wind and water, protecting the soil from being washed or blown away and preserving the physical and hydrographic balance of nature. Also the removal of forest cover to clear up area for agriculture has also led to soil erosion or loss of top soil especially for terrace farming in hilly region.

Desertification

Desertification is the washing away of earth's top soil due to various factors. That is what is now happening in many areas. Nowhere is the problem more acute than in arid, semi-arid and dry sub-humid areas which cover more than one-third of the earth's surface. In these areas, human activity may stress the ecosystem beyond its tolerance limit, resulting in degradation of the land. By pounding the soil with their hooves, lives stock compact the substrate, increase the proportion of the fine material and reduce the percolation rate of the soil, thus encoring erosion by wind and water. Grazing and the collection of firewood reduce or eliminate plants that help to bind the soil.

This degradation of formerly productive land or desertification is a complex process. It involves multiple causes and it proceeds at varying rates in different climates. Desertification may intensify a general climatic trend toward greater aridity, or it may initiate a change in local climate. Through desertification, susceptible areas lose their productive capacity.

Increased population and livestock pressure on lands has accelerated desertification. In some areas, nomads moving to less arid areas, disrupt the local ecosystem and increase the rate of erosion of the land. Nomads are trying to escape the desert, but because of their land-use practices, they are bringing the desert with them.

It is a misconception that droughts cause desertification. Droughts are common in arid and semi-arid land. Well managed land can, however, recover from droughts.

Indiscriminate Use of Chemical Fertilizers and Pesticides

Fertilizers: The crops require energy, basic foods and nutrients for their growth. While they get sunlight as prime source of energy, water and CO_2 as basic food, they even need inorganic substances like nitrogen, calcium, potassium, phosphorus, sulphur, etc., as nutrients. These, most of time, are not in sufficient quantities in the soil so they have to be supplied externally through substances called as fertilizers. These are the chemicals that stimulate growth of plants and increase the yield but these fertilizers are synthetic and do not decompose into the soil but remain there. The indiscriminate use of fertilizers lead to following disadvantages:

- They contaminate surface and ground water resources and cause many water borne diseases like blue baby syndrome, stomach cancer, etc.
- The quality of drinking water gets deteriorated due to disposal of fertilizers into land fill sites and lands.
- Reduces the fertility of land.
- Reduces the proportion of organic matter in the soil.
- Disturbs the entire ecosystem of lakes/ponds/rivers and underground water due to accumulation of chemical fertilizers in them and in soil.
- Some formulae of fertilizers cause acute acidification of soil depleting their nutrients, ultimately rendering them unfit for cultivation. They also disrupt the natural cycles of soil affecting the functioning of the entire soil ecosystem, leading gradually to its degradation or by turning it dependent on chemicals entirely. It is said that if the concentration of phosphates and nitrogen increase one part and thirty parts per, hundred million parts of water it causes eutrophication.

Pesticides: Pesticides are chemicals that are used to kill pests. Pests are the creatures that damage the crop and reduce their yields. Common pests are insects, rats, mites, birds and disease causing organisms like bacteria, fungi and viruses. The pesticides are often sprayed in liquid form on the crop plants that kill the specific pest. Common pesticides are malathion, BHC, disyston and DDT. There are certain other chemicals that kill the insects called as insecticides and others that kill the weeds or other undesirable vegetation that compete with the crops for resources and are unyielding. These useless plants are called weeds and these chemicals are called weedicides or herbicides. They all are grouped under pesticides. They have very harmful effect on man when used non-judiciously or indiscriminately.

General disadvantages of pesticides are:
- The non-targeted organisms are also killed and injured.
- The pests that do not die after the spray become resistant and produce the pesticide resistant generation.
- Due to killing beneficial pests, which actually get killed due to the use of broad spectrum pesticides and which are helpful in controlling the dangerous pests, the newer problematic pests are evolved.
- Reduces the fertility of the soil.
- Ecology of food chain and food web are disturbed, thus, resulting in disturbance in entire soil ecosystem or terrestrial ecosystem.
- Causes illness and slow poisoning in human beings on short duration exposure.
- Causes fatal disease like cancer, genetic defects, immunological and other chronic diseases on long duration exposure.
- Environment detriments due to solubility and mobility of toxic pesticides.

The cumulative effects of fertilizers and pesticides have turned into certain phenomenon described as under:

Eutrophication: This is a process by which the content of oxygen gets depleted in the waterbodies. This occurs either naturally or due to human activities like when human add excessive amount of plant nutrients especially nitrogen, carbon and phosphorous rich nutrients into streams and lakes through various activities. Run off from agricultural fields, domestic sewage, industrial effluents, fertilizers, etc., act as powerful stimulant to algae growth. These algae blooms change the quality of water and deplete the oxygen content for the aquatic system and also reduce the further penetration of oxygen, light and heat into the waterbodies. This causes the aquatic organisms to die and drains water of all its oxygen. The serious effect on aquatic life due to eutrophication are :

- Decrease in biodiversity.
- Changes in species composition and dominance.
- Toxic effects.

Bio-magnification: It is considered as a kind of pollution because in this process there is a tendency of pollutants to get concentrated in successive trophic or feeding levels of a food chain as they move up the food chain. The phenomenon of concentration of toxic deposition at the higher trophic level is known as bio-accumulation. This bio-accumulation takes place in different organisms. They accumulate in the tissues and internal organs of larger animals when they eat them and thus move up the food chain thereby increasing the concentration of the toxic compounds.

An example of Bio-magnification was seen in Illinois (USA) where Elm trees were sprayed with DDT and large number of robins died near due to DDT poisoning. The lethal dose came from the earthworms which they consumed. The earth worms had concentrated DDT residue by feeding on fallen Elm leaves.

General effects of agricultural practices on the ecosystem can be summarised as follows:
- Erosion of soil or loss of top soil cover.
- Increase in sedimentation towards downstream of a river.
- Fertilizer mixed sediments and other agricultural run-off in nearby water bodies can make the aquatic life toxic.
- Depletes the fertility of soil.
- Leads to desertification.
- Pollutes the air due to exhausts from tools, implements and machines and disturbs the life cycle of living beings around the area of the agricultural fields.
- Modify the chemical cycles such as :
    (i) O_2 cycle,   (ii) CO_2 cycle,   (iii) NO_2 cycle.
- Indiscriminate and non-judicious use of pesticides, insecticides, etc., destroy the useful microbes and organisms that are helpful in maintaining the fertility of soil.

LESSON AT A GLANCE

Ecosystem: Ecosystem is the basic fundamental unit of ecology which includes both the organisms and the non-living elements present in the environment each influencing the properties of the other and each is necessary for the maintenance of life.

Ecological imbalance in India

Ecological imbalance results from land degradation and soil erosion, deforestation, faulty utilisation of water and mineral resources.

Animals life plays an important role in maintaining the forest. Destruction of this forest for construction of dams leads to extinction of species.

(i) *Degradation of land and soil erosion;* (ii) *Deforestation;* (iii) *Faulty utilization of water resources;* (iv) *Environmental problems from faulty practices;* (v) *Industrial and atmospheric pollution;* (vi) *Infrastructural and domestic pollution*

Impact of Agricultural Practices on the Ecosystem:

Construction of Dams—Loss of Habitat Species:

Soil Erosion: The cutting away of valuable top soil *i.e.,* plant food nutrients by natural agents like rain, wind currents , etc. It may also be due to the coming up of injurious salts or sand through water-logging or desert spreading.

Causes of Soil Erosion: (i) Intensive irrigation; (ii) Jhoom farming; (iii) Nature of crops; (iv) Faulty land use practices; (v) Indiscriminate cutting of trees.

Desertification: All the causes of soil erosion leads to desertification.

Indiscriminate Use of chemical fertilizers and pesticides : It reduces the fertility of the soil.

QUESTIONS

A. Short Answer Questions
1. What do you mean by ecological imbalance?
2. What is deforestation?
3. Write down three points which causes extinction of species.
4. How does the temperature effect in the extinction of species?
5. What are the disadvantages of pesticides?
6. What is ecosystem?
7. Mention the main causes behind soil erosion.

B. Long Answer Questions
1. Discuss in detail the ecological imbalance in India.
2. What are the two agricultural practices that leads to soil erosion?
3. What do you mean by desertification?
4. How does the construction of dams causes loss of species?
5. How does the fertilisers affects agriculture?
6. Describe briefly some activities of man that are either causing harm to aquatic plants and animals or that are making grounds for future harm of them.

09 Measures to Check Ecosystem

GOVERNMENT INITIATIVES
Not Building Large Dams

OVERVIEW
Government has taken initiatives for ensuring minimum displacement and proper rehabilitation and resettlement caused by building of large dams. Some of the measures to check soil erosion are discussed in this chapter.

Though, hydropower is one of the cheapest and cleanest sources of power and dams are the generator of hydropower, yet large dams could have environmental and social repercussions which may outrun the benefits as they create an adverse impact on ecosystem. Besides the loss of habitat species, one of the major drawbacks of huge dams is the displacement of people who are natives of that place. Apart from the locational loss to such displaced people, the large dams give occupational loss, social loss and emotional loss to the residents of the area. Sometimes it may lead to loss of historical entities too. So the government has to take measures to rehabilitate them.

In the last 70 years, more than 50 million people in India have been estimated to be affected by the construction of dams. People have been displaced from their ancestral homes to other dwellings and this cuts them off their community life, social interaction, mutual transactions, interaction with environment, role in the society and traditional occupation and creates severe psychological and socio-economic impacts. The Hirakund Dam displaced about 20,000 people living in about 250 villages.

Since 1950, out of the millions of people who have been displaced by various development projects, only 25 per cent of such evicted people have been estimated to have been rehabilitated and resettled.

In view of these problems associated with large dams, experts have advocated the construction of smaller dams. New environmental laws to safeguard the planet from the effects of global warming have made smaller hydropower projects more viable.

Till date India has no resettlement and rehabilitation policy. Only Maharashtra, Madhya Pradesh and Punjab have state-wide Resettlement and Rehabilitation (R&R) policy.

Environmental Impact Assessments (EIAs) for large dam projects have been routine administrative procedure in India since the late 1970's. In 1985, the Ministry of Environment and Forests issued its "Guidelines for Environmental Assessment of River Valley Projects", which were updated in 1989 and specified the various studies that must be carried out under an EIA. Furthermore in 1994, the Ministry of Environment and forests issued a notification under the *Environmental Protection Act,* making EIAs a legal requirement for large dams.

The Government takes the responsibility to provide new places for settlement of the displaced people (resettlement) as well as support them to start their day to day activities (rehabilitation). Generally, the following are provided to people when they are displaced:

- Land as per records in their village to landholders and landless people.
- Compensation to be given in monetary terms to anyone who refuses to take land.
- Land for cattle.
- Transport facility.
- Civil amenities including drinking water supply from wells or other means, a Samaj Mandir, school with playground, internal and approach roads, electric supply, community toilets, etc.
- The landless families should also be given subsistence allowance.
- To ensure minimum displacement and proper rehabilitation and resettlement, the government has recently come up with the following policy.
- There should be minimum resettlement. Non-displacement and least displacement alternatives should be identified.
- People should be informed and involved in a project ever since it is being planned.
- An assessment of the needs of the community and the area has to be done.
- The people who are likely to be affected should have a decisive say in the entire process.
- The process must be well-defined and transparent.
- The people should have maximum possible information pertaining to the project.

SOIL CONSERVATION

Soil erosion is a serious problem and serious steps have to be taken to prevent it. It has to be a top priority to conserve the soil. According to Indian Department of Agriculture, *"Soil conservation is a composite approach to an efficient use of land and water resources so as to get optimum production from them, to preserve them from deterioration and improve them for future."*

METHODS OF SOIL CONSERVATION

(A) AGRONOMIC METHODS

Agronomic measures of soil and water conservation consist of those practices which help to intercept rain drops and reduce the splash effect. It also helps to reduce and run off through the use of mulching, strip-cropping and contour farming.

1. Mulching: The process in which a mixture of wet straw and leaves are spread over the land to protect roots of newly planted trees is known as Mulching. It reduces evaporation from the soil and improves the soil structure and yield.

2. Strip-Cropping: It means cropping on long narrow piece of land. For example:

(i) **Contour Strip Cropping:** It means growing of a crop in strips of suitable horizontal widths across the slopes on contour, alternating with strip of soil, protecting and erosion resisting crops.

(ii) **Field Strip Cropping:** It means planting of farm crops in more or less parallel strips across fairly uniform slopes but not on exact contours.

(iii) **Wind Strip Cropping:** It includes planting tall growing crops like jowar, bajra or maize and short-growing crops in alternatively arranged straight and long but relatively narrow, parallel strips laid out right across the direction of prevailing wind, regardless of the contour.

(iv) **Permanent/Temporary Buffer Strip Cropping:** In this case, the strips are established to take off eroded slopes in fields under contour strip cropping.

(v) **Mixed Farming:** This system of farming refers to the growing of mixture of crops alongwith rearing livestock to get better results in farming as the remains of the crop may become feeding material for livestock, while the livestock excreta become natural manure for the soil fertility.

3. Contour Farming: The soil cannot absorb all the rain when it falls particularly during intense rain storms. The excess water with the top soil flows down the slope under the influence of gravity. To stop such water run off contour farming has been found very helpful which reduces run-off and erosion. Contour farming refers to growing the crops perpendicular to a slope or on horizontally cut levels across the slope rather than up and down the slope.

(B) Mechanical Methods

These methods are also known as engineering measures. They help in intercepting the water run-off and providing an opportunity for the percolation or infiltration of water deep into the land. Besides, it reduces the velocity of the run-off, thus prevents soil erosion. They also include the methods that check the soil degradation.

1. Alternative Cropping/Crop Rotation: Alternative cropping is a technique of growing a crop for a few seasons and then alternating it with some other crop. If the same type of crop like paddy, wheat, jute, potato, sugarcane or sunflower is produced continuously in the same plot year after year the fertility of that plot of land gets depleted and the soil becomes prone to erosion. Fertility and soil binding capacity can be kept intact by practicing alternate cropping technique.

Crop rotation is one of the ways to restore fertility and conserve soil. Normally growing leguminous crops like grass, lentil, mung, etc., bring back the fertility as in the roots of leguminous plants, root nodules are found which are a symbiotic association between a bacteria called rhizobium and the roots of a plant. These bacteria are capable of fixing the gaseous form of nitrogen from the air into the usable form in the soil and make a natural fertilizer. This increases the fertility of the land.

Inter Cropping: The practice of raising two or more crops in the same field at the same time to improve productivity and conserve soil is called inter cropping. Soil is conserved because different crops trap different nutrients and moisture from different depths of soil profile, thus entire profile of soil does not get exhausted of one nutrient and at one level. For example, in Northern India mustard is planted together with wheat. In fruit orchards leguminous crops are planted to increase the yield of the land. In South India, coconut trees are planted on borders of rice fields to reduce the impact of water logging.

2. Shelter Belt: In this belt thick bushes and trees are grown in the boundary of fields at right angle to the direction of air, because of this shelter belt, the speed of air slows and stops erosion.

3. Plantation and Conservation of Grass Land: Afforestation and Agrostology comes under this category. Soil erosion is increased, where forests are removed. By developing vegetation near roads, railway canals and public places the roots of vegetation helps to bind soil particle, increases fertile capacity and reduces the speed of water. When such afforestation efforts are taken on the periphery of a desert, the expansion of the desert may be reduced and rather reversed. So, soil erosion can be reduced by afforestation and planting grass.

INDISCRIMINATE USE OF CHEMICAL FERTILIZERS AND PESTICIDES

With the advent of Green revolution in 1960s, the use of chemical fertilizers and pesticides has increased a lot in the agriculture but this has led to the degradation of ecosystem in the following manner:

Fertilizers: The crops require energy, basic foods and nutrients for their growth. While they get sunlight as prime source of energy, water and CO_2 as basic food they even need inorganic substances like nitrogen, calcium, potassium, phosphorus, sulphur, etc., as nutrients. Most of the times these are not in sufficient quantities in the soil so they have to be supplied externally through substances called as fertilizers. These are the chemicals that stimulate growth of plants and increase the yield but these fertilizers are synthetic and harmful as they do not decompose into the soil but remain there. This reduces the soil fertility in the long run.

Pesticides: Pesticides are chemicals that are used to kill pests. Pests are the creatures that damage the crop and reduce their yields. Common pests are insects, rats, mites, birds and disease causing organisms like bacteria, fungi and viruses. These pesticides are often sprayed in liquid form on the crop plants and they kill the specific pest. Common pesticides are malathion, BHC, disyston and DDT.

There are certain other chemicals that kill the insects called as insecticides. On the other hand, the chemicals that kill the weeds or other undesirable vegetation that compete with the crops for resources are called weedicides or herbicides. They all are grouped under pesticides and exerts very harmful effect on man when used non-judiciously or indiscriminately.

Both the fertilizers and pesticides are non-biodegradable chemicals and their concentration in soil goes on increasing with successive application. Certain varieties of fertilizers and pesticides contaminate ground water so much that they get consumed through drinking water and adversely affect the human nervous system.

NEED FOR ECO-FRIENDLY FERTILIZERS AND PESTICIDES

Many of the first generation pesticides like lead, arsenic and mercury are all inorganic chemicals and are extremely toxic. They lead to accumulate in soils to the point of inhibiting plant growth. New pesticides or second generation pesticides are found in synthetic organic chemicals. They are man-made chemicals with carbon as a principal component. The most famous second generation pesticide is DDT. But it has also many harmful effects.

After the banning of DDT, several substitutes were tried continuously one replacing the other but not with much success. A natural control method keeping in mind the eco-system balance is also suggested. In this natural control method, pests are considered as organism with in the ecosystem and hence the damage by them to crops is controlled through ecosystem management without completely eradicating them. Natural control may be through any of the following three methods:

(a) Biological control where pests control is achieved through a viral or bacterial disease;

(b) Genetic control, which implies introduction of lethal genes into pest population;

(c) Cultural control creates an environment unfavourable to the pest.

Hence, the harmful impacts of chemical fertilizers and pesticides can be eliminated by using more and more of natural agents to increase the fertility of soil and save the ecosystem. These natural agents are manure, green manure, bio-fertiliser, bio-pesticide and compost. A brief introduction of each of them is presented here:

(i) *Manure:* Manure is the organic matter which is derived from animal excretion. Manure from animal feces increase the fertility of the soil by adding organic matter and nutrients such as nitrogen, carbohydrates, fats and proteins, etc.

(ii) *Green Manure:* Green manure, also called a cover crop is a great way to add nutrients to the soil. Green manure includes the plants or crops which have been used by planting them back into the soil to increase its fertility. Normally leguminous crops like grass, lentil, mung, clove, etc., are used as green manures.

(iii) *Bio-fertilizers:* Bio-fertilizers refers to the material which contain living microorganism that when applied to a crop help the crop plants to receive the nutrients by their interactions in the rhizosphere or the interior of the plant. The microorganisms in bio-fertilizers help in stimulating plant growth through the synthesis of growth-promoting substances and developing the soil's natural nutrients through the natural processes of nitrogen fixation.

(iv) *Bio-pesticides:* The bio-pesticides are certain types of pesticides which are derived from the natural materials such as animals, plants, bacteria and certain minerals, etc. These natural materials may be certain types of bacteria, fungi, viruses, some natural substance like baking soda, etc.

(v) *Compost:* Compost is the decomposed remnants of organic materials like leaves, grass, vegetable peelings, bread, cereals, tea bags, old herbs and spices, etc. The compost is an excellent recharger of soil nutrients.

LESSON AT A GLANCE

Government Initiatives: Not Building Large Dams: Development projects like construction of dams displace people from their homes and force them to settle somewhere else. Similarly, dams create the problems of water logging and salinity. Therefore, construction of big dams has been discouraged by Government and initiated to construct water reservoirs.

Methods of Soil Conservation: Agronomic Methods: Agronomic measures of soil and water conservation consist of those practices which help to intercept rain drops and reduce the splash effect. It also helps to reduce and run off through the use of mulching strip-cropping, mixed cropping and contour farming.

Mechanical Methods: These measures are followed to supplement the agronomical practices when the latter are not much effective. It includes (i) Alternative cropping/crop rotation, (ii) Shelter belt, and (iii) Plantation and conservation of grass land.

Need for Eco-friendly Fertilizers and Pests: Indiscriminate use of chemical fertilizers and pesticides reduce the fertility of the soil therefore, manures, green manures, bio-fertilizers, etc., should be incorporated into the soil to increase its fertility.

QUESTIONS

A. Short Answer Questions
1. Name three states which have R & R policy?
2. What does EIA stands for?
3. What do you mean by soil conservation?
4. Name the different types of strip-cropping method.
5. What do you mean by contour farming?
6. What do you mean by shelter belt?
7. What do you mean by green manure?

B. Long Answer Questions
1. What initiatives have been taken by the Government to overcome the problem of building large dams?
2. Explain the methods for the conservation of soil.
3. Explain how the soil fertility can be increased by using eco-friendly fertilizers and pests.

10
Impact of Industrial Practices on the Ecosystem

Industrialization has the potential to help achieve a variety of social objectives such as employment, poverty eradication, gender equality, labour standards, and greater access to education and healthcare. At the same time and on the negative side, industrial processes play a major role in the degradation of the global environment, causing deforestation, loss of hydrological resources, air and water pollution and extinction of species. These threaten the global environment as well as economic and social welfare. In this chapter, we will discuss the impact of various industrial practices on ecosystem and the use of eco-friendly technologies for the sustainable ecosystem.

OVERVIEW

In his quest for more comforts, man has taken great strides in technological advancement and has indulged in rapid industrialization overlooking its impact on nature and existing ecological balance. This has played havoc with earth's environment and ecosystem resulting in massive deforestation and contamination of river waters. World's scientific community is forced to standup to the new challenges like global warming and melting of glacier.

How the activities of human society have degraded the environment physically, chemically, biologically and ethically is shown below:

IMPACT OF MINING

Mining activities adversely affect the local landscape due to large scale digging up process. Mining may result in many negative effects such as water contamination, subsidence of land, air pollution and desertification. Large amount of waste generated during mining operations often contaminate the soil with toxic heavy metals and acids which can lower the pH of the soil, preventing plants and soil micro-organisms from thriving, and can also react with various minerals in the soil that are required by plants, such as calcium and magnesium.

It also causes a loss of moisture in the soil leading to desertification. An example of this is Goa, where manganese is found on the ground surface or a few meters below. This surface soil is stripped off for extracting the minerals and this has left a desert-like landscape behind.

Mining has considerable adverse effects on environmental elements like air, water, land, soil and biotic components. The large scale digging process makes the following impact in local landscape.

(A) Physical Impact

Mining wastes liberate chemicals that are harmful to our environment as they cause pollution of different environmental components.

(1) **Pollution of Air:** Various processes involved in mining such as drilling, blasting, road haulage, crushing, etc., produce dust and suspended particulate matter (SPM) in the air thereby polluting it. Furthermore, while converting coal into coke, roasting of sulphide ores, coal seams on fire generate sulphur-di-oxide and other toxic gases.

(2) **Pollution of Water:** Different mines release different types of chemicals that pollute the water bodies:

(a) **Coal Mines:** The coal mines release waste water that consist of coal dressing, mine water that contains a large quantity of suspended solids.

(b) **Metal Mining Industry:** The mines where metals are extracted discharge waste water like mine water from smelters. This water is highly acidic and is rich in suspended solids.

(c) **Petroleum and Natural Gas Industry:** There are wells from which these fuels are extracted. The drilling of these wells produce waste mine water that contains large quantities of salt.

(3) **Soil Pollution:** The mining and mineral extraction industry utilizes many hazardous chemicals like salts of cyanide for the extraction of precious metals like gold and silver from their ores.

(4) **Noise Pollution:** Noise pollution caused by mining operation is dangerous. The process from blasting to crushing and cleaning the equipment, drilling, dumping, etc. causes a lot of noise which imposes a threat to the human habitation. Noise causes tension, hypertension, changing breathing patterns, fatigue and interrupts the process of blood circulation, etc.

(5) **Harm to Forest Cover and Vegetation:** Roads are constructed to make the mines accessible to the peasants, settlers, miners which eventually results in destroying the forest/ vegetation cover.

(B) Social Impact

Mining causes the entry of labourers, technicians, etc., from adjacent areas to the mining zone to work, this causes the region to become overcrowded. thus, the infrastructure gets overburdened to meet the requirement of so many people, like provisions of water supply, electricity, housing, medical facilities, management of sanitation and sewage disposal. Also the farming land is taken for habitation uses resulting in destruction of forests.

After the mining is finished *i.e.,* the natural resources exhausted and there is nothing much left to be extracted, the mines become useless for the miners, and they close down or abandon the mines. This process is referred to as dereliction of mines.

Dereliction too has many harmful effects

1. It makes the land waste, as it is no more suitable for either industrial or agricultural purposes because its fertility is lost.
2. There is a spoilage of landscape.
3. It causes health hazards.

An important point of concern is reclamation of land in surface mining that can lead to ecological crisis. The drastic disturbance of overburdened land changes the physical and chemical property of the soil, thus, making it hostile for seed germination and plant growth. The area becomes highly acidic, loses a proper texture and fertility, reduces infiltration, erosion and slides. Till the time the soil becomes capable of bearing any vegetation, the entire area can almost be exposed to rapid erosion of both land and water, further polluting surrounding water bodies with its sediments.

Case: Displacement of people from their land due to mining in Jharia.

Mining consumes several thousand hectares of land and thousands of people have to be evacuated. The Jharia coal fields in Jharkhand had to be evacuated by its local residents due to the threat of underground fires. Almost 0.3 million people were supposed to be shifted to an alternative site and almost ₹ 115 crores have been used since 1976 to suppress these fires. It is predicted that approximately ₹ 18,000 crore would be spent to shift the population of Jharia.

IMPACT OF INDUSTRIES

Industry is an enterprise that manufactures goods or provides service to human beings. Industries use land for factories, roads, open places and housing areas. Besides natural resources other resources of energy like coal and petroleum are exploited unequitably leading to their depletion. Waste generation and industrial pollution also cast an irreversible impact on ecosystem (especially on human health and environment).

The industries are often concentrated in urban areas. They all put a stress on land and along with unbalanced urbanization they create a disastrous impact on ecosystems. Different industries release different kinds of pollutants. Tanneries, metal plating industries, oil refineries contribute pollutants likes dioxins, pesticides, oil, acid and heavy metals etc. Industrial water pollution is also an important source of destruction of aquatic ecosystem due to the discharge of hazardous effluents.

No doubt industrialization has contributed to the growth of civilization and people are enjoying high standards of life, but we have got an unbalanced ecosystem along with it. The people from nearby areas especially rural areas migrate to the areas where industries are located thereby putting a stress on the natural resources of that area. The industries discharge their effluents in air, water and soil. The excessive CO_2 emissions released from industries contribute to the greenhouse effect or global warming, which finally impacts the pattern and growth of natural vegetation and agricultural crops.

Accidents are quite possible to occur in industrial areas that results in the loss or injury of life and damage of property over a wide area. The incidents that took place at Bhopal with a leakage of methyl-isocyanate gas from the union carbide plant is still having its impact on people generation after generations.

Industries contribute to generation of waste from various types of operations. The gaseous pollutants like SO_2 and NO_2 are responsible for causing acid rains.

IMPACT OF ENERGY GENERATION

Electricity generation is the process of converting non-electrical energy to electricity. Today we rely mainly on conventional sources of energy like coal, petroleum, natural gas and hydroelectric sources to generate electricity and for running our factories, various equipments and automobiles. All of these are exhaustible and are depleting at a rate of 1,00,000 times faster than they are being formed due to their over consumption. Big dams are also not environmentally viable. They submerge the agricultural lands and displace people. In India, the estimates of displaced people range between 14 and 50 million.

Dams prevent rivers from flowing in their course. This affects the water table, preventing the river water from flowing into underground areas. A dam blocks the sediments and nutrients, blocks migration of fish, alters the river temperature and chemistry and upsets the natural balance. Hence, we need to look at alternative sources of energy such as solar energy, biomass, tidal harnesses, wind generators and geothermal sources.

The main purpose to construct a dam is to provide security for water resources but it does not actually serves its purpose, it rather causes pollution. The Hirakund Dam displaced about 20,000 people living in about 250 villages. The Bhakra Nangal Dam was constructed during 1950's and displaced a number of people.

Environmental consequences of energy generation from fossil fuels:
1. Combustion of coal in thermal power plants takes place in presence of oxygen and it releases CO_2 which is a greenhouse gas that increases the temperature causing melting of glaciers and rise in sea and river levels.
2. The gas which is released when combustion of coal takes place in insufficient supply of O_2 is carbon monoxide. It damages the nervous system causes unconsciouness and can be even fatal.
3. The black soot released from thermal power plant increases the quantity of SPM in air and gets deposited over buildings, structures and nearby vegetation spoiling the aesthetics of the environment.

Environmental consequences of energy generation from petroleum:
1. Petroleum exhausts produce gases like NO, NO_2 that cause corrosion, attacks, skin and lung congestion.
2. During transportation of oil, there is a danger of oil spills in oceans, lakes and streams. Oil spills are hazardous to aquatic life.
3. Thermal pollution is caused when fossil fuels burn in thermal power stations thereby increasing air and water temperatures. This kills many aquatic species as they are not resistant to this high temperature.

IMPACT OF AUTOMOBILES

Automobiles or vehicles are mainly responsible for more than 80 per cent of total air pollution. The major pollutants released from automobiles, locomotives, aircrafts, etc., include CO (carbon monoxide) due to the incomplete combustion of fuel, the unburnt hydrocarbons and nitrogen monoxide. In the cities like Delhi, Mumbai and Kolkata vehicular exhaust comprises of 75 per cent of entire CO released, 45 per cent of all hydrocarbons, 40 per cent of all oxide and 30 per cent of all SPM (suspended particulate matter).

They also release volatile hydrocarbons like methane, acetylene, ethylene etc. Ethylene can undergo chemical reactions with NO (nitrogen oxide) in presence of sunlight and can release ozone which is a photochemical pollutant and is very harmful. Fuel combustion also produces nitrogen dioxide.

The gasoline powered motor vehicles are a principle source of sulphur dioxide, carbon monoxide and lead whereas the diesel powered engines emit significant quantities of SPM, SO_2 and NO. These cause adverse effect on the people who inhale them, symptoms such as cough, headache, nausea, irritation in eyes, poor visibility and bronchial outcome is the result of the gaseous emissions like CO, unburnt hydrocarbons, lead compounds, soot, aldehydes, etc. This has even affected the presence of flora and fauna in the areas which are densely populated and are saturated with automobile exhausts. In places like Los Angeles a clear connection has been noticed between air pollution and population. In this city combustion products from millions of automobiles are exhausted into Los Angeles Basin. In addition other industries too contribute to some amount of CO_2. Due to temperature inversion that takes place in this basin the pollutants are compressed closer to the ground level, reacting with sunlight and causing photochemical smog. As a result the residents of this city are exposed to severe air pollution. Similar happenings took place in many cities of China, New Delhi and some cities of Uttar Pradesh in the winters of 2016-17 when air pollution mixed with fog called smog created severe health problems for the residents of these places.

IMPACT OF URBANISATION

The migration of people from rural areas to urban areas in search of good living conditions and opportunities related to employment have made the cities over populated, thereby stressing all its resources. The land resources for settlement, water and food resources for living, energy resources for transportation and running appliances and maintaining life quality are under severe stress. All these activities and stress have resulted in the depletion of resources. It is an irreversible process that is costing too much on our environment. The main impact of urbanisation on plants and animals is the loss of their habitat and this happens due to pollution, construction activities and change in local climate.

The growing urbanisation and overpopulation raises an enhanced demand for building more dwelling units, but at the same time more and more land for cultivation is also required as agricultural produce has to be increased to feed so many mouths. The land is scarce and the demand is more. This finally leads to an escalation of land value. Urbanisation has even led to the encroachment of water bodies and forests. Urban run offs pollute water ways too. Forests are being lost due to forest fragmentation and deforestation. This is the result of shifting cultivation, expansions of agricultural lands, forest fires and illegal logging. All these activities have led to the shifting of agricultural land to the area which may be less fertile, thus resulting in less productivity. Urbanisation has led to changing the pattern of land use. The people generate better facilities for themselves, *i.e.,* better houses, better means of transport and communication and also of recreation and the consequence is the defacement of land. This leads to developing negative impact on the entire biosphere which is a large ecosystem. Urbanisation creates environmental, social and economic problems. They are:

- Defacement of land.
- Exploitation of ground and surface water resources.
- Over crowding.
- Increased pressure on services.
- Unemployment.
- Every kind of pollution.
- Health and sanitation problem.
- More generation of wastes.
- Stress on energy generation or energy crisis.
- Loss of habitat for many animal and plant species due to deforestation.

To add to this problem there are squatter settlement of poor and migrant population which turns a city's open areas to squalid slums. This is also a cause of defacement of land. For example, Dharavi in Mumbai is Asia's largest slum spread over 4.5 sq km of prime land in Central Mumbai. It used to be a creek land which has now been gradually occupied by garbage dealers, rag pickers and scrap dealers.

IMPACT OF DEFORESTATION

Forests are a renewable resource which play a vital role in enhancing the quality of environment as they are a part of life support system. They play an important role in affecting the climate, water and soil cycles. The productivity of the forests is means of livelihood for many. Lately, anticipating the commercial gains, man started indiscriminate use of forests and irrationally cutting down trees for their selfish purpose. This detrimental activity is called as deforestation. By deforestation we mean the ruthless demolition of trees and plants, for personal economic gains.

Causes of Deforestation

Main causes of deforestation can be enumerated as follows:

1. Need of land to accommodate increasing population and expanding urbanisation.
2. Economic gains by selling timber and using wood as fuel.
3. Industrial growth such as establishing a new power project, a new industry, a corporate office, etc.
4. Acquiring land for constructing dams and irrigation canals.
5. Mining and quarrying for minerals, oil exploration, etc.
6. Promotion of production of new agriculture items *e.g.,* fruit trees, palm trees, rubber plants, etc.

Besides above, some other causes of deforestation are as follows :

1. Overgrazing by domestic animals
2. Commercial logging, and
3. Shifting cultivation.

Effects of Deforestation

1. **Rise in Global Warming**: Forests help to maintain the temperature at a lower level and prevent them from rising. Firstly, they reflect a portion of sun rays reaching the earth's surface back into outer space and absorb the rest. This lowers the temperature of the earth, but in absence of forests this phenomenon does not takes place, thus leading to a rise in temperature.

    Secondly, the ultra violet rays from the sun are absorbed by the ozone layer, but due to certain pollutants like chlorofluorocarbons, the ozone layer is becoming thin or holes are formed in the ozone layer. Under such conditions the forests would serve as a natural filter for the ultra violet radiation that threatens the health of the people, but due to absence of forest now, it is becoming impossible to prevent the UV rays from penetrating the ecosystem of the biosphere thus inducing global warming.

2. **Increase of CO_2 in Atmosphere and Rise in Climatic Temperature:** The destruction of forests could change the global climate and de-stabilize polar ice caps. The tropical rain forests are reservoirs of carbon, which is stored in living vegetation. Releasing this

carbon by cutting trees and then burning them or leaving them to decay will add to the concentration of CO_2 in the atmosphere which would increase the temperature of the atmosphere. All these factors are responsible for the rise in global warming. This is also called as the green house effect as there would be less trapping of CO_2 by the forest cover leading to rise in global temperature.

3. **Loss of Rainfall and Change in the Pattern of Rainfall:** When large areas of forests are destroyed, then less rain falls on the deforested region. Deforestation removes the sponge that holds rain water and sends half of it back to the atmosphere directly by transpiration.

4. **Irregular or Non-regulated Water Cycle:** One method by which forests influence human activities, indirectly but strongly, is through the part they play in regulating the water cycle. The maintenance of dense and uniform woodland, particularly over hilly areas, is a major factor which can guarantee water supply during the dry season and also the best means of preventing floods in drainage basins at other times. Countries situated in the Mediterranean climates as well as those in tropical countries, especially India, and the Far East, have long experienced disastrous floods, caused by unwise deforestation of the slopes above river valleys.

5. **Soil Erosion:** Forests protect the soil. Deforestation causes soil erosion. When trees are felled and the root mat is destroyed, the soil is subjected to erosion by the full force of the rains and wind as there are no trees to bind the soil.

   The soil is exposed to sun, wind and rain for a long time and the top layer of the soil is lost. Thus, deforestation accelerates soil erosion.

6. **Degradation of Land:** Heavy rain removes nutrients by washing away the thin top layer of soil and by leaching nutrients deep into the sub-soil thus making it unavailable to plant roots. In the process, it compacts the soil and squeezes out the air pockets. Air is as much important to soil-quality as mineral nutrients and compacted soil poses serious threat to environment in the form of land degradation.

7. **Increase in Concentration of Pollutants in Environment:** Forests help to minimise the impact of air pollution and water pollution by maintaining the flow of rivers, reducing sedimentation in rivers and streams, by reducing surface run-off of rain water and reducing silting of reservoirs. Thus, the forests to a great extent, protect the habitat from serious water pollution problem. Similarly by its protection against the physical violence of winds, the air pollution effects are reduced. Forests maintain CO_2 and O_2 balance in the atmosphere, maintain water sheds in optimum condition and conserve soil.

   Since, forests exert a tremendous influence in maintaining ecological balance, they need to be protected. Afforestation projects should be given priority.

DETERIORATION OF HYDROLOGICAL RESOURCES

Water is a pure natural resource and satisfies human needs. Fresh water is available from the ice caps of glaciers and snow peaks, ground water and surface water. The global warming due to excessive emission of carbon dioxide is causing the snow peaks to melt fast, thus, affecting the storage of water and flooding low lying areas. The loss of forest and vegetation cover has hampered the percolation of rain water underground to the aquifers due to fast run off. Thus, water is extracted from aquifers faster than it is replenished due to natural recharging.

Thus, we see that with the increase in population, irrigation and industrialization, the demand for water has gone up to a large extent. The hydrological resources have been deteriorated due to following reasons :

- Over exploitation of underground water that has resulted in lowering of the water table.
- The loss of vegetation causes drought and reduction of rainfall causes a lowered water table.
- Irrigation uses approximately 85 per cent of total fresh water.
- Our water sources like underground water, river, lakes, etc., get polluted and their water can hardly be used without an adequate treatment.

LESSON AT A GLANCE

Different industrial practices are producing harmful impacts on the environment.

Impact of Mining: Mining operations and wastes cause following impacts— **(A) Physical impacts:** (i) Pollution of air, (ii) Pollution of water, (iii) Soil pollution; (iv) Noise pollution; (v) Harm to forest cover and vegetation **(B) Social impacts:** like overcrowding and over burdening of infrastructure, displacement of local populace, etc.

Impact of industries: They pose a threat on human health and environment. It causes : Pollution of air, water, soil and radioactive pollution; Leads to degradation of land or soil, forests, biodiversity; Depletion of resources; and Excessive CO_2 emissions contribute to green house effect or global warming

Impact of Energy Generation: Energy moves the world. Today, we rely mainly on conventional sources of energy like Coal, petroleum, natural gas, nuclear fuel, etc.

Energy is generated in two types of plants:

(i) **Thermal Power Plants:** Produce energy by burning fossil fuels like coal, petroleum.

(ii) **Hydroelectricity Plants:** Produce energy by the flowing water by the construction of dams.

(iii) **Thermal Power Plants:** Release smoke, soot, dust, gases like NO_2 and SO_2 etc., oil spills are caused which are dangerous. Hydroelectricity plants result in loss of habitat for species, loss of forests and soil erosion.

Impact of Automobiles: Result in excessive air pollution by releasing carbon dioxide, carbon monoxide, SPM (Suspended Particulate Matter), SO_2, NO, ozone and certain lead compounds with soot. Causes many health hazards.

Impact of Urbanisation: It is the undue growth of population in urban areas. It results in undue felling of trees, loss of agricultural land, stressed natural and energy resources, encroachment of water bodies and forest, defacement of land, pollution, etc.

It puts a stress on the resources like air, water, minerals and energy. It results in irregular and inequitable use of resources that causes their depletion.

Impact of Deforestation: Forest affects climate, water and soil cycle. Reason for Deforestation—Increased population, industrial growth, mining, irrigation, overgrazing, commercial logging.

It causes: (i) Rise in global warming; (ii) Increase of CO_2 in atmosphere and rise in climatic temperature; (iii) Loss of rainfall and change in pattern of rainfall; (iv) Irregular or non-regulated water cycle; (v) Soil erosion; (vi) Degradation of land; (vii) Increase in concentration of pollutants in environment.

Deterioration of Hydrological Resources: Due to the industrialization, demand for water has gone up to a large extent.

QUESTIONS

A. Short Answer Questions
1. Write down any three causes of harmful effects of mining.
2. Name a few pollutants released from different industries.
3. Write two environmental consequences of energy generation from fossil fuel.
4. Write a few problems caused due to Urbanisation in our ecosystem.
5. How is deforestation resulting in increase in concentration of pollutants in ecosystem?

B. Long Answer Questions
1. Describe the physical and social impacts of mining.
2. Describe briefly about any two important areas where people have been affected by mining.
3. What are the different effects of industries on our ecosystem?
4. What is the importance of energy in our lives? How are the sources of energy responsible for causing pollution?
5. Hydroelectricity is a clean fuel generating process but it creates a great socio-economic damage to a few. Justify this statement.
6. What are the environmental consequences of energy generation from petroleum?
7. Write down different pollutants that are emitted by automobiles and how do they effect us.
8. Urbanisation is an irreversible process that is costing too much on our environment. Justify the statement.
9. What does deforestation mean and what are the main causes of deforestation?
10. What is global warming and how is deforestation responsible for it?
11. How are our hydrological resources getting deteriorated?

11
Impact of Industrial Wastes & Its Accumulation

INDUSTRIAL WASTES

Wastes that result from different types of small and large industries are called industrial wastes. These are materials that cannot be utilized by any process in that industry. The wastes can be in organic or inorganic form, for *e.g.,* wastes like fibres, crushed grass, pathogenic organisms, remnants of flesh, etc., are organic wastes that come out of various food processing, packaging units, slaughter houses, etc. while chemicals like arsenic, lead, mercury, fly ash, dust, etc., are discharged from various metallurgical or manufacturing industries. Following are few types of industrial wastes:

OVERVIEW

Industrial wastes are a major hazard to the existing ecosystem. However, advanced they become, there is a tendency in the industry to get rid of the wastes generated in their production activities without any thought about the damage it will cause to the environment. The main culprits are mining, construction, oil refining and cement factories.

(A) Mining Wastes

The expansion of technology and industrial revolution has increased the need for resources like coal and minerals that have caused the ten-fold increase in mining activities. Wastes that are generated during the entire mining process *i.e.,* extraction, benefication and processing are called mining wastes. These substances inflict slow degradation of ecology and usually include hazardous wastes. Wastes from the extractive operations involve materials that must be removed to gain access to the mineral resource, such as topsoil, overburden and waste rock, and tailings that remain after the mineral have been largely extracted from the ore.

Mine Tailings: Large dumps of wastes that are piled up in the locality of the mining area pose an environmental threat. These are generated after mining and quarrying. These dumps release toxic elements that produce slag.

Following is a list of various wastes from different mines:

1. Slag from primary zinc, copper, lead processing, phosphorous production.
2. Red and Brown muds from Bauxite refining.
3. Phosphogypsum from phosphoric acid production.
4. Gasifier ash from coal gasification.
5. Process waste water from coal gasification.
6. Calcium sulphate sludge from primary copper processing.
7. Fluorogypsum from hydrofluoric acid production.
8. Residue from roasting/leaching of chrome ore.
9. Sludge from carbon-steel production.

Some of these wastes are inert and hence not likely to represent a significant pollution threat to the environment but they cause smoothening of river beds and possible collapse if stored in large quantities. However, other fractions, in particular those generated by the Non-Ferrous Metal Mining industry, may contain large quantities of dangerous substances, such as heavy metals. the extraction and subsequent mineral processing of metals and metal compounds result in the generation of acid or alkaline drainage. Moreover, the management of tailings is an intrinsically risky activity, often involving residual processing chemicals and elevated levels of metals. In many cases tailings are stored in heaps or in large ponds, where they are retained by means of dams.

Mining operations cause leaching of metals into the acidic effluents thus adding to the metal content in river, lakes and ground water. For *e.g.,* discharge of mercury from gold mining activities had polluted some streams in Brazil and Equador and created serious health problems.

Similarly, the mining processes release harmful chemicals like mercury and cyanide into local streams and rivers polluting both water and land. It exposes the buried metal sulphides to the environment causing run off of strong sulphuric acid and metal oxides into local water ways.

Smoke, dust, fumes and particulate matter are released in the air due to the activities like drilling, blasting, road haulage, crushing and screening.

Sulphur dioxide, carbon dioxide and other toxic gases are liberated during processing of minerals in open Bhattas to convert coal into coke, roasting of sulphide ores and oxidation of mine dumps and coal scans. Mining of coal, mica produce acidic waste. Lead is released as a result of the process of smelting of lead bearing ores and metals and this can enter water and soil resource and can accumulate in the biological system. Metals like lead, nickel, arsenic, beryllium, tin, vanadium, titanium are released in air as solid particles, liquid droplets and gases in areas where mining and metallurgical processes are carried on. Hazardous materials like cyanide salts are released when used to extract gold and silver from their ores. Sometimes methane gas leakage is seen during the course of mining.

(B) Wastes From Cement Factories

Cement manufacturing is one of the largest mineral commodity industry.

The principal chemical elements required for the production of cement are calcium, silicon, aluminum and iron. Calcium is provided typically from limestone usually mined on close to the plant site.

Silicon and aluminium come from clay, shale, slate, and/or sand. Iron can come from a variety of sources including iron ore or steel mill scale.

Cement is considered as one of the most important building materials around the world. It is mainly used for the production of concrete. Concrete is a mixture of inert mineral aggregates, *e.g.,* sand, gravel, crushed stones and cement. Cement consumption and production is closely related to construction activity, and therefore to the general economic activity.

Cement is one of the most produced materials around the world. Due to the importance of cement as a construction material, and the geographic abundance of the main raw materials, *i.e.* limestone, cement is produced in virtually all countries. The energy consumption by the cement factory is estimated at about 2 per cent of the global primary energy consumption, or almost 5 per cent of the total global industrial energy consumption. Due to the dominant use of carbon intensive fuels, *e.g.,* coal, in clinker making, the cement factory is also a major source of CO_2 emissions. Besides energy consumption, the clinker making process also emits CO_2 due to the calcining process. The cement factory contributes 5 per cent of total global carbon dioxide emissions.

The cement factories emit dust and smoke which contains carbon, metals and other solid materials that pollute the air. Some of them remain suspended in the air. So they are called as Suspended Particulate Matter (SPM). Cement factories also produce sulphides with cement lime dust and carbon soot too.

The waste waters from cement factories generally contain large quantities of suspended solids.

Cement factories during their manufacturing process produce hydrogen sulphide, sulphur oxide, fluorides and dusts.

All these pollutants create a harmful impact on animals, plants and humans. For e.g. the cement dust gets deposited on leaves, when moistened, it gets encrusted and plug the leaf openings. The pollutants from cement factories pollute water bodies and harm aquatic life, *i.e.,* one such example is pollution of River Sone at Dalmia Nagar (in Bihar). Various coarse and fine particles in cement dust are a potential health hazard as they block and disturb the nasal and respiratory tract. The stone crushers and the hot mix plants too create a menace. The SPM levels in the areas of stone crushing are more than five times the industrial safety limits.

It is beyond doubt that cement factory is an important manufacturing factory as cement becomes the most important component of infrastructure development which is an important aspect of growth and progress of industrialization, but the level of pollution should be checked for the harmful emissions.

(c) Wastes From Construction Industry

The pressure of exponential growing population is increasing on the resources. To provide dwelling units to this growing population, forests are denuded and the area is developed to create housing projects. Not only houses but for a better living more and more roads, bridges, flyovers, railway stations, tracks, airports, work places *i.e.*, offices and industrial units are constructed too. The waste generation does not restrict to construction process but also come out from the old and demolished buildings.

Construction waste consists of unwanted material produced directly or incidentally by the construction industries.

Construction and demolition waste is generated whenever any construction/ demolition activity takes place, such as, building roads, bridges, flyover, subway, remodelling, etc. It consists mostly of inert and non-biodegradable materials such as concrete, plaster, metal, wood, plastics, etc. This also includes building materials such as insulation, nails, electrical wiring and rubber, as well as waste originating from site preparation such as dredging materials, tree stumps, and rubble, etc.

A part of this waste comes to the municipal stream. These wastes are heavy and having high density, often bulky and occupy considerable storage space either on the road or in communal waste bin/container. It is not uncommon to see huge piles of such waste, stacked on roads especially in large projects, resulting in traffic congestion and disruption.

Waste from small units like individual house construction or demolition, finds its way into the nearby municipal bin/waste storage depots, making the municipal waste heavy and degrading its quality for further treatment like composting or energy recovery. Often it finds its way into surface drains, choking them. It constitutes about 10-20 per cent of the municipal solid waste (excluding large construction projects).

It is estimated that the construction industry in India generates about 10-12 million tonnes of waste annually. Much building waste is made up of materials such as bricks, concrete and wood damaged or unused for various reasons during construction.

Certain components of construction waste such as plasterboard are hazardous once landfilled. Plasterboard is broken down in landfill conditions releasing hydrogen sulphide, a toxic gas.

Construction waste may contain lead, asbestos, or other hazardous substances.

This category of waste is complex due to the different types of building materials being used. The most commonly occurring hazardous materials found in construction and demolition waste are:

- Adhesives
- Asbestos
- Asbestos Materials
- CFC - refrigerants and foam
- Treated timber
- Emulsions
- Solvent-based concrete additives
- Resins
- Some scrap electrical and electronic material
- Bituminous compounds used for roofing
- Some packaging associated with hazardous substances

It is important to safely dispose and treat these wastes, but the best way is to prevent the harmful pollutants to spoil the environment.

There is a potential to recycle many elements of construction waste. Often roll-off containers are used to transport the waste. Rubble can be crushed and reused in construction projects. Waste wood can also be recovered and recycled.

Government or local authorities should make rules about how much waste should be sorted before it is hauled away to landfills or other waste treatment facilities. Some hazardous materials may not be moved, before the authorities have ascertained that safety guidelines and restrictions have been followed. Proper handling and disposal of such toxic elements as lead, asbestos or radioactive materials should be their primary concern.

(D) Wastes From Oil Refineries

Petroleum is a dark oily liquid with an unpleasant odour. It is not soluble in water and floats on it. The word '*Petro*' means rock and '*oleum*' means oil. The name petroleum indicates that this oil is obtained from rocks. It is present between two non-porous rock layers deep inside the earth. Holes are drilled through these rock layers into the earth's crust. It provides energy as fuel to most of the automobiles and also for heating houses. The petroleum obtained from the earth's crust has many impurities in it and is called as crude oil. This crude oil is taken through pipes to the oil refineries and purified to obtain the useful products in fractions. Thus, the process is called *fractional distillation*. Petrol, diesel, kerosene and petroleum gas are main petro chemicals obtained from the crude oil. The crude oil releases many toxic chemicals in the environment during the process of purification. So it is responsible for generating many harmful wastes or pollutants.

The smoke coming out of refineries has particles of carbon, metals, solids, etc. Because sulphur and nitrogen are introduced in various stages of the process, sulphur dioxide (SO_2) or nitrogen dioxide (NO_2) emerge as major pollutants. On combining with rain water and oxygen they form sulphuric acid (H_2SO_4) and nitric acid (HNO_3) and fall down as acid rains that have a devastating effect not only on the biotic components but also the articles, rock, stones, etc. Since the crude oil is a mixture of hydrocarbons hence during the refining process many types of hydrocarbons are also released in the form of gases called volatile organic compounds (VOCs) and ozone too. Ozone is a photochemical oxidant emitted directly from combustion sources. It is also a dangerous pollutant. The other pollutants besides unburnt hydrocarbons, VOCs, SO_2, NO_2 include carbon dioxide (CO_2), carbon monoxide (CO), soot, dust and suspended particulate matter (SPM), cyanides, oils and alkalis, etc. A foul smelling gas known for its rotten egg like odour called hydrogen sulphide (H_2S) is also emitted from the petroleum refineries. The organic or hydrocarbon vapours include a large number of chemical compounds like paraffin, olefin, aromatic hydrocarbon and chlorinated hydrocarbon. They also contribute to the formation of smog along with some fluorides and dust. Smog can result in severe sight and respiration problems and even may be carcinogenic (cancer producing) these all are together called as hazardous air pollutants, posing an acute threat to health and life of people.

Acid Rain: The oil refining process produces sulphur and nitrogen which reacts with oxygen and are converted to their respective oxides *i.e.*, sulphur dioxide (SO_2) and nitrogen dioxide (NO_2) which are soluble in water. During rainfall these oxides react with large volumes of water vapour in atmosphere to forms acids like sulphuric acid (H_2SO_4), nitric acid (HNO_3) and nitrous acid (HNO_2). When these acids precipitate together they create acid rain.

The Taj Mahal, one among the seven wonders of the world, the beauty in white has now turned yellow due to the effect of the pollutants from Mathura Oil Refinery that is located 60 kms away from the Taj Mahal. The oil refinery daily emits 25-30 tonnes of SO_2. SO_2 precipitation together with humidity and low wind speed has caused the disfiguration of marble termed as '*cancer of the stone*' or '*stone cancer*'. The sulphuric acid (H_2SO_4) of the acid rain reacts with calcium carbonate ($CaCO_3$) in the marble to form calcium sulphate ($CaSO_4$) which causes pitting in the Taj and discolouration of the white marble surface. Chipping and breaking edges of the marble slabs, marble at some places has also developed cracks and thus this beautiful monument is getting deteriorated.

Different Kinds of Waste Generated by Petroleum Refineries

Pollution	Approximate Quantities
1. Cooling systems	3.5-5 m^3 of waste water generated per ton of crude phenol 20-200 mg/l
2. Polluted waste water	oil 100-300 mg/l (desalted water)

	oil 5000 mg/l in tank bottom benzene 1-100 mg/l heavy metals 0·1-100 mg/l
3. Solid waste and sludge	3 to 5 kg per ton of crude (80% should be considered as hazardous waste because of the heavy metals and toxic organic presence)
4. VOC emissions	0.5 to 6 kg/ton of crude BTX (Benzene, Toluene and Xylene) 0.75 to 6 g/ton of crude sulphur oxides 0.2-0.6 kg/ton of crude
5. Other emissions	Nitrogen oxides 0.006-0.5 kg/ton of crude

Smoke is formed when the burning mixture contains insufficient oxygen or is not sufficiently mixed. Modern furnace control systems prevent this from happening during normal operation.

Smells are the most difficult emission to control and the easiest to detect. Refinery smells are generally associated with compounds containing sulphur, where even tiny losses are sufficient to cause a noticeable odour.

Water: Aqueous effluent's consists of cooling water, surface water and process water contaminate and degrade environment.

IMPACT OF WASTE ACCUMULATION

Spoilage of Landscape: Spoilage of landscape is directly related to improper disposal of wastes. The waste accumulation not only ruins the natural beauty of the land but also provide a home to rats and other disease carrying organisms. Sources of these wastes may be excess heaps from mines, paper mills, fertilizers manufacturing units, and the groceries from domestic waste like food scraps, vegetable remains, plastics, cans, construction waste, etc. Every year several tonnes of solid waste is dumped along the highways and other places. This not only destroys the greenery of that area but also reduce the area where children can play. Also, the soil on which the garbage is thrown becomes infertile and toxic in nature due to changes in the physio-chemical and biological characteristics of the soil, thereby spoiling landscape.

Health Hazards of Pollution: Waste accumulation is not only responsible for creation of health problems, but also equally responsible for environmental pollution of any type *viz.* soil, water and air. Burning of fuel in industries, thermal power plants and vehicles generates huge amount of smoke and other pollutants that release toxic substances into the environment leading to air pollution. These toxic pollutants remain suspended in air and are called Suspended Particulate Matter *i.e.* SPM. While disposal of large amount of waste from industries, agricultural practices and domestic sewage into land, ponds, lakes, streams or river leads to water and soil pollution. The following are the hazards of waste accumulation on human health:

Effects of Air Pollutants on Human Health

The toxic gases present in air enter human body through inhalation or breathing. Let us now discuss the health effects of waste accumulation of air pollutants:

Air Pollutants	Health Effects
1. Nitrogen oxide	Asthma, bronchitis, impairs functioning of lungs.
2. Sulphur dioxide	Burning of the nose and throat, breathing difficulties.
3. Ozone	Causes cough, dryness of throat and headache
4. Carbon monoxide	Effect nervous system, increases respiratory problems, continuous inhalation can cause death.
5. Chlorofluoro-carbons (CFCs)	CFCs can destroy ozone layer which allow more of harmful UV radiation to reach us, thus causing, skin cancer.

Effects of Soil and Water Pollutants on Human Health

The waste from Industries and Agriculture practices are often discharged into land, rivers, ponds, etc. When these toxic pollutants, present in waste enter human body through food chain it leads to harmful health effects as they contain heavy metals and chemicals. Let us now discuss the health effects of waste accumulation of water and soil pollutants :

Lead: Lead is hazardous to health as it accumulates in the body and affects the central nervous system. Children and pregnant women are most at risk.

Fluoride: Excess fluorides can cause yellowing of the teeth and damage to the spinal cord and other crippling diseases.

Nitrates: Drinking water that gets contaminated with nitrates can prove fatal especially to infants that drink formula milk as it restricts the amount of oxygen that reaches the brain causing the '*blue baby*' syndrome. It is also linked to digestive tract cancers.

Chlorinated Solvents: These are linked to reproduction disorders and to some cancers.

Arsenic: Arsenic poisoning through water can cause liver and nervous system damage, vascular diseases and also skin cancer.

Mercury: Contamination containing mercury may result into minamata disease, mental disorders, etc.

Other Heavy Metals: Heavy metals cause damage to the nervous system and the kidney, and other metabolic disruptions.

Pesticides: Certain chemicals present in pesticides affect and damage nervous system. Some pesticides contain cancer causing elements.

Sewage: Sewage contains harmful pathogens which include virus, bacteria, protozoa, and parasitic worms. Contaminated water contains many of these pathogens and its consumption causes various water-borne diseases.

Water-borne Diseases	Symptoms
1. Typhoid	Diarrhoea, vomiting, inflamed intestine
2. Cholera	Diarrhoea, vomiting, dehydration
3. Hepatitis	Headache, fever, abdominal pain, enlarged lever.
4. Dysentery	Diarrhoea, fatal in infants.
5. Gastroenteritis	Nausea, vomiting, acute stomach pain.

EFFECT ON TERRESTRIAL AND AQUATIC LIFE

Wastes accumulate in the environment and pollute the air, water and soil resources. This in turn causes extinction and death of plants and animals that live on land as well as in water. Some effects on terrestrial and aquatic life are summarized as follows:

- Acid rain (formed in the air) destroys fish life in lakes and streams. Acid rain can kill trees, destroy the leaves of plants, can infiltrate soil and making it unsuitable for purposes of nutrition and habitation. Chemical contamination has been known to cause declines in frog biodiversity. Oil pollution (as part of chemical contamination) can negatively affect development of marine organisms, increase susceptibility to disease and affect reproductive processes.
- Elevated concentration of metals such as mercury and cadmium can occur in the flesh of large and wide ranging predatory fishes, dolphins, sea birds, etc.
- Thermal pollution has a significant impact on the distribution and abundance of native fish species in estuaries and coastal systems. Their changed behaviour may include their reduced breeding by preventing migration to spawning sites.
- The presence of excess amount of free chlorine in streams or rivers completely destroys the aquatic life including fish.
- Bio-accumulation in sea-birds and marine mammals has been linked to reduced breeding success.

LESSON AT A GLANCE

Industrial Wastes: Wastes that result from different types of small and large industries are called industrial wastes. They can be both organic and inorganic and cannot be further used in that industry.

Industrial waste are of following types:

Mining Wastes: Result during the mining activity:

- Mine tailing are the large dumps of wastes piled up in mining areas, contain toxic waste that produce slag.

- The effluents are highly acidic or alkaline.
- Mining causes leaching of metals into acidic effluents and adds the metals into water sources.
- They expose the buried metal sulphides.
- Mining releases dust, smoke, fumes, CO_2, SO_2, NO_2 in air and lead, arsenic, mercury, cyanide, etc., in water.

Waste from Cement Factories : Cement is one of the largest mineral commodity:
- Requires elements like calcium, silicon, aluminium and iron, lime stone, clay, etc.
- Emit dust, smoke, SPM, sulphides of metals, hydrogen sulphide, sulphur oxide, fluorides.
- These pollutants harm plant, animal and human life on land and in water.

Wastes from Construction Industry: It includes the unwanted material produced during construction and demolition both. It consists of mainly inert and non-degradable material like plasterboard, asbestos, CFC, treated timber, emulsions, resin, etc.

Wastes from Oil Refineries: Petroleum is a dark oily liquid with an unpleasant odour. It is extracted in form of crude oil that has many impurities in it, so it has to be processed in oil refineries to extract clean petrol.

Refineries emit smoke, dust, carbon, metals, SO_2, NO_2, etc. SO_2 and NO_2 react with atmospheric moisture to form acid rains.

Acid rains and SO_2 from Mathura Refinery have caused the cancer of stone or yellowing of stone on the Taj Mahal.

It also released certain VOCs (Volatile Organic Compounds).

Impact of Waste Accumulation:

Various diseases spread on an epidemic scale due to waste accumulation on land and water bodies. Vectors like files, mosquitoes, rodents and pet animals transmit these diseases.

QUESTIONS

A. Short Answer Questions
1. How does leaching of metals caused by mining affect the environment?
2. Categorize the wastes produced by mining in a tabular format under the categories.

Solid effluents	Liquid effluents	Gaseous effluents

3. How does waste discharged from cement factories affect leaves?
4. How does the waste from cement factories affect human health?
5. Why was requirement of coal and mineral exceeded lately?

6. What role can government authorities play in managing waste generated due to construction activities?
7. What is smog ? How is it caused and what are its effects?
8. What is acid rain and how is it caused?
9. Write a short note on stone cancer of Taj Mahal.
10. What are the gases included in VOCs?

B. Long Answer Questions

1. What are industrial wastes? Name a few industries that produce wastes.
2. What are mining wastes and mine tailings? How do mine tailings affect the environment?
3. List a few effluents that are discharged during mining activity.
4. Write a note on waste caused due to mining.
5. What are elements basically required to manufacture cement and what are the other requisites to manufacture cement?
6. What kind of pollutants are emitted from cement industries?
7. Define construction wastes and in which areas do we normally find these? Why do you think a lot of construction wastes are generated these days?
8. What kind of wastes are released from construction industries and where are these wastes normally disposed off?
9. What is petroleum and in what form is it obtained? What are oil refineries?
10. Briefly describe the pollutants that are emitted from refineries and how do they affect the environment?

12
Eco-friendly Technologies

The industrial revolution has been a major landmark in the history of mankind. Although, technology has made human life better but the indiscriminate manufacturing and use of industrial products has produced a lot of toxic pollutants and tonnes of waste which is very harmful for our environment. Hence, it has become very important to replace the old and harmful technology with the efficient and eco-friendly technology. This will not only improve production, but also lessen the damage to the environment along with facilitating ecologically sustainable development.

OVERVIEW
Due to technological advancement and industrial revolution, ecological balance is disturbing. This ecosystem can be preserved by replacing harmful technologies with the efficient and eco-friendly technologies.

ECO-FRIENDLY TECHNOLOGY

The goal of any technology is to make our lives better. The phrase environmental friendly is used to refer to goods, services or practices considered to inflict little or no harm on the environment. Eco-friendly technology (also known as sustainable technology) is based on use of renewable resources as raw material and energy and their transformation through highly efficient biotechnology to produce environment friendly products. Solar power and wind power are some of its outstanding examples. Eco-friendly technology looks to improve situations in two major areas:

1. Eco-efficiency
2. Reduction of harmful waste.

The term eco-efficiency was coined by the World Business Council for Sustainable Development (WBCSD) in its 1992 publication "*Changing Course*". It is based on the concept of creating more goods and services while using fewer resources and creating less waste and pollution. Eco-efficiency is increasingly becoming a key requirement for success in business because this will improve the image of company in the eyes of consumer. According to the WBCSD, critical aspects of eco-efficiency are:

- A reduction in the material intensity of goods or services;
- A reduction in the energy intensity of goods or services;
- Reduced dispersion of toxic materials;
- Improved recyclability;
- Maximum use of renewable resources;
- Greater durability of products;
- Increased service intensity of goods and services.

WAYS TO IMPROVE EFFICIENCY OF EXISTING TECHNOLOGIES

1. **Reduction in the Amount of Raw Material Used:** This will reduce the amount of raw materials used, which is depleting rapidly. The wise use of raw materials will lead to less wastage and less pollution and thus eco-efficiency can be achieved.
2. **Reducing Pollution:** This will reduce the hazardous effects of pollutants on environment. The present technology must be used judiciously and proper maintenance of equipment and machines will definitely lead to relatively lesser pollution. There are many eco-friendly technologies that pollute less. Solar power, wind power, bio-cleaner and bio-gas are some of the examples of eco-friendly technology.
3. **Recycling Material:** This will reduce the amount of waste, landfill spaces and the pressure on using newer resources. Man generated waste products can be recycled. For example, recycling of vehicle tyres will reduce the use of natural rubber for producing new tyres. This will save the raw material and cost production.

> **Advantages of Eco-friendly Technology:** It allows improvement in economic performance while minimizing harm to the environment by:
> - Increasing the efficiency in the selection and use of materials and energy sources;
> - Designing out the need for toxic substances;
> - Reducing toxic emissions, and increasing the recovery and reuse of *"waste"* material;
> - Development and permanent impro-vement of cleaner processes and products;
> - Eco-marketing—Increased profits by developing innovative products and increasing market share; and
> - Greater durability of products.

4. **Use of Renewable Resources:** Renewable resources of energy are inexhaustible *i.e.*, we can use it repeatedly without depleting it and polluting it. Uses of sunlight, wind, flowing water, etc., are some of the examples of renewable source. They are often described as clean and green forms of energy because of their minimal environmental impact compared to fossil fuels.
5. **Ensuring that Goods are Durable:** A durable good is a good that does not quickly wear out and can be used for a longer time. This, in turn, will ensure that raw materials are saved by not making the product number of times. An example of durable eco-friendly product is Eco-furniture because it made with endurable material and can be recycled.

IMPLEMENTING NEW ECO-FRIENDLY TECHNOLOGIES

Since the use of renewable energy resources is a part of achieving eco-efficiency so UNEP (United Nations Environment Programme) and GEF (Global Environment Facility) has begun a project called SWERA (Solar and Wind Energy Resource Assessment) which helps to facilitate investment in large scale use of solar and wind energy in developing countries.

To ensure that the products reaching the consumers are technically correct the Bureau of Indian Standards (BIS) certifies them with ISI Mark. Similarly, an Eco-Mark Scheme of labeling those products that are eco-friendly is started by CPCB (Central Pollution Control Board) and the Ministry of Environment and Forests with the help of Bureau of Indian Standards. Products like toilet soaps, detergents, other toiletries, edible products, oils, packaging materials, etc., are generally marked with an Eco-Mark.

Many companies have started adopting and encouraging eco-efficient technologies because such technologies improve environmental performance and reduce the rapid depletion of resources. Let's discuss some of the examples of eco-friendly technology that already exist in brief:

1. Solar Energy: The energy from the sun is the ultimate source of energy. India mostly receives almost 5,000 trillion kwh per year in around 300 sunny days. We need to harness this solar energy by using various eco-friendly products like solar cookers, solar heaters, solar cells, etc. Solar collectors that face the sun, trap the energy of sun. This technology is eco-friendly as compared to conventional heating systems because it is pollution free and uses renewable source of energy. The basic principles on which the various solar devices work are:

(1) Concentrating sunlight

(2) Converting light to heat

(3) Trapping heat.

2. Windmills: Windmill is eco-friendly as it uses the renewable source of energy *i.e.*, wind. It converts the energy of wind into rotational energy by means of vanes called sails or blades. Originally, windmills were developed for milling grain for food production but these days they are also used to pump water and for generating electricity.

3. CNG: Compressed Natural Gas (CNG) is used as fuel in automobiles. This gas is eco-friendly as it is cheap and emits fewer pollutants as compared to petrol and diesel.

4. Biogas: Biogas is produced from the anaerobic digestion of organic matter such as animal manure, sewage and municipal solid waste. After it is processed to required standards of purity, biogas becomes a renewable substitute for natural gas and can be used to fuel natural gas vehicles. Along with the biogas slurry is also produced which is a good fertilizer.

5. Bagasse: It is the fibrous matter that remains after sugarcane or sorghum stalks are crushed to extract their juice. It is currently used as a biofuel and in the manufacture of pulp and paper products and building materials.

6. Gasohol: The fermentation of sugar (anaerobic respiration by the micro-organisms) produces ethanol and this is mixed with petrol to produce a liquid fuel called gasohol which is used to run vehicles. This is emerging as another pollution free alternative source of energy. In the present context, the ethanol is being mixed with petrol to decrease the pollution as well as import bill.

7. Biomass Gasification: This technology uses agro-waste *i.e.*, animal and crop waste to generate energy based on gasification process to convert solid fuel into gaseous fuel which can be used to serve domestic and agricultural purposes. The biomass gasifiers convert these wastes by removing carbon monoxide and hydrogen sulphide from the crude biogas and process it with steam to produce hydrogen rich, clean and pollution free gas. This gas is very useful in generating electrical power for rice mill, maize mill, groundnut mill, etc.

8. **Lightweight Materials:** The uses of magnesium alloy and plastics have improved fuel efficiency and reduced the weight of automobiles. This has decreased the fuel consumption. Though, there are so many technologies, they still haven't gained popularity as many of these technologies still need to be developed and made more efficient.

USE OF ENERGY EFFICIENT TECHNOLOGY IN VARIOUS INDUSTRIES

Industrial waste or industrial pollution is a major source contributing to increasing environmental hazards. If eco-friendly technology is used in industries then it would generate less waste and pollution. A few industries that have taken up this step are:

(1) **Automobile Industry:** The use of magnesium alloy and plastics have improved fuel efficiency and reduced the weight of automobiles. This has decreased the fuel consumption.

(2) **Leather Industry:** Instead of processing the leather by using salt and hazardous chemicals, leather is now processed by using the leather processing enzymes. This has resulted in less generation of waste and increased output.

(3) **Fertilizer Industry:** Instead of chemical based fertilizers that are a major cause of effluents, polluting our soil and water, scientists are getting inclined towards developing organic fertilizers with the help of microbes. The scientific researchers are developing new methods of employing various microbes or culturing them. they either breakdown organic wastes to produce organic fertilizers or act like fertilizers themselves. These facilitate a higher crop yield. It better quality of produce and acts like a soil conditioner and sometimes bio-remediator. For example, the mass production of mycrohiza, that is a microscopic fungi, found in root modules is facilitated by TERI. This is a biofertilizer and is multifaceted specifically in improving the nutrition of the soil. It is pollution free and is widely used in economic plantations, forestry and horticulture. It helps in soil reclamation. Similarly a few fertilizer industries have started using their effluents in phosphatic plants.

Reusing Wastes

If there are devices and techniques that can convert the waste into a raw material to other industries then a lot of effluents passing into the natural resources can be hindered. several areas where wastes can be reused are:

(1) **Agro-based Industries:** A lot of solid wastes and waste water is released while processing agro products. These wastes can be decomposed and reused, like molasses and bagasse are released while processing sugar cane in sugar mills. By little treatment these can be used in distilleries and pulp and paper industries. The same can be achieved by treating Jute wastes which have a lot of cellulose so that it can be used in paper industry. Technology has been developed that can use rice husk to make strong particle board.

(2) **Silk Industry:** In silk industry the waste pupae can be used as poultry feed as it is rich in animal protein.

(3) **Automobile Industry:** The metal part of old car or vehicles can be extracted and recycled to make new car.

(4) **Plastic Industry:** Researches are carried on and technologies are being developed by which plastics can be recycled to be used in the manufacture of glass fibres.

STRATEGIES TO PROTECT ENVIRONMENT FROM INDUSTRIAL WASTE

The non-recyclable plastics that cannot be destroyed have become a threat to our global environment as they are a big source of pollution. Industrial ecology should be observed to prevent this, as it helps to transform it into by-products that can have both a market value and an environmental value. Green marketing should be practiced that means marketing of eco-friendly products. For example, Thermoplastics *i.e.,* PVC, poly propylene, Teflon, etc., are finding more and more applications in the engineering world as they can be recycled again and again. These are also known as green plastics. A specific and distinctive marking can be made on various products that can identify that the goods are eco-friendly. This helps to encourage the manufacturers to use eco-friendly materials in their products. It also helps to create a green world. This is quite similar to the Eco-Mark scheme that is mentioned in the chapter earlier.

Similarly, proper waste disposal practices may be adopted by identifying the organisations which recycle scrap and waste. There are many organisation in metropolitan cities who have initiated to collect e-waste, plastic waste to process them to be recycled if they can be or dispose them securely without any harm to the environment. Such kind of organisations must be encouraged to develop further and expand in all the areas of the country.

LESSON AT A GLANCE

Eco-friendly Technology: It is based on use of renewable resources as raw material and energy and their transformation through highly efficient biotechnology to produce environment friendly products.

Ways to Improve Efficiency of Existing Technologies: (i) Reduction in the amount of raw material used; (ii) Reducing pollution; (iii) Recycling material; (iv) Use of renewable resources; and (v) Ensuring that goods are durable.

Eco-mark scheme: This scheme is used to label eco-friendly products which do not cause pollution. We must use solar energy, wind energy, tidal energy i.e., all the renewable and cleaner energy resources to run our appliances.

Implementing New Eco-friendly Technologies: (i) Solar energy; (ii) Windmills; (iii) CNG; (iv) Biogas; (v) Bagasse; (vi) Gasohol; (vii) Biomass gasification; and (viii) Lightweight materials.

We must use eco-friendly technology is different industries like automobile, leather, fertilizer industries, etc.

QUESTIONS

A. Short Answer Questions

1. Why it is important to adopt efficient and eco-friendly technology?
2. What are the different ways to achieve eco-efficiency?

3. Write down the full forms of :
    (i) WBCSD
    (ii) CPCB
    (iii) UNEP
    (iv) GEF
4. What is the 'Eco-mark' scheme?
5. What are the advantages of eco-friendly technology?
6. Give two uses of Bagasse.
7. What is gasohol?
8. Name two materials used in the manufacture of light weight material.
9. What is the use of eco-friendly technology in leather industry?

B. Long Answer Questions
1. What is meant by the term 'eco-efficiency'? Explain the ways to achieve eco-efficiency.
2. Explain with the help of examples how eco-friendly and efficient technology helps to prevent and reduce pollution.
3. Mention about the industries, where waste can be reused.

13
Waste Disposal Methods

Since the beginning, humankind has been generating waste. With the progress of civilization, the earth itself became more polluted with the generation of non-biodegradable solid waste. The increased urbanization was also largely responsible for the increase in solid waste. The local corporations have adapted different methods for the disposal and recycling of this waste. Recycling involves the collection of used and discarded materials, processing these materials and utilising them into new products. It reduces the amount of waste that is thrown into the community dustbins thereby making the environment cleaner and the air fresher to breathe. Studies have revealed that 7 per cent–15 per cent of the waste is recycled. If recycling is done in a proper manner, it will solve the problems of waste or garbage.

OVERVIEW
Waste disposal methods include various methods like segregation, dumping, composting, drainage and treatment of effluents before discharge, etc.

METHODS OF WASTE DISPOSAL

We live in a world where nearly everything is considered disposable. Waste Disposal refers to the '*different treatments which are given to the waste for avoiding environmental and health hazards*'. It is the most important element as it includes planning, administrative set up, finance, technology support and their interdisciplinary relationships. There are several methods for waste disposal:

1. Segregation
2. Dumping
3. Composting
3. Drainage
5. Treatment of Effluents.

SEGREGATION

Waste segregation is the process of dividing garbage and waste products in an effort to reduce, reuse and recycle materials. Certain things that are not needed around the house are kept aside to be sold to the kabadiwala. These items are newspapers, used bottles, magazines, carry bags, aluminum foils, plastics, metal, glass, old exercise books, oil cans, etc. This is the form of dry waste and this kind of segregation is done as a routine in all households in India. Wet form of waste consists of leftover foodstuff, vegetable peels, etc., which should be put in a compost pit and the compost could be used as manure in the garden.

On the basis of degradation, waste can be segregated as:

1. **Biodegradable:** Biodegradable waste include organic waste, *e.g.* kitchen waste, vegetables, fruits, flowers, leaves from the garden and paper.

2. **Non-biodegradable:** Non-biodegradable waste can be further segregated into :
   (i) Recyclable waste—plastics, paper, glass, metal, etc.
   (ii) Toxic waste—old medicines, paints, chemicals, bulbs, spray cans, fertilizer and pesticide containers, batteries, shoe polish, etc.
   (iii) Soiled—hospital waste such as discarded syringe needles, bandages, swabs, plasters, cloth soiled with blood and other body fluids, etc.
   Toxic and soiled waste must be disposed off with utmost care.

These days Indian government is also giving too much emphasis upon the segregation of waste into dry waste which may be recycled and wet waste which can be converted into compost. For this purpose, special promotional drives and education programmes are being organised by the government.

DUMPING (LAND FILLING)

Dumping or Land filling is an old way of disposing off wastes. It is an easy method of disposal of dry refuse. In this process, solid wastes are dumped in a low lying area and as a result of bacterial action, refuse decreases considerably in volume and are converted gradually into humus. The advantage of landfill is that it is a simple and easy method of disposing off wastes. Dumping have major disadvantages, however, especially in heavily populated areas. This happened in the Gazipur area of East Delhi in September 2017 where the dumping resulted into

Fig.: Dumping Site

collapse of garbage mound which killed at least two people. Toxic chemicals can also filter down through a dump and contaminate groundwater. The liquid that filters through a dump or landfill is called leachate. Dumps may also generate methane, which at times is fatal. Early landfills had significant problems with leachate and methane, but those have largely been resolved at facilities built since about the early 1970s. Well-engineered landfills are lined with several feet of clay and with thick plastic sheets. Leachate is collected at the bottom, drained through pipes and processed. Methane gas is also safely piped out of many landfills.

COMPOSTING

Composting is a process in which, various micro-organisms, including bacteria and fungi, break down organic matter into simpler substances under controlled aerobic conditions (requires oxygen). It is nature's way of recycling. Organic waste, *i.e.*, food waste, manure, leaves, grass trimmings, paper, wood, feathers, crop residue, etc., are dumped in large pits called compost pit. After few

Fig.: Composting

days, these materials biodegrades and turns it into a valuable blackish soil like structure called compost. It is a good organic fertilizer and also makes the soil sticky. The effectiveness of the composting process is dependent upon the environmental conditions present within the composting system *i.e.*, oxygen, temperature, moisture, material disturbance, organic matter and the size and activity of microbial populations. The composting process is carried out by three classes of microbes:

- Psychrophiles-low temperature microbes
- Mesophiles-medium temperature microbes
- Thermophiles-high temperature microbes

Generally, composting begins at mesophilic temperatures and progresses into the thermophilic range.

Advantages of Composting

1. Reduces need for landfill space, thereby, reducing the production of leachate and methane gas.
2. It reduces the volume and weight of organic waste as the composting process converts much of the biodegradable component to gaseous carbon dioxide.
3. It converts organic matter into stable compost that is odour and pathogen free, and can be used as manure in various agriculture practices.
4. It is a clean, healthy and inexpensive method to eliminate wastes.
5. Reduces the need for fertilizers and pesticides.
6. Assists pollution remediation.

Compost: Some Benefits
- It supplies part of the 16 essential elements needed by the plants.
- It helps to reduce the adverse effects of excessive alkalinity, acidity or the excessive use of chemical fertilizer.
- It makes soil easier to cultivate.
- It helps to keep the soil cool in summer and warm in winter.
- It aids in preventing soil erosion by keeping the soil covered.
- It helps in controlling the growth of weeds in the garden.

DRAINAGE

Drainage is removal of undesirable excess water from a region, *i.e.*, crop land, city streets, dwelling place, playground, airport, etc. Many agricultural soils need drainage to improve production or to manage water supplies. The overflowing of surfaces during rainy season essentially needs proper drainage. Drainage can be broadly split into two categories: foul water and surface water. Foul water is domestic, municipal and industrial waterborne waste, and is drained exclusively by piped sewers. Surface water means run-off from roofs, roads, gardens and agricultural land, etc. It is drained by both piped sewers and open watercourses. Thus, drainage helps in removing excess water and excess salts from the land surface and from the crop root zone soil, to provide an environment conducive to good crop growth and yield.

TREATMENT OF EFFLUENTS

It is the process of removal of unwanted foreign material from waste water or sewage. Effluent is the waste water that comes out from residences, businesses and industries in a community. It is 99.94 per cent but the remainder contains some ions, suspended solids and harmful bacteria that must be removed before the water is released into the sea. Waste water treatment plants handle sewage in a step-by-step process:

1. **Preliminary Treatment:** Large solids (plastics, rag, toilet paper residues) are removed first by mechanical screens. Traditionally, screening was used to remove only large solid material (> 25–30 mm) in order to protect downstream operations.

2. **Primary Treatment:** The sewage passes into large sedimentation tanks. Most of the solids settle to the bottom of the tanks and form a watery sludge, known as "*primary sludge*", which is removed for separate treatment. The sewage remaining after settlement has taken place is known as "*settled sewage*".

3. **Secondary (Biological) Treatment:** Settled sewage then flows to an aerobic biological treatment stage where it comes into contact with micro-organisms which remove and oxidise most of the remaining organic pollutants.

4. **Final Settlement:** Following secondary (biological) treatment, the flow passes to final settlement tanks where most of the biological solids are deposited as sludge (secondary sludge) while the clarified effluent passes to the outfall pipe for discharge to a watercourse. The secondary sludge from biological treatment also requires separate treatment and disposal and may be combined with the primary sludge for this purpose.

5. **Tertiary Treatment:** In circumstances where the highest quality of effluent is required, a third (tertiary) stage of treatment can be used to remove most the remaining suspended organic matter from the effluent before it is discharged to a watercourse.

LESSON AT A GLANCE

Wastes are polluting our nature due to urbanization and industrialization.

Methods of Waste Disposal:
   (i) **Segregation:** Waste is divided into (a) biodegradable, (b) Non-biodegradable.
   (ii) **Dumping:** Simple and easy method of disposing of waste.
   (iii) **Composting:** Microbes break down the organic compound into simpler substance under aerobic conditions.
   (iv) **Drainage:** Removal of undesirable excess water.
   (v) **Treatment of Effluents:** Removal of unwanted material from waste steps:
1. Preliminary treatment; 2. Primary treatment; 3. Secondary (biological) treatment; 4. Final settlement; 5. Tertiary treatment.

QUESTIONS

A. Short Answer Questions
1. What do you mean by recycling of waste?
2. What does wet waste consist of?
3. What are the disadvantages of Dumping?

4. Name the three classes of microbes, which carry out the process of composting.
5. In which two classes drainage can be categorized?
6. Explain the primary process of treatment of effluents before discharge.

B. Long Answer Questions

1. What is meant by 'Wet Waste'? Define waste categories on the basis of degradation.
2. Write short notes on:
    (i) Segregation
    (ii) Dumping
    (iii) Composting
3. Write in brief the advantages of composting.
4. Write a short note on the process of treatment of effluents before discharge.

14
Abatement of Pollution

Pollution may be described as any addition to air, water or soil that deteriorate their quality and threatens human life or other living organisms. It can be understood as the unfavourable change of surrounding which takes place mainly because of human activities.

OVERVIEW
Setting standards and implementing them, using technical devices to reduce air pollution.

The concern for environmental quality has been an issue of concern in the backdrop of increasing urbanization, industrial and vehicular pollution as well as pollution due to discharge of waste without confirming to the environmental norms and standards. Realizing the trend of pollution in various environmental media like air, soil, etc., Ministry adopted policy for abatement of pollution, which provides multi-pronged strategies in the form of regulations, legislations, agreements and other measures to prevent and abate pollution. To give effect to various measures and policies for pollution control, various steps have been initiated which include strict regulations, developmental environmental standards, control of vehicular pollution, spatial environmental planning including disposal of solid wastes. In this chapter, we will discuss methods for abatement of air and soil pollution.

ABATEMENT OF AIR POLLUTION

Abating air pollution is a challenging task as there are diverse pollutants and emissions and their varying quantities in the air, emerging from various industries and other sources. The first step is to set up the standard for permissible emissions in the air to make the monitoring and control of pollution possible.

Setting Ambient Air Quality Standards: The Central Pollution Control Board (CPCB) has set up National Ambient Air Quality Standards (NAAQS) that uses Air Quality Index (AQI) to assess the quality of air of a particular area by detecting the pollutants present in the air along with their concentration and their retentivity in the atmosphere.

National Ambient Air Quality Standards (NAAQS) Concentration in Ambient Air (Annual)

Pollutant	Sensitive Area	Industrial Area	Residential, Rural & Other Areas
Sulphur dioxide (SO_2)	15 mg/m^3	80 mg/m^3	60 mg/m^3
Oxides of Nitrogen (NO_2)	15 mg/m^3	80 mg/m^3	60 mg/m^3
Suspended Particulate	70 mg/m^3	360 mg/m^3	140 mg/m^3
Lead (Pb)	0.50 mg/m^3	1.0 mg/m^3	0.75 mg/m^3
Carbon monoxide (CO)	1.0 mg/m^3	5.0 mg/m^3	2.0 mg/m^3

Note : 24-hourly/8-hourly values should be met 98% of the time in a year.
Source: Air quality status and trends in India, CPCB.

METHODS TO CONTROL AIR POLLUTION

The best way to control pollution is to use control techniques and methods at different stages of manufacturing process in the industries.

(A) Using Control Techniques at Source

Here the formation and emission of pollutants is controlled at the source itself through proper design and development of equipments and implementing strategies and methods that do not add to air pollution.

This entire process takes place through following steps:

1. Using Pre-combustion Techniques by Changing the Raw Material: There are certain raw materials that cause a lot of air pollution but they should be substituted with other raw materials which cause less pollution *i.e.*, reduction in sulphur, dust, ash, etc. For example, use of TEL (Tetra Ethyl Lead) has been almost reduced or eliminated in many countries as on its combustion it produces lead which is a toxic substance. The use of nuclear power and natural gas (CNG) is preferred so as to reduce atmospheric emission, same happens with urban areas where distillate oil is used for energy generation instead of coal or diesel to reduce undesirable fumes and particulate matter. The same happened few years back in Agra (U.P.) and Firozabad (U.P.) where coal furnaces were replaced with gas furnaces to abate the pollution in these areas.

2. Using Combustion Modification Techniques by:
   (i) Changing the process.
   (ii) Modifying the existing equipments.
   (iii) Maintaining the equipments.

(i) Changing the process: The introduction of new processes of production reduce industrial emissions and thus lower the pollutants in the atmosphere. For example, the emission of sulphur dioxide can be reduced from metallurgical industries, by using low temperature hydro metallurgical techniques. The fly ash emissions can be reduced from the processes that use coal by washing coal before pulverizing it. catalytic reduction is a technique to reduce nitrogen oxide emissions. The emissions of nitrogen oxide, carbon monoxide and hydrocarbons can be reduced from motor vehicles by using three way catalytic converter.

Table 14·1: Sector-wise Summary of Key Actions that could help in Improving Air Quality

Intervention Type	Industry	Urban	Transport
Clean fuels	Switching to cleaner fuels (reduction in sulphur, gaseous alternatives)	Increasing share of domestic and commercial users of cleaner fuels (gas and kerosene for cooking, electricity for heating)	Use of cleaner fuels (gasoline lead elimination, suphur reduction in liquid fuels, use of gaseous fuels) Better lubricant quality and only pre-mixed 2T oil for two and three wheelers.

Improved technology	More efficient and cleaner combustion technology	Better road infrastructure (road widening, traffic management, new flyovers)	Scrappage of old commercial vehicles and their replacement with a new fleet
Stronger and better enforced regulation	Tightened and better enforced emission norms leading to installation of pollution control devices	Enforcement of land-use zoning regulations (closure and relocation of industry from non-conforming areas, development of green belts/areas)	Introduction of new and more stringent emission norms for new and in-use vehicles

(ii) **Modifying the existing equipment:** By using modern equipments in place of the traditional equipments in industrial processes, the pollutants can be reduced to certain extent. For example, the amount of these pollutants can be reduced by the use of electric furnaces or gas furnaces or controlled basic oxygen furnaces. In petroleum refineries due to evaporation there is a loss of hydrocarbons from storage tanks which can be reduced by designing storage tanks with floating roof cones.

(iii) **Maintaining the equipments:** A lot of pollutants are emitted due to the lack of maintenance of equipment. Many disastrous accidents in industrial areas can take place if enough care is not taken to maintain the machinery. The same is with vehicles where non-maintenance or poor maintenance results in the emission of pollutants in high quantity.

3. Using Post-combustion Control Techniques: This includes use of various pollution control equipments like gravitational settling chambers, electrostatic precipitator, cyclone separators, bag filters, etc., to remove pollutants from fuel gases and vehicle exhausts.

(B) Using Pollution Control Equipments

The air pollution can be minimized by using various control equipments. There can be two kinds of pollutants that are normally found in air:
- Particulate contaminants.
- Gaseous contaminants.

The particulate matter consists of tiny suspended particles that need special control equipments which depends upon volume of particulate matter emitted, the properties or nature of the particulate matter along with its size, the temperature and humidity of the medium, its toxicity and inflammability.

Installation of Devices: The following devices are useful for air pollution control:

1. Fabric Filters (Baghouse Filters): Filters are used to sieve the particulate matter from the gases and trap them and let the clean air pass through. In this system the attached bags trap the particulate matter which form a dust mat on the inside of the bag, which further acts as a filtering medium to remove more particulate matter (almost up to 5 mm) and lets the clear air to pass through.

2. Cyclone Separators: The polluted air is passed through a metallic cylinder rotating at a high speed. Using the centrifugal force, the particulate matter is separated which is thrown outwards towards the wall of separator and fall down.

3. Gravitational Setting Chamber: The polluted gas laden with particulate matter is made to enter from one end of huge rectangular chambers. The horizontal velocity of the stream is lowered so as to help the particulate matter to settle at the bottom due to gravity.

4. Electrostatic Precipitator: This is a special device that helps to control pollution by removing chemicals using the principle of electrostatic precipitation. In this, the particulate matter is electrically charged and is separated as it precipitates from the gas stream under the effect of electrical field. It removes chemicals like lime salts, soot, dioxins, activated charcoal and fly ash that contains metals like lead, cadmium and nickel.

5. Scrubber: It is a device used to spray water to catch pollutants during missions. Wet lime power is sprayed into the hot exhaust chamber to remove pollutants. It is a well scrubber. Acid gases are removed by dry scrubbers.

LESSON AT A GLANCE

Abatement of Air Pollution: Abatement of pollution is an issue of concern. National Ambient Air Quality Standards (NAAQS) have been set by Central Pollution Control Board (CPCB)

Methods to Control Air Pollution:
  (A) Using Control Techniques at Source: This consists of following steps:
   (i) Using pre-combustion techniques by changing the raw material.
   (ii) Using combustion modification techniques: Consists of three sub processes:
       (a) Changing the process; (b) Modifying the existing equipments;
       (c) Maintaining the equipments.
   (iii) Using post-combustion control techniques.
  (B) Using Pollution Control Equipments: (i) Fabric filters; (ii) Cyclone separators; (iii) Gravitational setting chamber; (iv) Electrostatic precipitator; (v) Scrubber.

QUESTIONS

A. Short Answer Questions
  1. Give the full form of:
     (i) CPCB   (ii) AQI
  1. Write a short note on:
     (i) Cyclone separator   (ii) Gravitational setting chamber
     (iii) Scrubber
  2. Name any two methods to Control Air Pollution.

B. Long Answer Questions
  1. How can using control techniques at source help to abate the pollution?
  2. Explain any three devices which are helpful for controlling air pollution.

15 Infrastructure of Indian Economy

For day-to-day working and expansion of our economy, we require a strong infrastructure. the weakness of the infrastructure is clearly visible in slow growth and economic development of the country. No doubt, we have made some progress in building up a sound infrastructure but still much more remains to be done.

INFRASTRUCTURE

Infrastructure is defined as capital of a society or a *social capital*. It must be differentiated from the capital structure of the economy which simply means factories, machines, farms and tractors and all forms of equipment required for the production of goods and services. Infrastructure includes transport and communication, energy and electricity and other public services like water supply, etc. It also includes health, skills and other qualities of the working population. Infrastructural facilities do not produce commodities directly. They facilitate the general economic activities. As such they are known as 'social overhead capital' or 'social overhead costs'.

OVERVIEW

The facilities, services and activities which support the development, expansion and operation of other sectors of economy (particularly agriculture and industry) is called as infrastructure. There has been a significant development and expansion of infrastructural facilities in our country since Independence. It may be divided into Social and Economic infrastructure. Social Infrastructure includes education, training and research, health and family welfare, housing water supply and other civic amenities.

The working of any economy depends on the development and expansion of infrastructural facilities, e.g., power, irrigation, transport, communication, banking and financial services.

These services or facilities are required for a healthy socio-economic structure which can easily be turned into the developed economic structure with the passage of time.

Apart from the production of goods and commodities, the economy generates services as well. Some services are necessary for easing and facilitating the processes of production, *e.g.*, transportation of raw materials. Transportation of the finished product and advertisement of the goods are the services which add to the value of the finished goods after the actual process of production is over. All such services are called '*productive services*'.

As against productive services we have '*consumption services*'. Transport of passengers from one place to another through rail, road, sea or air; provision of medical facilities and provision of educational facilities are services that are consumed directly by us like any other commodity. These services are called '*consumption services*'.

Types of Infrastructure

For economic development, a sound infrastructure is required which may be social as well as economic. '*Social infrastructure*' is the one which contributes to economic processes indirectly and from outside the system of production and distribution by improving the quality of human resource. The network of schools, colleges, hospitals, etc., are examples of social infrastructure. *Economic infrastructure* is one which is mainly within the system of production and distribution and helps the economic process for the growth of the economy by improving the quality of all the economic resources.

Importance of Infrastructure

The working of any economy depends on the expansion of infrastructure. Infrastructure works as the base of an economy. It is the transport, which moves men and materials from one place to another for production, distribution, consumption, and investment. Electricity provides a driving force for machines and meets the lighting requirements of factories, offices and homes. Public utilities like water supply, etc., are necessities for all economic activities. In short, better the infrastructure, better will be the opportunities for production and investment. The under-developed economies of the world generally have very limited infrastructural facilities.

Infrastructure is a component of social capital stock. An increase in capital stock promotes development. It creates new opportunities for investment. Social overhead capital is a precondition for accelerating the growth. The development of an economy is determined by the infrastructure facilities available and to accelerate our economic development, we must further strengthen the infrastructural facilities. In brief, infrastructure is of great importance to an economy as it facilitates functioning of an economy, promotes economic development, improve the quality of human resources, etc.

SOCIAL INFRASTRUCTURE

Social infrastructures include Education, Health, Water, Supply, Housing, Sanitation, etc., which helps in improving living standards.

EDUCATION

Education is universally recognized as a central component of '*Human Capital*'. The role of education as a contributor to economic growth and its impact on population control, life expectancy, infant mortality, improving nutritional status and strengthening civil institution is well recognized.

Role of Education

Education moderates the behaviour of human-being. Education is an important factor for the development of human resources. Education—general, technical and medical improves upon the level of understanding. It also adds to the capacity of human stock to produce more. It increases the mental efficiency of the people. According to **Prof. Strumilin**, "*Primary education causes an increase of 40 per cent in labour productivity, secondary education 100 per cent and higher education 300 per cent.*" According to **Prof. Secomski**, "*Primary education plays a very vital role in the initial stages of development, particularly in the modernization of agriculture and in speeding up the rate of industrialization.*"

Importance of a rational education system is summarized herewith:
- It modifies our behaviour.
- It produces skilled and trained workers.
- It promotes science and technology and develops scientific outlook.
- It enlarges mental horizon of people.
- Education modernizes the attitudes and behaviours of the people.
- Education develops personality.
- Education generates sense of national consciousness and provides sound structure for rapid economic growth.

Expansion of General Education

Over the decades, literacy rates have shown a substantial improvement. The total literacy rate which was only 18.33 per cent in 1951, rose to 64.84 per cent in 2001 and further increased to 74.04 per cent in 2011. According to the census of India, 2011, the literacy rate has gone up to 82.14 per cent for males and 65.4 per cent for females. During the last decade, female literacy rate has shown much higher growth, increasing by 11.24 per centage points as against 6.29 for males; thus, reducing the male-female differential in literacy rates from 21.70 per cent in 2001 to 16.74 per cent in 2011.

Table: Literacy Rates in India (1951–2011) in Per centage

Census Year	Persons	Males	Females	Male-Female gap in literacy rate
1951	18.33	27.16	8.86	18.30
2001	64.84	75.85	54.16	21.70
2011	74.04	82.14	65.4	16.74

Source : Economic Survey of India 2006-07 and Census 2011.

The number of primary schools increased from 6,38,738 in 2000-01 to 8,23,162 in 2009-10. The number of upper primary schools increased from 2,06,269 in 2000-01 to 3,67,745 in 2009-10. The ratio between upper primary schools and primary schools was 1 : 2 in 1999-2000 as against 1 : 3 in 2000-01. The total enrollment at the primary and upper primary school levels in India witnessed a steady increase. During 1999-2000 and 2000-01, the growth rate of enrollment for girls at the elementary level was higher as compared to that for boys. Participation of girls at all levels of school education has improved appreciably over the years.

Development of Research Facilities

There has been considerable progress in the development of research facilities since 1950-51. Research organizations, facilities and personnel have greatly multiplied. Research in science and technology is being undertaken by universities, institutes of technology, professional colleges and specialized research laboratories.

Problems of Educational Development

Education has made all round significant progress since independence. Inspite of the many sided progress, educational reform and development remains a major problem of Indian socio-economic development.

The major current problems of educational system in India are given below:
- It involves tremendous wastage of resources as the *drop-out rate is still very high* at all levels of general education.
- School education has been divided into *two distinct streams i.e., Public school education*, which is very expensive, hence meant for the elites. *State-aided ordinary schools* are meant for common masses.
- *Illiteracy among the adults* continues to be high in most states.
- Considerable *disparities in educational standard* among different regions and institutions persist.
- The educational system at all levels remains *examination-oriented*, where cramming is more important than understanding.
- A large number of full-time teachers at all levels are engaging themselves in *non-academic activities*. Private tuition-work, coaching in unrecognized academies and writing sub-standard help-books to supplement their income, is the common feature.
- There is a *discipline problem* in colleges and universities. Students, teachers and the non-teaching employees' unrest, result in disturbance in universities over a major part of the academic session. This adversely affects teaching, research works and conducting of examination.
- Educational institutions are lacking in funds to equip themselves with adequate buildings, libraries, laboratories and sport facilities.
- Modern *research is very expensive*.
- The country still depends largely on expensive imported technology.
- Technical and professional *education is very expensive*. It is beyond the reach of poor students.

Thus, we can conclude that the educational reforms and development continue to face tough problems. The traditional educational system should be reshaped and reconstructed according to the needs and requirements of the Indian economy and society.

HEALTH AND FAMILY WELFARE

Health is a factor, which indirectly support the economic development. As we know that for the progress of a nation, its citizens must be fit physically as well as mentally. Thus, health-care-services play a vital role in any economy.

Increased access to quality health care services has been one of the thrust areas of the social development programme undertaken in the country. Health means a state of complete physical, mental and social soundness. It should not be taken as the absence of illness and infirmity. The government of India has evolved a national health policy, which lays down stress on the preventive, *promotive and rehabilitative aspects of health care.*

Role of Health Services: Better health services improve the productivity, efficiency of worker, enhances economic advancements, leads to healthy ideas and dynamism in the people, necessary for better utilisation of physical and natural resources.

Healthy population helps directly and indirectly in the economic development of the country. Human element is the essential factor of production. Inspite of all technological development, the importance of human force cannot be undermined. All machines, equipments and tools require men to operate them. Health is the essential requirement for making efficient, active and competent working force. *There is always a sound mind in a sound body.*

We should try our best to improve the health standard of the citizens. It requires eradication of all diseases such as malaria, small-pox, tuberculosis, filaria, leprosy, blindness, cholera, diptheria, veneral diseases, tetanus, polio and whooping cough, etc.

Illness is the part of human life, so there should be sufficient number of hospitals and dispensaries to cure ailing patients. Diseases are also caused by unbalanced diet, dusty, dirty and suffocating atmosphere. Refreshing atmosphere improves the standard of our health.

Health helps indirectly the economic development by supplying active, energetic and healthy working force, which activates the entire production process.

Standard of Health Before independence

The average standard of health in India was very poor on the eve of adoption of planned development. The death rate had been 7.273 per thousand population per year in 2019. The infant mortality rate in 2019 was 28.3 per thousand per year. The life expectancy was 67·4 years for males and 70·2 years for females as per National Health profile 2019. Mother mortality rate was 20 per thousand. Approximately 100 million persons (10 crores) were affected by malaria and about a million of them died every year. Some 2·5 million persons were suffering from T.B. (Tuberculosis). Epidemics like cholera and small-pox were wide spread due to unhygienic environment, inadequate diet and poor nutrition, lack of proper housing, safe water supply, proper removal of human wastes and health education.

There was inadequate preventive arrangement of curative measure of health care. There was one doctor for every 6,300 persons, one nurse for every 3,200 persons, one trained midwife for every 60,000 persons. Most of the trained health personnel served in the urban areas and only a negligible per centage of these trained personnel worked in the rural areas.

Progress of Health Development since 1950-51

There has been a very considerable progress in health development in the sense of avoidance of diseases since 1950-51. The death rate declined from 27·4 during 1950-51 to 7·2 per thousand during 2010-11. The infant mortality rate had declined from 183 in 1951 to 28.3 in 2019. The life expectancy had gone up from 32·45 years in 1951 to 69·50 years in 2019.

This progress in health development has been made possible by:
- Effective implementation of the programmes for control of communicable diseases.
- Creation of a structure of health care institutions in rural areas.
- Expansion and re-orientation of medical education and research.
- Effective implementation of family welfare programme to reduce birth rate.
- Large increase in health facilities.
- Large increase in medical and para-medical personnel.

The National Health Policy (NHP) was formulated in 1983. It provides a reliable and relevant policy framework for improving health care and measuring and monitoring the health care delivery systems and health status of population.

New Health Policy 2017 Objectives are—

NHP 2017–Goals to be Achieved

- Reduce IMR to 28 by 2019.
- Increase public health facilities by 50% from current level by 2025
- Access to safe water and sanitation to all by 2020
- Increase the share of state on health to more than 8 per cent by 2020.
- Eliminate status of Leprocy by 2018, Kala-Azar by 2017 and Lymphatic filariasis by 2017.

HOUSING

Housing is an important organ of socio-economic structure. Individuals cannot live alone, so they live in a family. Members of family require a shelter to live in. In ancient days, people lived in forests. With the progress of civilization they built their houses and society.

Citizens require house to live peacefully. House fulfills our basic needs of shelter. They protect us from heat, rain and cold. After working for our livelihood, we want certain place to rest and refresh ourselves for next day's job.

Housing does not directly contribute to our economic development. It provides us refreshed working energy which is needed again and again for hard and efficient working. House building is itself an industry which directly adds to our economic prosperity. Our government has adopted social welfare as its goal, as such it has launched many rural and urban housing schemes to fulfill its social commitments and to provide houses to every family.

Role of Housing : Indian economy suffers from the shortage of proper housing facilities quantitatively and qualitatively both. Reasonable housing facilities helps in economic development through:

- Improving standards of living of common man.
- Providing sanitation and immunity from water and air borne diseases.
- Improving efficiency and productivity of labour.
- Promoting social understanding among residents.

Housing Schemes

Urban population has been growing faster, because of continued rural-urban migration. The government has launched various housing schemes to meet the increasing need for housing. The public agencies have, however, played a growing multi-dimensional role to complement and supplement the private efforts in housing development.

CIVIC AMENITIES

In addition to education, health and housing facilities, the citizens of the country require certain other civic amenities. These facilities may be regarding water supply, sanitation, parks, sewage and drainage system, etc.

Cleanliness keeps our surrounding clean and fresh. Civic amenities are not directly related to production but affect the productivity of our working force. The absence of civic amenities either to the industrial workers or to the agricultural labourers reduces their productivity and thus production suffers. It is accepted fact that the low productivity of Indian worker is also due to the improper civic amenities.

WATER SUPPLY

Urban Water Supply

Safe drinking water supply is an essential requirement for life, health and efficiency. Water supply in urban areas was not paid serious attention up to the fourth plan. Much greater attention was paid and much larger financial provision was made for water supply during 5th plan, but the position remained unsatisfactory, 1027 towns had no piped water supply facilities out of 3119 towns in the country by 1980. Even the situation did not improve till 2011 and in a survey of 1405 cities in 12 states, it was found that almost half of them did not have proper water supply.

The situation is much grave in smaller towns with less than 20,000 population, 902 towns were without water supply facilities out of 2097 towns. 110 class III towns, 13 class II towns and 2 class I towns are lacking in water supply facilities. The water supply in cities is generally restricted to a few hours a day. Urban water supply schemes are highly capital intensive. Greater attention was paid to water supply in small and medium-sized towns during sixth plan. There is unsatisfactory maintenance of water supply facilities due to the inadequate non-plan grants provided by the State Governments for the purpose. Urban water supply must be put on a sound financial footing. Distribution of households according to the primary source of drinking water reported by census 2011, nearly 70 per cent households have access to tap water, out of which 62 per cent have access to treated tap water.

Rural Water Supply

Development of rural water supply programme was not an independent programme up to the third plan. The rural water supply schemes were taken up under the community development programme. The scheme involved construction and renovation of wells and installation of hand pumps. Piped water supply schemes in rural areas of water scarcity and salinity were undertaken under the National water supply and sanitation programme of the Ministry of Health.

Census 2011 reported the coverage of households in India having access to tapwater from treated source at 32 per cent, comprising over 62 per cent of urban households and around 18 per cent of rural households. It is estimated that 52 per cent of rural households were served by a tubewell/hand pump, 13 per cent by a well, and 31 per cent by taps.

The Accelerated Rural Water Supply Programme (ARWSP) currently implemented through the Rajiv Gandhi National Drinking Water Mission in the Department of Drinking Water Supply, has been in operation since 1972-73 to assist the States and Union Territories to accelerate the pace of coverage of safe and adequate drinking water supply facilities to the rural population.

SANITATION

Sanitation means the arrangements for removal of human excreta, drainage of rain water and effluents, and collection and disposal of garbage and sewerage. Proper sanitation is an essential condition for improvement in health, productivity, efficiency and quality of life.

Sanitation Facilities in Rural Areas

Sanitation conditions in the rural areas are not good. Simple pilot projects are being undertaken but the progress of rural sanitation will depend upon the co-operation of rural population and rural organisation. The Central Government supplements the efforts of the States in the field of rural sanitation under the Central Rural Sanitation Program (CRSP). This program was restricted in 1999 and Total Sanitation Campaign (TSC) was introduced. The TSC envisages a synergised interaction between the Government, people and active NGO participation, besides intensive Information, Education and Communication (IEC) campaigns, provision of an alternative delivery system and more flexible, demand-oriented construction norms. The revised Tenth—Five Year Plan strategy envisages a shift from allocation based program to a demand based project mode. Besides, the paradigm shift envisages a greater household involvement, intensive IEC campaigns, and stress on software and emphasis on school sanitation. The annual budgetary support for the TSC was increased from ₹ 202 crores in 2003-04 to ₹ 1,500 crores in 2011-12.

Sanitation Facilities in Urban Areas

Though the position of urban sanitation is comparatively better than rural sanitation, yet unsatisfactory. Only 198 towns out of 3119 towns had been provided with sewerage facility in 1980. More than half of class I towns were without sewerage arrangements. Only 30 per cent of the total urban population had access to sewerage facilities in 1989.

In a study it was found that more than 85 million people in India lack sanitation facilities in 2015-16. Almost 17 million urban households don't have adequate sanitation facilities along with approximately 15 million more households which have no toilets in urban areas. Almost 12·6 per cent of urban households defecate in open areas.

Sewerage programmes have been considered as an integral part of urban development. The *United Nations had declared the ten years from 1981 to 1990 as the international drinking water supply and sanitation decade.* India, being a signatory of the resolution, was required to mount a campaign to provide sanitation facilities for all people. Efforts have been made to evolve low cost techniques for urban sanitation with U.N. assistance. A programme of installing water-seal latrines in small towns in several states was launched during sixth plan. Upto March 31, 2004, 866 schemes in 1,534 towns have been sanctioned at a projected cost of ₹ 2,043 crores involving Government of India subsidy of ₹ 568 crores and HUDCO loan of ₹ 776 crores for construction/conversion of 36·75 lakh individual units along with 51·70 community toilets. ₹ 294 crores have been released to the states as GOI subsidy and ₹ 479 crores have been released as loan from HUDCO. 586 towns have been declared scavenger free. A National Action Plan for total eradication of manual scavenging by 2007 has been drawn up by the planning commission.

Arrangements for collection and disposal of garbage are unsatisfactory in villages, small towns and even in congested parts of large cities. Proper and adequate arrangements for the collection and disposal of garbage should be done to keep cities and villages clean.

Recently, the NDA government has started **"Swachh Bharat Abhiyan"** at the national level to collect and dispose off the garbage in the most eco-friendly manner. Efforts are being made at all levels to make people aware of the importance and methods of cleanliness. Its results are awaited to be seen.

Problems pertaining to lack of social infrastructure and their impact:

1. **Shortfall of Health Infrastructure:** Rural areas in India have a shortage of medical professionals. 74 per cent of doctors are in urban. Doctors do not prefer to work in rural areas due to insufficient housing, healthcare, education for their children, drinking water, electricity, roads and transportation facillities. Studies have indicated that the mortality risks before the age of five are greater for children living in certain rural areas compared to urban communities. Full immunization coverage also varies between rural and urban India, with 39 per cent completely immunized in rural communities and 58 per cent in urban areas across India. Poor health infrastructure results in high mortality rate, spread of epidemic and low life expectancy. Government launched a nationwide health care system known as the National Health Assurance Mission, which would provide all citizens with free drugs, diagnostic treatments, and insurance for serious ailments. In April 2018, the government announced the **Aayushman Bharat Scheme** that aims to cover up to R 5 lakh to 100,000,000 vulnerable families (approximately 500,000,000 persons – 40 per cent of the country's population). This will cost around $1.7 billion each year.

2. **Inadequate Access to Safe Drinking Water and Sanitation Facilities:** Rapid improvements are being made in supply of drinking water and sanitation in India, due to efforts by the various levels of government and communities. In 1980 rural sanitation coverage was estimated at 1per cent and reached 95 per cent in 2018. The share of Indians with access to improved sources of water has increased significantly from 72 per cent in 1990 to 92·67 per cent in 2019. A study by Water Aid estimated as many as 10 million Indians, or 5 per cent of Indians living in urban areas, live without adequate sanitation. India comes in first place globally for having the greatest number of urban-dwelling inhabitants living without sanitation. India tops the urban sanitation crisis, has the largest amount of urban dwellers without sanitation, and the most open defecators (urban) with over 5 million people. These results in large number of people are susceptible to water borne diseases.

3. **Low Gross Enrollment Ratio (GER) in Higher Education:** At present, in India, there are about 1.86 crore students enrolled in various streams of higher education. The gross enrolment ratio (GER) for higher education in India was 27.4 per cent in 2017-18. Our enrolment level is far below several other countries. For example, according to a Report, GER is 65.6 per cent for France, 49.1 per cent for China 51.3 per cent for Brazil, 60.6 per cent for U.K. 77 per cent for both Australia and Russia

and 88.2 per cent for the U.S. Government authorities are making efforts to increase the number of students by 2020 so as to reach GER of 30 per cent. As a positive step, for the remaining duration of Eleventh Five Year Plan, the Government has taken initiatives to incentivise States for setting up/expansion of existing educational institutions, establishment of 8 universities, expansion of colleges to achieve a target of 1 lakh students enrolment and schemes for setting up model colleges in regions which are below national average of GER. Despite the large number of students studying in various streams, there is no major shift in the productivity as skills and talents are deficient to support economic activities and, hence, there is a serious concern on employability of these educated persons in India.

4. **High Drop out Rate at Primary Level of Education:** Our education system is based on general education. The dropout rate is very high at primary and secondary level. Most of the students in 6-14 age groups leave the school before completing their education. It leads to wastage of financial and human resources. Primary education in India is ridden with too many problems. Large number of primary schools has no buildings, lack basic facilities like drinking water, urinals and electricity, furniture and study materials etc. Large numbers of primary schools are single teacher schools and many schools are even without teachers. So, the drop rate is very high and a cause of concern. Government has made efforts to reduce dropout rates by launching Mid-day meal scheme and giving children free dress and books.

Low level of education means low income earning capability and low level of health awareness. All these factors make them incapable of earning a minimum acceptable of income and sustain proper life.

5. **Growing Number of Homeless in India:** A homeless person is the one who cannot afford housing or are unable to maintain a regular and safe shelter. In India, there are about 78 million homeless people despite the country growing in global economic stature. According to census 2011, India has more than 1.7 million homeless residents, of which 938, 384 are in urban areas. This figures indicates the housing problems in the country. Homelessness is a result of large families migrating from rural areas to urban cities in search of employment. This creates not only a problem of social tension but also degrades the quality of life of urban poor. Prime Minister Narendra Modi has set a target for the nation – every Indian must have a house by 2022 with the construction of twenty million accommodations within that timeframe.

ECONOMIC INFRASTRUCTURE

Economic infrastructure includes Transport network, Communication network, Power, Irrigation facilities, Monetary and Financial Institutions, etc., which helps in accelerating the economic growth of a country.

TRANSPORT

A well-knit and a coordinated transport system plays an important role in the process of sustained economic growth in a developing country like India. The present transport system of our country comprises several modes of transport including railways, road, shipping and inland water transport, pipeline transport and air transport, etc.

The following chart represents the modes of transport with some detail:

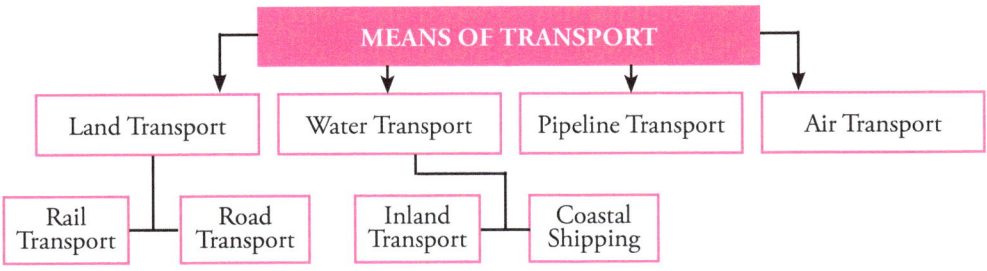

Significance or Advantages of Transport

The significance or advantages of transport system can be realized from the social and economical progress of the nation, which have been generated by this sector in India during the plan periods. The following points illustrate its significance :

Facilitates Production in both Agriculture and Industrial Sectors: Transport system has significantly helped in industrial and agricultural production by transporting raw materials and labour to the places of production and by carrying the products produced by these sectors to different corners of our country and abroad.

Reduction in Scarcity of Goods: Facilitating movement of goods and factors of production from one place to another, helps in solving the problem of scarcity of goods and factors in different regions, thus, maintaining stability of prices in the economy.

Reduction in Cost of Production: The proper transportation network reduces the cost of manufactured goods and equalizes their price in the market. With the help of efficient and cheap transportation system raw materials, fuel and machinery, etc., can be easily carried to factories where these are needed and which is the ultimate cause of the reduction of the cost of production.

Growth in Foreign Trade: Transport system provides a connecting network for transactions among different countries of the world. It helps in promoting foreign trade of the country. A country's exports/imports cannot be developed without good ports, shipping and cargo facilities.

Specialization of Labour and Mobilization of Resources: By the efficient and effective transportation system, the benefits of specialization of labour and proper mobilization can be achieved. Thus, an economic system grows and develops which makes the best use of resources.

Expansion of the Market: Markets for both industrial and agricultural products have increased, both on the domestic and international front with the expansion of transport network. For example, adequate links between different parts of India could be established through the expansion of road, rail and water transport during the plan periods. On the other hand, development of overseas transport system helped India in expanding its overseas market.

Promotion of Tourism: An ideal transport system promotes tourism system or services all over the country.

RAIL TRANSPORT

In India, Railway is the principal mode of transportation for freight and passengers. Indian Railways have now became a unified state enterprise. Indian railways had the modest beginning in 1853 when the first railway train covered a distance of 34 km. from Mumbai (Bombay) to Thane. Now, it is the fourth largest rail network after USA, Russia and China.

Indian Railways is among the world's largest rail network, and its route length network is spread over 1,23,236 kms, with 13,523 passenger trains and 9,146 freight trains playing 23 million travellers and 3 million tonnes (MT) of freight daily from 7,349 stations in the year 2019. India's railways network is recognised as one of the largest railway systems in the world under single management.

Railway Development in Recent Years

Indian Railways has developed very rapidly during the past few years. Some of important developments are enumerated here :

- Rail Vikas Nigam Ltd. (RVNL) was set up in January 2003 as an effort to create new institutional mechanisms for implementing railway projects through a blend of budgetary support and non-budgetary initiatives. It is implementing a part of the National Rail Vikas Yojana.
- Prime Minister inaugurated the commercial operations of Delhi Metro Rail on December 24, 2002. This train was started from Seelampur Station. In the first phase this Rail service has been provided between Tees Hazari and Shahadra w.e.f. 25 December, 2002. The entire project is completed by 2008. The estimated completion cost of the project will be ₹ 10,570 crores. Now such kind of projects have been initiated in many cities of the country.
- Safety on Indian Railways has been receiving the highest priority. Special railway safety fund—a non-lapsable fund—with ₹ 17,000 crores set up to wipe out the arrears in the renewal of vital safety equipment within a fixed time frame 5-7 years for replacing old assets including tracks, bridges, signalling equipments and other safety enhancement items. Bogie mounted brake system being introduced on wagons in place of the conventional pull/push road types air brake system. But a lot is required to be done on the safety front of trains.
- A new category of inter-city train services called as Jan–Shatabdi was also introduced during 2002-03.
- Later in years, the 2016-18 Deen Dayalu Coaches, Executives Lounges, Gatiman Express, CNG trains, Privatisation of catering, Talgo Bullet trains, Bio toilets in trains, were also introduced.

Advantages or Importance of Railway Transport

The main advantages of railway transport are following:

Development of Market and Specialization: Railways have extended the size of market and thus, stimulated the process of specialization. Heavy goods can easily be transported by railways.

Development of Agriculture: Contribution of railways plays a great deal to the development of agriculture. Before the development of railways, agriculture was largely subsistence-oriented. Railways have commercialized it as our cultivators do not produce for self consumption only but also for sale in the market.

Helpful in Internal Trade: By joining different corners of the country, railways have made internal trade more convenient as they carry freight and passengers to distant places easily.

Inter-connecting of New Sources and New Areas: Railways have connected new sources and new areas of production. They not only provided knowledge of the new areas, but also helped in reaching the inaccessible areas.

Mobility of Labour and Capital: Railways have increased the mobility of labour and capital which in turn has contributed to the rapid industrialization of the country.

Export Promotion: Railways also help to promote exports by carrying goods from the centre of production to the ports.

Elimination of Famines: Railways helped in minimizing the intensity of famines by carrying the food grains from surplus to famine-stricken areas.

Postal Services: In India, railways initiated postal services in 1909. At present, railways carry thousands of tonnes of posts from one place to the other. It has contributed to the progress of means of communication.

Employment: Railways are an important source of employment in India, lakhs of skilled and unskilled people are employed in its operation. In addition, they create so many ancilliary employment opportunities. They provide direct employment to more than 1·331 million people in the country.

Strategic Importance: Their strategic importance cannot be ignored. They are instrumental in providing internal security and efficient arrangements of defence of the country against any external threat.

Disadvantages or Problems of Railway Transport

Financial Deficits: One of the serious problem of Indian railways is that of deficits in the railway budgets. The gross earning and working expenses are both rising with the increase in the capital outlay. As a result, the dividends to be paid will also rise. To cover the deficits and to increase the revenue, the railways has been regularly increasing passenger fares and freight. Railways are not entirely a commercial concern, but they are a public utility concern. They are used by all sectors of the economy. Apart from these facts, the operational expenses for various commodities are also increasing, *e.g.,* coal, oil, and iron and steel prices are rising.

Slow Modernization: Modernization of Indian railway is slow when we compare it with the international standards. For example, only 45 per cent of total route length of Indian railways is electrified by the end of 2015-16.

Inadequate safety and Amenities: Inadequate safety and insufficient amenities are provided to the rail passengers. Therefore, Indian railways meet with frequent accidents.

Losses due to Negligence, Corruption and Theft: Railways are losing heavy sums due to widespread corruption and theft. Often rail staff is found to be involved in such malpractices. Railway properties are stolen due to negligence of the rail security staff. Ticketless travelling is also a major problem of the country. It is estimated that ticketless travelling causes a loss to railways to the tune of about ₹ 300 to ₹ 500 crores every year.

ROAD TRANSPORT

Road transport is one of the most promising and potent base for rapid industrial and agricultural development. It is suitable for movement of goods and people over short and medium distances.

India has the second largest road network in the world spanning a total of 5.89 million kms. and the most important advantage is that it connects even the remotest villages and hilly regions, which cannot be connected by railway network. They connect the villages with markets, developing towns, administrative centres, cultural and religious places, thereby keeping all these with the mainstream of national development. The roads play a very important role in national defence and internal security as a quick movement of forces and weapons is made possible.

In 1950-51, total road length was only 4 lakh kms and now in 2019, this length is approximately 142, 126 lakhs kms. The national highways carries nearly 40 per cent of the total road traffic.*

Road Development in Recent Years

Three initiatives in the road sector began in recent years: The National Highway Development Project (NHDP), Pradhan Mantri Bharat Jodo Pariyojna (PMBJP) and Pradhan Mantri Gram Sadak Yojana (PMGSY).

- NHAI (National Highways Authority of India) has been mandated to implement National Highway Development Programme (NHDP) which constitutes 4/6 Laning of Golden Quadrilateral Connecting Delhi–Mumbai–Chennai–Kolkata–Delhi and North–South and East–West corridors connecting Kashmir to Kanyakumari and Silchar to Saurashtra respectively and Salem to Cochin. In 2019, 10,855 km of highways were constructed.
- The recent Pradhan Mantri Bharat Jodo Pariyojana (PMBJP) involves development of 14,000 kms of roads. The project was started on January 14th, 2004. The estimated total project cost is around ₹ 65,000 crores.
- The Pradhan Mantri Gram Sadak Yojana (PMGSY) which was launched in December 2002, seeks to provide road connectivity to about 1·6 lakh rural unconnected habitations with a population of 500 persons or more by the end of the plan period *i.e.*, 2007. 11th plan will continue the special accelerated Development Road Programme.

Advantages or Importance of Road Transport

Transportation of Perishable Goods: According to *Road Reorganization Committee's Report,* means of road transport encourages the sales of perishable goods, such as vegetables, fruits, milk, butter, etc., in the markets wherefrom cultivators simultaneously attain a knowledge of fertilizers, implements and improved methods of agricultural production.

* Bharat 2012, P 1134.

Extension of Agriculture: In India, there are many areas lacking efficient means of transport. But these are efficient for growing all types of crops including cash crops. According to *"Indian Roads and Transport Development Institute"*, it is possible to increase cultivable areas by 25 per cent by extending roads to the rural regions.

Employment Generation: Road transport generates employment to large number of people. According to *"Road Transport Development Committee"*, an outlay of ₹ 3,500 crores on roads can provide employment to about 170 lakh persons.

Flexibility: It is a most flexible mode of transport. Motor vehicles can run not only between two places but also from door to door.

Less Capital: Roads need less capital than the railways. Therefore, our country gives more attention towards road development.

Saving of Time and Cost: Goods in small quantities can be transported regularly through quick means of road transport, whereas the railway department waits for full wagon load of goods.

Multipurpose Utility: Roads are built not only for specific vehicles. Various kinds of vehicles provide services through road transportation. Roads can be used by bullock carts, tongas, rickshaws, cycles, motors, etc., whereas rail tracks are used by railway trains of specific gauge only. Similarly, water and air transport are also meant for specific vehicles.

Development of Industries: In India, the roads have contributed significantly to the development of industries. They carry raw materials and other goods to the factories and the manufactured goods to different cities and ports.

Disadvantages or Problems of Road Transport

High Burden of Taxes: According to *'Road Transport Reorganization Committee'*, Road transport has been subjected to heavy taxation. Therefore, the committee suggested that small operators must combine themselves and form public limited companies with a view to run the services in an efficient manner.

Inefficient Management and Services: *'Road Transport Reorganization Committee'*, gave valuable recommendations for the efficient management of road transport. The Committee said that 90 per cent of the operators are small operators owning five or less vehicles. Owing to this large number, satisfactory and efficient service is not being provided to the people.

Indisciplined Driving and Accidents: Most of the drivers on the roads are unskilled and untrained. They also drink alcohol while driving. As such, road accidents are more frequent in India.

Rising Prices of Petrol/Diesel: Due to high prices of petroleum and diesel by the Government, operational costs of road transport is rising and making the mode of transport costlier.

Bad Conditions of Road: In India, roads are not well-maintained because there are no timely repairs which causes discomfort as well as quick depreciation of vehicles.

Water Transport (Shipping)

Shipping plays an important role in the transport sector of India's economy. Approximately, 95 per cent of the country's external trade by volume (70 per cent in terms of value) is moved by sea. India has the largest merchant shipping fleet among the developing countries and ranks 16th amongst the countries with the largest cargo carrying fleet with 10.67 million GRT (Gross Registered Tonnage) and the average of the fleet being 17 years. Indian maritime sector facilitates not only transportation of national and international cargo, but also provides a variety of other services such as cargo handling services, ship building and ship repairing, freight forwarding, light house facilities and training of marine personnel, etc.

India, with her 7,517 km long coastline studded with 13 major ports and 200 non-major ports providing congenial and favourable conditions for the development of this alternate mode of transport.

Coastal Shipping

Coastal shipping is an energy efficient, environmental friendly and economical mode of transport in the Indian transport network and a crucial component for the development of domestic industry and trade.

India's Coastal Shipping Tonnage as on 30 June, 2011 was 732 vessels with 10·35 million GRT. Action plan for the development of coastal shipping is already on the anvil with the Central Government. With a view to promote coastal shipping and sailing vessel industry, the home trade vessels and sailing vessels have been exempted from the payment of lighthouse dues under the provisions of the Lighthouse Act, 1927 and efforts are being made to develop minor ports, which would, in turn, develop coastal shipping.

Inland Water Transport

Inland Water Transport is a fuel efficient and environment friendly mode of transportation. India is richly endowed with navigable waterways, comprising rivers, canals, backwaters, creeks, etc. It is estimated that a total of 14,544 km of the waterways could be used for passenger and cargo movement. About 44 million tonnes of cargo is being moved annually by inland water transport. But, this means of transport is important only in few States, namely Assam, West Bengal, Bihar and Kerala. Also, it is operational only in restricted stretches of Ganga-Bhagirathi-Hoogly rivers; the Brahmaputra river; the Barak river; the rivers in Goa; the backwaters in Kerala; inland waters in Mumbai and the deltaic regions of the Godavari-Krishna rivers.

Besides, the capacity of this sector is under-utilized, because most navigable waterways suffer from hazards like shallow water and narrow width of channel during dry weather; silting of river beds and erosion of banks; absence of adequate infrastructural facilities like terminals for loading and berthing and surface road links.

Advantages or Importance of Water Transport

Expansion of Foreign Trade: Current volume of India's foreign trade is quite large and it is likely to further expand due to economic development of the country. Therefore, its importance cannot be under-estimated.

Cheapest Mode of Transport: Water transport is the cheapest mode of transport because oceans and rivers are the free gifts of nature, as the cost of construction is not involved in such transport.

Foreign Exchange: Foreign exchange is of utmost importance for country's economic development. Shipping enables the country to save enough of foreign exchange. National shipping makes significant contribution to the foreign exchange earnings of the country.

Transportation of Bulky Goods: Heavy and bulky goods can be transported at very low prices through water transport.

Defence: Development of shipping is also essential for the defence of the country. It is regarded as second line of defence.

Low Maintenance Cost: Compared to other modes of transport, cost of maintenance for water transport is very little.

Useful During Natural Calamities: During natural calamities like floods, heavy downpour, etc., rail or road transport is disrupted, water transport alone is possible.

Problems or Disadvantages of Water Transport

Inadequate Tonnage: The first major problem of Indian shipping is the inadequacy of tonnage capacity. At present, Indian ships carry only 29 per cent of the India's total sea-borne trade.

High Operating Costs: High operating costs are responsible for reducing the competitive strength of Indian shipping. Modern foreign vessels that have low operating cost, generally offer lower freight rates and better services. Consequently, they skim off a larger chunk of high value cargo from Indian ports.

Stiff Competition: India's geographical position is such that a number of foreign vessels are able to use Indian ports as wayside ports, when returning from gulf countries or sailing towards the far East. Thus, in the absence of proper policies, Indian shipping companies face stiff competition and discrimination from well-established international shipping companies.

Inadequate Infrastructure: Indian shipping suffers from inadequate infrastructure support like ship repair facilities, dry docking and cargo handling.

Containerization is Negligible: While the world is moving rapidly towards containerization, the Indian container fleet is almost negligible.

AIR TRANSPORT (CIVIL AVIATION)

It is the fastest mode of transport and most suitable for long distances and for those routes which have uneven and difficult terrain. It also provides a valuable relief service in case of natural calamities. During emergency, the civil aviation facilities (with personnel and organization) can be utilized for supporting defence forces.

With the long distances and good flying conditions, India has a good potential for the development of internal and international air services.

At the time of Independence, India virtually had no civil aviation. In 1946, the Government set-up the *Air Transport Licensing Board* which gave licenses to 11 companies to operate internal and external air services.

Now, India's aviation industry is the second largest in the world. It has been witnessing a boom due to exponential growth in the domestic passenger carriage, cargo movement and international air traffic. Airlines have carried nearly 90·5 million domestic passengers during the year 2011, as against 108·1 million during 2010, thus showing a growth of 19·4 per cent.

As far as the airlines are concerned, there are a number of companies, both public and private sector, which are providing passenger transport and cargo handling services in the country. In the public sector, there are Air India (Indian Airlines has got merged with Air India) and Pawan Hans Ltd. In the private sector, there are following airlines (passenger) namely, Jet Airways, Indigo, Spice Jet, Kingfisher Airlines, Paramount Airways, GoAir, Air

Asia and Vistara, etc. There is also a cargo private scheduled airline called as the Blue Dart Aviation Ltd.

Further, in order to increase international connectivity and facilitate foreign travel for passengers, India has entered into '*Air Service Agreements (ASA)*' with around 100 countries.

The Ministry of Civil Aviation is the nodal authority responsible for the formulation of national policies and programmes for development and regulation of the civil aviation industry in the country. Its functions also extend to overseeing airport facilities, air traffic services and carriage of passengers and goods by air.

The Ministry of Civil Aviation has the following public sector undertakings/ companies/ autonomous bodies under its administrative control:

Air India Limited: It is a company incorporated under the Companies Act, 1956 and has the functions and responsibilities of providing safe, efficient, adequate, economical and properly coordinated international and domestic air transport services.

Airports Authority of India (AAI): It was constituted in 1995 for creating, upgrading, maintaining and managing civil aviation infrastructure, both on the ground and air space of the country. It aims at providing world class airport services for efficient operation of air transport in the country. It manages 127 airports, which include 15 international airports.

Pawan Hans Helicopters Limited (PHHL): It was established in 1985 as the country's national helicopter company for providing helicopter support services to the Oil Sector; operate scheduled/non-scheduled helicopter services in inaccessible areas and difficult terrains; as well as provide charters for promoting of travel and tourism. It has a well balanced fleet of 42 helicopters.

Indira Gandhi Rastriya Uran-Akademi: It was established by the Government with the objective of improving the flying training standards in civil aviation and to impart line oriented flying training of international standards. It has been set up at Fursatganj in Rai Bareilly District of Uttar Pradesh. It is equipped with modern and sophisticated trainer aircraft, flight simulators, computer based training system, runway with modern navigational and landing aids and its own airspace.

With liberalization of the Indian economy and its global integration, continuous upgradation and modernization of the aviation sector has become critically important. Accordingly, the current policy focus of the Government is on modernization of the existing airports as well as the construction of new ones. For instance, the international airports in Delhi and Mumbai are being restructured through public-private partnership. The AAI has decided to develop and modernise 35 non-metro airports to world class standards. Also, the bilateral arrangements are being strengthened for ensuring better international connectivity.

Advantages or Importance of Air Transport

High Speed: It is a high speed mode of transport. Thus, it saves time that cannot be matched by surface transport over long distances. Passengers and freight can be transported speedily from one place to the other.

Minimum Cost of Construction: Unlike road and railway transport, there is no need to spend more money on the construction of road or track as one has to only construct airport.

Transportation of Expensive and Light Commodities: It is convenient to send expensive, light and perishable goods, like, diamond, gold, fruits, etc.

Removal of Geographical Constraints: Mountains, oceans and rivers create no obstruction to air transport.

Strategic Importance: It has great strategic significance. Soldiers, arms and ammunition can be airlifted to the troubled spots speedily.

Disadvantages or Problems of Air Transport

Huge Investments: Creation of aviation facilities require huge investments. Only the Government is capable of increasing the number of planes and airports in the country. The private sector has its own limitations in this regard. Also, with rising operational costs, air transport in India is becoming very costly day-by-day.

Staff's Non-cooperation: Indian aviation facilities regularly face problems due to non-cooperation of the staff, such as, strikes by pilots, etc.

Outdated Planes: Aviation technology is changing very fast. Our planes are outdated and not very safe. Indian airlines find it difficult to compete with the world airlines.

Inadequate Training Facilities: There are no adequate facilities for training a large number of pilots in the country. On privatization of airlines, we might face the problem of sufficient trained staff.

Risks Due to Crimes: In air transport, risks are increasing these days due to crime and terrorism, violence, hijacking, etc., all over the world.

PIPELINE TRANSPORT

Pipelines form an unique mode of transportation. They can move large quantities of certain types of commodities, mainly fluids, over long distances at relatively low cost. The operations are environment friendly, dependable and continuous. The pipelines can be laid on a wide variety of terrains without much difficulty.

Compared to normal surface mode like railways and road vehicles, the following advantages are particularly attractive:

- They do not require the return of *'empties'* to the starting point and as such are ideal for unidirectional traffic.
- They are insensitive to surface conditions such as storms, inclement weather, etc.
- Operating costs are low.
- Capital cost being the major cost of transportation, inflationary influences have a small effect on transport cost.
- They are environment friendly.
  The Indian Oil Corporation has constructed as extensive system of pipelines for crude oil and petroleum products.
- from Hazira via Bijapur to Jagadishpur (BHJ) carries natural gas.
- from Kudremukh ore mines to Mangalore port transport iron ore in slurry from.

Crude Petroleum transporting pipelines are:
- from Assam oil fields to Guwahati and Barauni.

- from West Coast to Koyali (near Vadodara in Gujarat)
- from Salaya Port to Mathura.

The Petroleum products from refineries are carried from:
- Barauni to Kanpur.
- Mathura to Delhi, Ambala and Jalandhar.
- Mumbai to Pune.

COMMUNICATION

Communication network has been recognized as an important tool for the socio-economic development of nation. It not only interlinks the people of a country, but also enhances global connectivity and competitiveness of the economy. However, transport and communication are closely interlinked, because all tangible messages can be sent by transport. Information through telephone or wireless can be communicated without assistance of transport. It is also important to note that the developments in communication system help to speed up transport and transport in turn speeds up communication and thereby accelerates economic developments. The most important means of communication are : postal services, telephones, fax and computers, radio and television.

Now-a-days modern technology has given a wide option to choose the means.

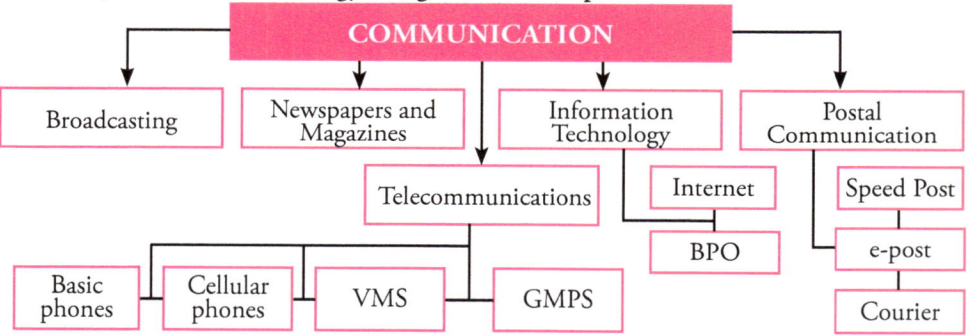

POSTAL SERVICES

The modern system of postal services in India began in 1837. Now, India possess the largest postal network in the world. Due to successive implementation of Five Year Plans, the number of post offices since Independence has increased from 22,116 to 1,54,965 as on March 2017, out of which 1,39,067 (89·86%) are in rural areas and 15,826 (10·14%) are in urban areas.

The postal network consists of three categories of post offices, *viz.*, Head Post Offices, Sub-Post Offices and Extra Departmental Post Offices. All categories of post offices offer similar postal services. In 1997-98, 402 Extra Departmental Post Offices (EDPOs) were opened. Expansion of the postal network especially in the rural areas, has to a great extent, been brought about by opening part-time. Extra Departmental Post Office, a system unique to the Department of Posts.

To facilitate better and quick services, the *Pin Index Number (PIN)* system and *Quick Mail Service* (QMS) has been introduced since 1972 and 1975 respectively.

The Business Development Wing of the Department is constantly striving to create new and better services for enhancing the revenue earning potential of the department.

The Department of Posts started computerizing its post offices from the early 1990's. The objectives of computerization and networking of post offices are improvement of quality of services, introduction of new value added services to meet the expectation of the customers and strengthening its financial position. For the Tenth—Five Year Plan the Government has approved a plan for induction of computers.

All these computerized Post Offices will be linked to a National Data Centre, to be set up by March 2007. Once the National Data Centre becomes operational, this would enable setting up of an efficient management information system for decision making and also improve the quality of Post Office Saving Bank, Postal Life Insurance, Money Order, Speed Post services, etc., by leveraging the networked environment.

Speed Post: Another mode of communication service known as *Speed Post* has also been introduced since 1st August, 1986, in which the articles are delivered within definite time period with money back guarantee against any service defect. The mechanization and computerization are also being introduced to provide much better services to the users. The Speed Post Network comprises 315 National and 986 state Speed Post Centres. This service is also available internationally to 97 countries.

e-Post: e-post service, launched on 30 January, 2004. People who do not normally have access to internet are able to send and receive e-mail messages without possessing an e-mail ID. To make it useful for business, a corporate version of e-post was also launched on 18 October, 2005 which allows simultaneous sending of e-post to a maximum of 9999 addresses.

Courier Services: Time was when one had to wait for weeks together to see the other person receive important document. The common man had no access to fax machines nor was he aware of its utility. Then came along the speed post, which too took about a week to deliver. The start of private courier services however changed all that. Documents could now reach within the day or by the next day. Moreover they are more reliable as changes of misplacement are minimal. Today businesses as well as individuals are increasingly dependent on the courier service.

TELE-COMMUNICATIONS

Tele-communication services were introduced in India soon after the invention of the telegraphy and telephone. At the time of Independence, there were only 321 telephone exchanges, 82,000 working connections, 338 long-distance public call offices and 3,324 telegraph offices. Now, India's tele-communication network is the 2nd largest in the world after China. It is also amongst the fastest growing markets in the world.

Tele-density, the most important factor in determining the penetration of telephone lines in a country has been increasing over the years, from 18·31 per cent in March 2007. to 76·86 percent in Dec. 2011. The overall Tele-density in India declined from 88·56 at the end of December to 87·45 at the end of Jan-20. India's telecom network comprises of 27,753 telephone exchanges, with a total equipped capacity of 272·17 lakh lines and 226·3 lakh working telephones.

Telecom Sector in India is undergoing rapid changes. New services like Broadband, WIFI, Mobile, VPN, etc., are becoming common. At the same time, number of service providers are also rapidly increasing subjecting BSNL to fierce competition.

In the field of international communications, India's overseas service carrier Videsh Sanchar Nigam Ltd. (VSNL) has made tremendous progress by using extensive infrastructure of satellite earth stations, state-of-the-art digital gateways, Optical Fiber Multi Media Submarine Cables and Multi Media Data Switches. Fully automatic International Subscriber Dialing (ISD) service is provided to almost all the countries in the world. Telecom Sector aims to make India, a global IT superpower and develop a world class telecom infrastructure in the country. It focuses on creating an environment, which enables continued attraction of investment into the industry. Towards this ends, the New Telecom Policy 1999 includes the following in the telecom service sector:

- Access Providers (Cellular Mobile Service Providers, Fixed Service Providers and Cable Service Providers);
- Radio Paging Service Providers;
- Public Mobile Radio Trunking Service (PMRTS) Providers;
- National Long Distance Operators;
- International Long Distance Operators;
- Other Service Providers;
- Global Mobile Personal Communication by Satellite (GMPCS) Service Providers;
- V-SAT based Service Providers;

As a result of all such initiatives, private participation is permitted in almost all the segments of telecom services, namely, international long distance, domestic long distance, basic, cellular, internet, radio-paging, and a number of value-added services.

With more players entering the market, the competition has grown stronger, catering to the demands of consumers. Vodafone, Airtel, and Reliance are doing very well.

The New National Telecom Policy 2012 has also made it its main objective to raise competitiveness of India Telecom Sector to make it a world leader. For this purpose, the policy intends to provide 1,200 million mobile connections by 2017 and mobile access to all villages, 175 million broadband connecting by 2017 and 600 million connections by 2020.

INTERNET

It not only interlinks the people of a country through a communication network, but also enhances global connectivity and competitiveness of the economy through world wide web.

Though e-mail and internet browsing remain the favourite purposes e-commerce and e-business have put their foot in. Banks have now facilitated Internet banking. The Indian Railways offers a computerized reservation system which enables a person to book his tickets online and from anywhere. It also provides other services like railway timetables and ticket availability. Airlines bookings, movie ticket bookings, hospital appointments and even consultations are widely available. Connectivity is fast spreading in all areas and the Internet is becoming more and more user friendly. The number of broadband users in

India was 284.23 million by the end of April, 2017. The NASSCOM has estimated the number of internet user in India to be 730 million by 2020.

BPO (Business Process Outsourcing)

The concept of BPO emerged when the market became more price sensitive and competitive. BPO services provide flexibility of working as per client's required timings and days, which make the business operations successful. The shift from low-end business processes to higher-value, Knowledge based processes or Knowledge Process Outsourcing (KPO) are having a positive impact on the overall industry growth.

ENERGY OR POWER

Power is an essential requirement for all facets of life and has been recognized as a basic human need. It is a critical infrastructural component on which the socio-economic development of a country depends. The availability of reliable and quality power at competitive rates is very crucial for sustained growth of all the sectors of the economy, that is, primary, secondary and tertiary sectors. This helps to make domestic markets globally competitive and thus improve the quality of life of the people.

The electric supply is a basic input for industrial sector and also for the agricultural growth. In order to have a continuous growth of industrial sector and agricultural sector, it is necessary to have consistent power supply.

Sources of Electric Power /Energy

India is the world's sixth largest energy consumer accounting for about 3.5 per cent of the world's total annual energy consumption. The thermal, hydro and nuclear energy are the major sources of generation of electricity in India. The all India installed power generation capacity has been 3,26,841 MW at the end of March 2017 consisting of 2,18,330 MW (thermal); 44,478 MW (hydro); 6,780 MW (nuclear); and 57,260 MW (renewable energy sources).

In India, the Ministry of Power is the nodal authority for the overall development of electrical energy in the country. It is concerned with perspective planning; policy formulation; processing of projects for investment decision; monitoring of the implementation of power projects; training and manpower development; as well as the administration and enactment of legislation in regard to power generation, transmission and distribution. The Ministry also provides research, development and technical assistance relating to hydro-electric and thermal power transmission and distribution system in the States/UTs as well as deals with all the matters connecting energy conservation.

Thermal Power

Thermal power is the major source of electric power in India. India is the seventh largest producer of thermal power. Thermal power in India is generated by Coal, Gas and Oil. The share of Thermal power in gross power generation in India was approximately 83 per cent in 2012-13. In absolute terms, the installed capacity of thermal power increased from 1.1 thousand MW in 1950-51 to 665 Billion KWH in 2010, which is 75.8 per cent of the total installed power generation capacity of India.

Hydroelectric Power

Hydroelectric power is a renewable natural resource. In 1950-51 installed capacity of hydropower was 10·6 thousand MW which increased to 114·26 Billion KWH in 2010-11.

Hydel power has several advantages:

- It is the most economical source of power.
- There is no problem of pollution of atmosphere or disposal of waste in generation of hydel power.
- Oil, coal and gas resources that are used for producing electricity; are in short supply and have implications in terms of high costs and exert great pressure on foreign exchange resources; these can be replaced by hydel power.

Inspite of these clear advantages claimed for hydropower, and despite the fact that only one-fifth of hydropower has been harnessed in the country. So far, the Government has been relying more on the thermal power to relieve the power shortage in India.

The Government of India has recently announced a policy on Hydroelectric Power Development with a view to exploit the vast hydroelectric potential available in the country at a faster pace.

Nuclear Power

Nuclear power is of recent origin and its supply accounts for only 26·2 Billion KWH in 2010 which comes to 3·1 per cent of the total installed capacity of electricity through 17 Nuclear Power reactors. The production of atomic power was 32·86 Billion kwh in 2012-13. According to Planning Commission, "*In relation to total capacity of the power systems in India and their rates of growth, the contribution of nuclear power will remain relatively modest in the coming two decades.*" Considering the relative failure of nuclear power in Russia and in other countries including India, nuclear energy is unlikely to make a significant contribution to power generation in the country.

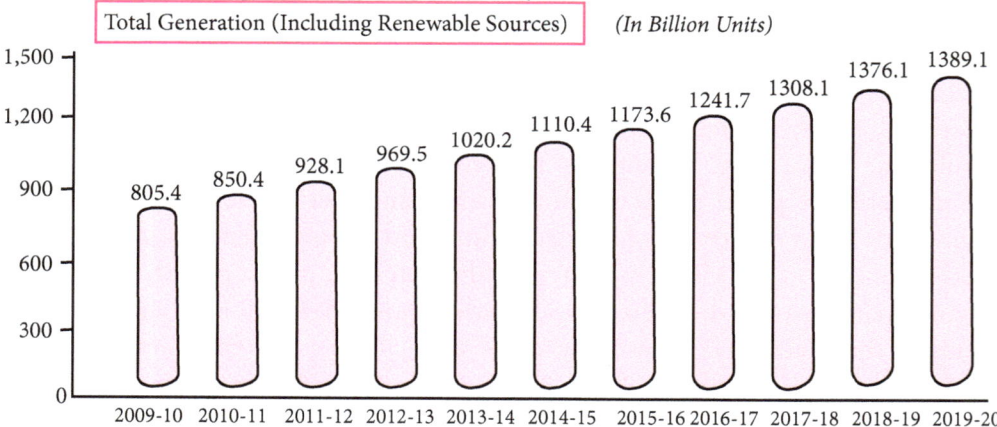

IRRIGATION

Both the agricultural production and productivity, depends upon the availability of water in sufficient quantity. Since the irrigation facilities in our country are not adequate and major part (about 2/3rd) of cultivated land depends upon rains for water requirements but the monsoons are unpredictable and hence it is essential to have proper irrigation system, so that agricultural production and productivity does not suffer. Therefore, development of this infrastructural facility is extremely important for India because its economy is based predominantly on agriculture.

India's irrigated agriculture sector has been fundamental to India's economic development and poverty alleviation. As according to Economic survey 2011-12, 14.5 per cent of India's Gross Domestic Product (GDP) and 58.2 per cent of employment is based on agriculture. Agriculture is the primary source of livelihood in rural areas, which account for 69 per cent of India's population and 80 per cent of its poor. And, in turn, irrigation is the base for about 84 per cent of total agricultural output. The rapid expansion of irrigation and drainage infrastructure has been one of India's major achievements.

Importance of Irrigation for our Country

Unpredictable Rains: In India, the rainfall is restricted to about four months only *i.e.*, during monsoon period mainly and it is not uniform throughout the country. Sometimes, the rains are delayed considerably and are insufficient. All these uncertainties make it very essential to have a proper and adequate irrigation system.

Higher Productivity: The productivity of irrigated land is almost double (93 per cent more to that of unirrigated land) than that of unirrigated land under identical conditions. Therefore, proper irrigation, either naturally or artificially, is highly essential to improve the productivity of land and to achieve greater agricultural production.

Possibilities of Multiple Cropping: Because of tropical and sub-tropical climate in India, there are great possibilities and potential to produce more than two crops. If we totally depend upon monsoons, only one crop will be possible and the remaining period of the year will be idle. With proper irrigation facilities, it is possible to grow different types of crops round the year. By changing the types of crops, the fertility of land can also be re-stored at proper level.

Implementation of Modern Techniques: The success of modern methods of agricultural practices, like using high yielding varieties of seeds and use of sufficient fertilizers, etc., largely depend upon the timely availability of ample supply of water to crops. This is one reason why the HYVP remained confined to only those areas which have adequate irrigation facilities throughout the year.

Help in Correcting Imbalances: The rainfall in our country is not proper and uniform, resulting in an uneven distribution at different places. In fact, India's climatic geography is governed by its location in the tropical and sub-tropical zones while others are dry areas. These regional imbalances can only be narrowed down by artificial means of irrigation.

Avoids Imports of Foodstuffs: In India, growing population has a great demand of foodstuff for its consumption. In the absence of foodgrains, imports are to be made. That means, import of foodgrains makes the balance of payments unfavourable. To curb imports, the country should be self-sufficient in foodstuffs. This can be achieved by raising agricultural production through increasing irrigation facilities to the maximum.

Other Benefits: Irrigation facilities help in controlling floods and famines by diverting excess water to deficient areas through canals, etc. Development of irrigation facility creates new employment opportunities due to more land under cultivation.

Sources of Irrigation

Canals: India has one of the world's largest canal system. Since 1950-51, canal irrigated area has increased from 8.3 million hectares to 15.5 million hectares during the last four decades. Canals are of two types, *viz.*, (i) Inundation canals which are taken out from rivers without any regulating system, (ii) Perennial canals are taken out from perennial rivers or reservoirs. The important canals are Western Jamuna Canal, Sirhind Canal, Upper Bari Doab Canal, Ganga Canal, etc.

Wells: These are generally constructed in soft soil and sub-soil, where water is not too deep. The tubewells are operated with the help of animal power or by electric power. Since 1950-51, it is well irrigation, particularly tubewell irrigation which has made the most spectacular progress. In 1960-61, only 0.1 million hectares were irrigated by tubewells, but in 1990-91, it is increased to over 14 million hectares. Well irrigated area has increased from 6 million hectares to 24 million hectares during the last 40 years. Wells and tubewell irrigation in 2005-06 accounted for 58.8% of the total irrigated area as compared to only 29 per cent in 1950-51.

Tanks: Tank irrigation is widely practised in the state of Tamil Nadu, Karnataka and Orissa. Tanks are constructed for storing water in rainy season and subsequently used for irrigation purposes in scarcity. At present, about 3.3 per cent of the total irrigated areas is irrigated by tanks. Construction and maintenance of different tanks are the responsibility of individual, Panchayati Raj institutions and Government. Since the introduction of canal irrigation, the proportion of tank irrigation has considerably fallen, but it is high time to renovate it and expand the tank irrigation system, as it is cheap and fulfill the local needs conveniently.

Development of Irrigation and Government's Policy

Government took sincere measures in different plan periods for providing various facilities to agricultural sector on priority basis and irrigation was one of these facilities. The outlay/expenditure in First Plan was ₹ 446 crores, which increased to ₹ 9,318 crores in Sixth Plan and ₹ 84,735 crores during Tenth Plan. The important projects include valley projects like Bhakra Nangal, Sutlej-Beas, Hirakund, Damodar Valley Corporation and Nagarjunsagar. Besides, the minor irrigation projects scattered throughout the country continued to occupy significant position by contributing about 50 per cent of the total irrigation potential.

The New Agricultural Strategy and use of HYV seeds demand highly adequate irrigation facilities. Accordingly, the comprehensive programme was introduced in Fifth Plan, in which 38 command area development authorities were constituted covering 50 irrigation projects. However, before implementation of new comprehensive programme, all works previously taken up were allowed to be completed by the end of Fourth—Five Year Plan.

During the Ninth Plan, 57.90 million hectares of irrigation potential was created and in Tenth Plan a target of 63.71 million hectares of irrigation potential is fixed.

The Government of India in July, 1996 has announced the setting up of an Infrastructure Development Finance Company for the development of infrastructural network in the country with an authorized capital ₹ 5,000 crores.

In January 2006, a centrally sponsored scheme on micro irrigation was launched for promoting water use efficiency through drip and sprinkler irrigation.

LESSON AT A GLANCE

Infrastructure: Infrastructure is defined as capital of a society or a social capital. It must be differentiated from the capital structure of the economy which simply means factories, machines, farms and tractors and all forms of equipment required for the production of goods and services. Infrastructure includes transport and communication, energy and electricity and other public services like water supply, etc.

Types of Infrastructure: There are two types of infrastructure: (i) Social Infrastructure; (ii) Economic Infrastructure.

Social Infrastructure: It includes Education, Health, Water supply, Housing, Sanitation, etc., which helps in improving living standards.

Economic Infrastructure: It includes Transport, Communication, Power, Irrigation facilities, Monetary and Financial institutions, etc., which helps in accelerating the economic growth of a country.

PROJECT WORK

1. Write a report on 'The availability of some infrastructural facilities in a region.'
   - At first select any particular town or district or State for your study.
   - **Collect the information like:** (i) number of railway stations in that region; (ii) availability of electric power and the sources of this power in that region; (iii) the length of motorable roads/highways in the said region; (iv) non-conventional sources of energy used in that region (say, solar energy, bio gas, etc.) for power generation; (v) irrigation facilities available in that region through major, medium and minor irrigation projects; (vi) availability of water transport facilities in that region; (vii) whether the interior parts of the said region are well connected with other parts of the country through the transport system.
   - Try to evaluate the importance of this economic infrastructure/transport and communication network in the economic development of the given region.
   - Give your suggestion for improving the infrastructural facilities in that region.
2. Prepare a report on 'The Functioning of an Air Transport.'
3. Prepare a report on 'The Functioning of the Shipping Corporation of India.'
4. Prepare a report on 'The Functioning of any Multipurpose River Valley Corporation' (say, Damodar Valley Corporation or DVC).

In the given projects 2-4, you have to examine their roles in supplying infrastructural facilities for the industrial and agricultural development. You may also explain the problems faced by these Institution and give suggestions to overcome these problems.

QUESTIONS

A. Short Answer Questions

1. What do you mean by infrastructure?
2. What is the importance of infrastructure? Discuss its components.
3. What do you mean by social infrastructure?
4. State the importance of education.
5. Give any two problems of educational development.
6. What is the importance of health in economic development?
7. State any two factors that contributed in the development of health facilities.
8. Why housing is important for socio-economic structure?
9. What is meant by civic amenities?
10. State the position of sanitation facilities in rural areas.
11. What is meant by the economic infrastructure of an economy? Mention its principal components.
12. What are the main means of transport in India?
13. State significance of transport in brief.
14. Railways are considered as a better mode of surface transport for bulk of heavy goods over long distances. Explain.
15. Mention four advantages of road transport in India.
16. State two problems of road transport.
17. Mention two advantages of water transport in India.

OR

Mention two factors which make water transport superior to other modes of transport.

18. Distinguish between Economic and Social infrastructure.
19. Briefly describe the progress of shipping in India.
20. Mention any two problems of water transport.
21. What do you understand by 'civil aviation'?
22. What are the different corporations of air transport in India?
23. State two advantages of air transport.
24. Explain briefly the problems of air transport.
25. What do you understand by pipeline transport in India?
26. What do you mean by communication? Name any two important means of communication in India.
27. Name new projects launched by the Government in telecommunication network.
28. Mention the important sources of powers.
29. What are the advantages of hydroelectric power?
30. What are the three important advantages of irrigation to economic growth in India?
31. Mention the important sources of irrigation in India.
32. Give a brief account of progress of irrigation facilities since Independence in India.

33. Give two advantages of irrigation.
34. Give full form of B.P.O. and K.P.O.
35. State any four benefits of pipeline transport.

B. Long Answer Questions
1. What role does infrastructure play in the economic development of a country?
2. Explain any four social infrastructure facilities.
3. Discuss the problems of educational development.
4. Why are health facilities essential for the economic development?
5. Write a note on: (i) Housing facilities, (ii) Environment.
6. Write a detailed note on the sanitation facilities available in India.
7. Examine any four reasons for the importance of a good transport system in a growing economy like that of India.
8. How railways are the principal mode of transport for goods and passengers?
9. Describe four beneficial effects of railways.
10. State disadvantages of railway transport.
11. Give three reasons, why the railways should be protected against road transport?
12. What are the main disadvantages of road transport?
13. Write a note on the development of coastal shipping and inland water transport.
14. State the disadvantages or problems that arise in the transportation of goods through water.
15. Air transport plays a significant role in the Indian economy. Explain.
16. Write a note on 'pipeline transport'.
17. What do you mean by communication? Describe briefly two important methods of communication.
18. Write a short note on the telecommunication system in India.
19. Write a note on telephone and Internet service.
20. Write a note on the development of : (a) the telephone system, and (b) the postal services.
21. Describe three important sources of power.
22. Explain the sources of irrigation adopted for the agricultural development.
23. What is the importance of irrigation in our economic life?

16
Consumer Awareness

CONSUMER

Consumer is a person who has indicated his/her willingness to obtain goods and services from a supplier with the intention of paying for them.

The word *"consumer"* has been defined under Consumer Protection Act of 2019 as follows:

"Consumer" means any person who—

(i) Buys any goods for a consideration which has been paid or promised or partly paid and partly promised, or under any system of deferred payment and includes any user of such goods other than the person who buys such goods for consideration paid or promised or partly paid or partly promised, or under any system of deferred payment, when such use is made with the approval of such person, but does not include a person who obtains such goods for resale or for any commercial purpose; or

(ii) Hires or avails of any service for a consideration which has been paid or promised or partly paid and partly promised, or under any system of deferred payment and includes any beneficiary of such service other than the person who hires or avails of the services for consideration paid or promised, or partly paid and partly promised, or under any system of deferred payment, when such services are availed of with the approval of the first mentioned person, but does not include a person who avails of such service for any commercial purpose.

OVERVIEW

Indian Market is generally a seller's market and it is very easy to dupe the innocent consumers. India is a very big country where majority of consumers are poor and helpless. Also Indian consumer is not well informed of his rights. An important socio-political environment confronting the business is the growth of consumerism and legislative measures to protect the consumers. Now there has been growth of consumer awareness in most of the countries leading to growth of consumerism and growing demand for consumer protection. A consumer is exposed to several difficulties like physical, environmental and exploitation due to unfair trade practices. He should be informed of the negative impacts of consuming adulterated eatables, expired or sub-standard medicines or paying more for a product or service. To protect the consumers from such hazards, consumer rights and duties have to be spread amongst consumers.

CONSUMER EXPLOITATION

When the producers cheat consumers of their hard earned money and hurt them either physically, mentally or financially by selling adulterated or defected goods or poor services to them is called consumer exploitation.

In other words, consumer exploitation means the practices (which are unscrupulous, exploitative and unfair) used by the producers or sellers to cheat consumers, ignoring their interest, with an objective to maximise their profits.

Ways in which a consumer gets exploited

Some common ways by which consumers are exploited by manufacturers and traders are given below:

Under Weight and Under-Measurements: The goods being sold in the market are sometimes not measured or weighed correctly.

Sub-Standard Quality: The goods sold are sometimes of sub-standard quality. Selling of consumables beyond their expiry dates and supply of deficient or defective home appliances are generally the regular grievances of consumers. This also includes the sales of medicines after expiry date and selling spurious drugs (sub-standard drugs).

High Prices: Very often the traders charge a price higher than the prescribed retail price.

Duplicate Articles: In the name of genuine parts or goods, fake or duplicate items are being sold to the consumers.

Adulteration and Impurity: In costly edible items, such as oil, ghee and spices, adulteration is made in order to earn higher profits. Adulteration of foods causes heavy loss to the customers; they suffer from monetary loss as well as spoil their health.

Lack of Safety Devices: Electronic goods, electrical devices or other appliances produced locally, lack the required inbuilt safeguards. This causes accidents to the consumers.

Artificial Scarcity: In order to make illegitimate profit, businessmen create artificial scarcity by hoarding. They sell the products at a later stage at higher prices.

False or Incomplete Information: Sellers easily mislead consumers by giving wrong information about a product, its price, quality, reliability, life cycle, expiry date, durability, its effect on health, environment, safety and security, maintenance costs involved, and terms and conditions of purchase. Cosmetics, drugs and electronic goods are common examples where consumers face such problems. Some producers promote goods that are injurious to public health through surrogate advertising. For instance, advertisement of a soda brand may be carried out to promote the sale of liquor with the same brand name, advertisement of fairness cream containing no chemicals guaranteeing to make the user fair within a week.

Unsatisfactory After-sales Service: Many of the high cost durable items, such as electrical or electronic equipments, home appliances and cars, need adequate after-sale care. The suppliers do not provide the satisfactory after-sale services despite the necessary payments made by the consumer. For example, non fulfillment of guarantee or warranty, etc.

Unpleasant and Rough Behaviour and Undue Conditions: In matters related to procuring LPG gas connection, fixing of a new telephone line, procurement of licensed items, etc., consumers are often harassed and undue conditions are put before them. Supply of blood from a blood bank infected with AIDS or other diseases, death of a person due to medical negligence of a doctor, advertisement with false claims etc., are all included in consumer exploitation.

Hidden Price Component: A lot of companies give offers that invites the consumers to buy products at very low prices or they make exchange offers or offers like buy one get one, which are good enough to lure the innocent consumers but have some or the other hidden price component attached to it which the consumer is forced to fulfill and he gets cheated.

Environmental Hazards: The producers may cause ecological and environmental hazards for the consumers and society by causing water, air and noise pollution.

Other Ways: There are few other ways by which consumers are cheated, like:
- Variations in the content filled in the packaged goods.
- Illegal fixation of maximum retail price (MRP) and selling above MRP.
- Non-compliance with the terms and conditions of sales and services and not providing after-sales services.
- Shifting the liability of tax payment levied on producers/service providers on to innocent consumers.

Reasons or Factors Causing Exploitation of Consumers

Limited Information: Producers provide incomplete and incorrect information about various products.

Limited Supplies: When goods and services are hoarded by producers/suppliers with an intention to create short supply, then prices shoot up.

Limited Competition: Single producer may manipulate the market in terms of price and stocks i.e., when seller enjoys monopoly in the market.

Low Literacy: Illiteracy leads to exploitation. Lack of consumer awareness is the root cause for exploitation.

Lack of Bargaining Power: This results among consumers due to lack of market information.

Irregular Prices Offered: Sellers often manipulate the pricing of the product in absence of government control and there is price discrimination by the seller.

Misleading Advertisements: Form a basic reason causing exploitation of a consumer. They have been designed and projected in such a way that the consumer gets carried off and gets trapped in the mesh of hidden costs, etc.

For example: The producers may advertise a low price for the goods on offer. But when one goes to purchase the goods, he ends up paying more than the advertised price because it did not include the price of accessories or other things that are necessary to use the goods.

Lack of Unity: consumers lack courage and unity to voice against the exploitation, irrespective of the rights issued to them by our government.

Cumbersome and Time Taking Legal Proceedings: Our legal procedures are critical and cumbersome. This puts off the courage in people to file any complaint against exploitation.

CONSUMER AWARENESS

Consumer: Someone who purchases goods for personal use.

Awareness: Having knowledge of; state of elementary or undifferentiated consciousness.

Consumer awareness is the knowledge that a consumer should have about his/her legal rights and duties. It is a must for a consumer to follow these rights. It is implemented for the protection of the consumer, so that the consumer is not exploited by the seller of the products.

Growth/Rise of Consumer Awareness

Kautilya was one of the earliest to write in his Arthasastra about the need for consumer awareness and protection. With the growth of private sector, there is a greater need for discipline and regulation of the market. The process of development, along with globalisation and liberalization process has increased the number of consumer related issues.

Today consumers have become aware of the sale and purchase of goods, the health and security aspects also. They try to ensure the safety of food items sold in the market which is essential these days.

Consumer protection has earned an important place in the political, economic and social agendas of many nations. In India, the Government has taken many steps including legislative, to protect consumers like The Contract Act 1982, The Sale of Goods Act 1930, The Essential Commodities Act 1955, The Consumer Protection Act 1986 , etc.

Media is playing an important role in accelerating the growth of consumer awareness. Advertisements of 'Jaago Grahak Jaago' is aired on national television and broadcasted on Radio also.

World Consumers Right Day is celebrated on 15th March every year. National Consumer Day is celebrated on 24th December every year. Many consumer organisations and NGO's have been formed which contribute a lot to the growth of consumer awareness.

One of the most important method by which consumer awareness is growing and can further grow is enabling people with consumer education.

The most important step in consumer education is awareness of consumer rights. However, consumer education is incomplete without realizing the responsibilities and duties of consumers, and this influences individual behaviour to a great extent.

Consumer education also involves environmental education as it deals with the importance of conserving (natural resources) and sustaining (recycling and reusing) the environment, including the direct health effects of environmental pollution and toxic products on consumers. Schools must incorporate consumer education into school curriculum.

Consumer Rights

In the 20th century, the presence and influence of the market grew dramatically in consumer life. We began to purchase things from the market for a price. Soon, mass production and industrial production came into being, giving the consumer world an entirely new dimension. Have you ever wondered how much urban consumers depend on the market for fulfillment of even their basic needs. This over-dependence on the market and the inherent profit motive in mass production and sales has given manufacturers and dealers a good reason to exploit consumers. As a consumer, you would know how market products are constantly under-weighted, of inferior quality and do not prescribe to quality standards specified by quality-control agencies. Consumers do not get value for their money and often have to suffer losses and inconvenience due to market manipulations.

Consumer rights are now an integral part of our lives like a consumerist way of life. They have been well documented and much talked about. We have all made use of them at some point in our daily lives. Market resources and influences are growing by the day and so is the awareness of one's consumer rights. These rights are well-defined and there are agencies, like the government, consumer courts and voluntary organisations that work towards safeguarding them. While we all like to know about our rights and make full use of them, consumer responsibility is an area which is still not demarcated and it is hard to spell out all the responsibilities that a consumer is supposed to shoulder. In this chapter, we will give an overview of the 8 consumer rights, their implications and significance for a developing country like India, and also define the various aspects of consumer responsibility.

The consumer rights are as follows:

Right to Safety: Means right to be protected against the marketing of goods and services, which are hazardous to life and property and it includes concern for not only meeting their immediate needs, but also fulfills long-term interests. Before purchasing, consumers should be informed of the products and services. They should preferably purchase quality marked products, such as ISI, AGMARK, etc.

Right to be Informed: Means right to be informed about the quality, quantity, potency, purity, standard and price of goods so as the consumer should insist on getting all the information about the product or services before making a choice or a decision to enable him to desist from falling prey to high pressure selling techniques.

Right to Choose: Means right to be assured, wherever possible, of access to variety of goods and services at competitive price, satisfactory quality and service at a fair price. It also includes right to basic goods and services. This is because of denial for the majority of its fair share. This right can be better exercised in a competitive market where a vast variety of choices are available to the consumer. The producer/supplier should not force the customer to buy a particular brand only.

Right to be Heard: Means that consumer interests will receive due consideration at appropriate forums. It also includes right to consumer welfare. The consumers should form non-political and non-commercial consumer organizations and other bodies to give them unity and a platform to voice their problems.

Right to Seek Redressal: Means right to seek redressal against unfair trade practices or unscrupulous exploitation of consumers. Consumers must make complaint for their genuine grievances. Many a times their complaint may be very large. They can also take the help of consumer organisations in seeking redressal of their grievances.

Right to Consumer Education: Means the right to acquire the knowledge and skill to be an informed consumer throughout life. Ignorance of the rights is responsible for their exploitation. They should know their rights and must exercise them. Only then consumer exploitation will be prevented.

Apart from the above six rights two additional rights are recommended by the UNO. These are:

Right to Basic Needs: Every citizen has the right to fulfill the basic needs—food, clothing, health care, drinking water, sanitation, education, etc., to survive and have dignified living.

Right to Healthy Environment: According to this right, the consumers and all the citizens have the right to be protected against environmental pollution and protected against environmental degradation.

Thus, the concern of consumer protection is to ensure fair trade practices; maintain quality of goods and efficient service quantity, potency of the product, composition and price for their choice of purchase. Such a consumer protection policy would enable consumer satisfaction from the delivery of goods and services needed by them.

CONSUMER BEHAVIOUR IN MARKET

Consumer behaviour is the study of when, what, how, where and why people do or do not buy products. It blends elements from psychology, sociology, social psychology, anthropology and economics. It attempts to understand the buyer decision making process, both individually and in groups.

Consumer awareness has grown in recent years influencing his behaviour and response in the market. The consumer wants to verify the quality, quantity and correct price of the product. They also bargain on the MRP of the products.

Consumers still behave to be attracted towards numerous discount offers and sales, but they do try to know about the hidden price components also.

Consumer has become more informed about his rights, duties and responsibilities. Consumer's behaviour in the market has become more responsible. A few of consumer responsibilities affecting consumer behaviour are as follows:

CONSUMER RESPONSIBILITIES

- Get a bill for every important purchase and also the Warranty card.
- Check the ISI mark or AGMARK on the goods.
- Form consumer awareness groups.
- Make a complaint on genuine grievances.
- Consumer must know the way to exercise their rights.
- Shop carefully and wisely.
- Understand the terms of the sale.
- Read and follow instructions.
- Get guarantees in writing.
- Save receipts.
- Ask questions at point of sale.
- Keep informed about new products (Quality consciousness).
- Respect the environment and avoid waste littering.
- Discourage black marketing, hoarding and choose only legal goods and services.

CONSUMER PROTECTION

Consumer dissonance is the root cause of consumer exploitation. This refers to the purchase doubts, dissatisfaction, disillusion and disappointment. Consumer protection is essential for a healthy economy. save him from unfair trade practices of producers and traders. The consumer should be provided with the complete information about a product or services so that a proper decision about availing a product or service can be made.

NEED FOR CONSUMER PROTECTION

Consumer's choice is influenced to a great extent by the effect of mass media and other aspects of consumer behaviour. He usually does not know that for whatever he pays for is worth it or not, for *e.g.,* whether the food stuff has the correct nutritional value or not or any electrical goods he buys is safe by all standards or if it causes any environmental hazards, etc. So he needs to be protected.

Consumer protection is not only important for the consumer but to the business as a whole.

Consumer protection is needed for the following reasons:

1. **For the Physical Protection of a Consumer:** Against the products that are unsafe or harmful to the health and welfare of a consumer.
2. **For Protection Against Unfair Trade Practices:** Consumer should know about his rights and in case of any exploitation, due to supply of sub-standard, defective goods, etc., and he should know the means to redress against frauds.
3. **Protection Against Environmental Hazards:** Use of chemical fertilizers and certain refinery complexes pollute air, water and food and they cause a threat to human life, thus, protection is needed for it.
4. **Protection from Deceptive Advertising:** Some producers give incorrect information about their products and the consumer is misled by these fake advertisements which costs hard on their pockets. There should be certain measures which can prevent consumers from such misleading advertisements.
5. **Un-Organized Consumers:** India is a country that has population from various socio-economic backgrounds and the consumers are highly unorganized. consumer organizations are working in this direction, so consumer protection is important to safeguard the interest of the consumers.
6. **For the Growth of Business:** It is ultimately in the interest of business community to protect and serve the consumers. Due to economic liberalisation and globalisation, Indian firms are facing competition from multinationals. In order to survive and grow in future, business firms in India must become consumer oriented.
7. **Other Reasons:** For protection of poor illiterate, ignored consumers, for moral and ethical justification.

WAYS/METHODS OF CONSUMER PROTECTION

There are following ways of protecting the consumers.

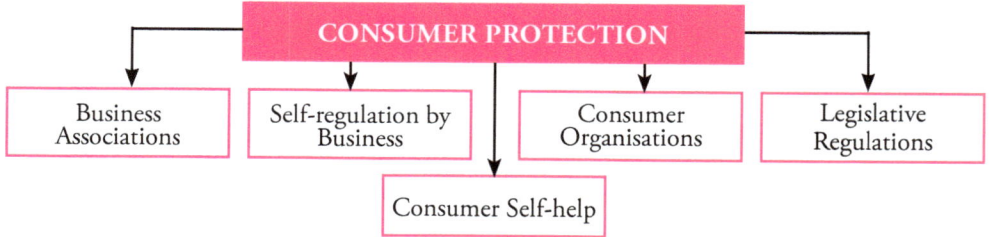

1. **Self-regulation by Business:** Business community can help to achieve protection and satisfaction through disciplining itself by adopting higher ethical standards. The trade associations and chambers of commerce can regulate the unfair trade practices used by some businessmen.
2. **Consumer Self-help:** Consumer should make efforts to know about his own rights. He should not allow the shrewd businessmen to cheat him.
3. **Legislative Regulations:** Consumer associations, consumer right groups, consumer protection act, consumer protection councils are the bodies which help to regulate consumer protection.
4. **Business Associations:** The association of trade, commerce and business like CII, FICCI may lay down code of conduct for their members.

5. **Consumer Organisations:** These organisations can force businessmen/ business firms to avoid malpractices and exploitation of consumers and spread consumer education.

CONSUMER PROTECTION ACT, 2019

The Consumer Protection Act, 2019 received the President's assent on 9 August 2019 and has replaced the Consumer Protection Act, 1986 to protect and strengthen the rights of the consumers by establishing authorities, imposing strict liabilities and penalties on product manufacturers, electronic service providers, misleading advertisers, and by providing additional settlement of consumer disputes through mediation. It extends to the whole of India except the State of Jammu and Kashmir. The basic aim of the Consumer Protection Act, 2019 is to save the rights of the consumers by establishing authorities for timely and effective administration and settlement of consumers' disputes.

Mentioned below are some rights that consumers are entitled to under the Act:
1. The right to be protected against the marketing of goods, products or services which are hazardous to life and property;
2. The right to be informed about the quality, quantity, potency, purity, standard and price of goods, products or services, as the case may be, so as to protect the consumer against unfair trade practices;
3. The right to be assured, wherever possible, access to a variety of goods, products or services at competitive prices;
4. The right to be heard and to be assured that consumer's interests will receive due consideration at appropriate forum;
5. The right to seek redressal against unfair trade practice, restrictive trade practices or unscrupulous exploitation of consumers; and
6. The right to consumer awareness.

Under the Consumer Protection Act, 2019, the following remedies are available to the aggrieved consumer:
1. Refund of price paid to the seller.
2. Removal of defects in the goods or services bought.
3. Replacement of defective goods with new goods.
4. Payment of compensation by seller for loss incurred by consumer.
5. Withdrawal of hazardous goods from the market.
6. Discontinuance of unfair and restrictive trade practices.

If a trader or person against whom a complaint is made, fails or omits to comply with any order made by a redressal agency, he shall be punishable with imprisonment upto three years or with fine not less than ₹ 25,000 extendable to ₹ 1 lakh, or both.

CONSUMER DISPUTES REDRESSAL AGENCIES

The Consumer Protection Act, 2019 sets up a three-tiered system of consumer
Disputes redressal agencies which are given below:
A. District Commission: The State Government shall, by notification, establish a District Consumer Disputes Redressal Commission, to be known as the District Commission, in each district of the State:

The State Government may establish more than one District Commission in a district, if it deems fit.

Each District Commission shall consist of:
(a) A President; and
(b) Not less than two and not more than such number of members as may be prescribed, in consultation with the Central Government.

Jurisdiction: Subject to the provisions of this Act, the District Forum will have Jurisdiction to entertain complaints where the value of goods or services and the compensation of any claim does not exceed ₹ 1 Crore.

B. State commission: Each state commission shall consist of :
(a) A President; and
(b) Not less than four or not more than such number of members as may be prescribed in consultation with the Central Government.

Jurisdiction: Subject to the provision of the Act, the state commission has the jurisdiction:

(i) To entertain complaints where the value of goods or services or compensation claimed is between ₹ 1 Crore and ₹ 10 crore.

To entertain appeals against the orders of any District Forum within the state, and

(ii) To call for the records and pass appropriate orders in any consumer dispute that is pending before or has been decided by any District Forum within the State, where it appears to the State commission that such District Forum has exercised jurisdiction not vested in it by law or has failed to exercise a jurisdiction so vested or has acted in exercise of its jurisdiction illegally or with material irregularity.

C. The National Commission: The National Commission will consist of:
(a) a President; and
(b) not less than four and not more than such number of members as may be prescribed.

Jurisdiction: The National commission shall have jurisdiction :
(i) To entertain complaints where value of the goods or services and the compensation if any claimed exceeds ₹ 10 crore.
(ii) To entertain appeals against the orders of any state commission, and
(iii) To call for the records and pass appropriate orders in any consumer dispute which is pending before or has been decided by any State Commission where it appears to the National Commission that such state commission has exercised a jurisdiction not vested in it by the law, or has failed to exercise a jurisdiction so vested or has acted in the exercise of its jurisdiction illegally or with material irregularity.

Importance of Educating Consumers of their Rights

In an ideal and theoretical situation, the relationship between a consumer and a producer arises out of a voluntary act between equal parties. In practice, however, just as in any relationship, one of the parties may be more empowered and can wield its power and impose its will on the other party in an unfair manner. In consumer-producer relationship, it is usually the producer who is more empowered and can commit some excesses. There may of course be a few exceptions where the boot is on the other leg. Therefore it is necessary to make the consumer aware of his rights.

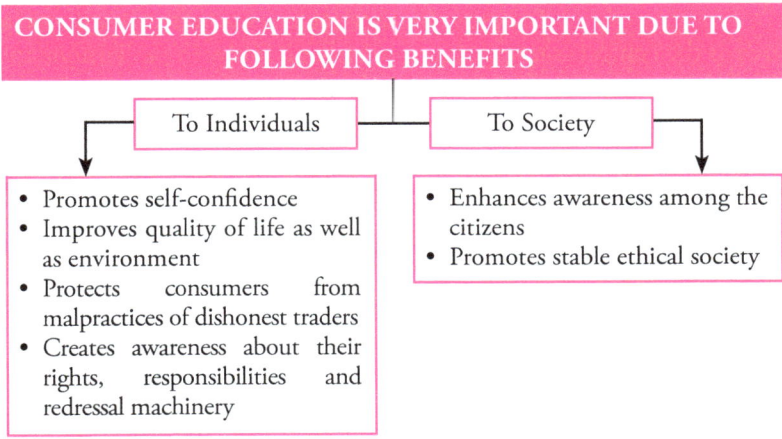

Education and Information Programmes: Governments should develop or encourage the development of general consumer education and information programmes, bearing in mind the cultural traditions of the people concerned. The aim of such programmes should be to enable people to act as rational consumers, capable of making an informed choice of goods and services, and conscious of their rights and responsibilities. In developing such programmes, special attention should be given to the needs of disadvantaged consumers, in both rural and urban areas, including low-income consumers and those with low or non-existent literacy levels.

Consumer education should, where appropriate, become an integral part of the basic curriculum of the education system, preferably as a component of existing subjects.

Consumer education and information programmes should cover such important aspects of consumer protection as the following: (a) Health, nutrition, prevention of food-borne diseases and food adulteration; (b) Product hazards; (c) Product labelling; (d) Relevant legislation, how to obtain redress, and agencies and organizations for consumer protection; (e) Information on weights and measures, prices, quality, credit conditions and availability of basic necessities; and (f) As appropriate, pollution and environment.

Governments should encourage consumer organizations and other interested groups, including the media, to undertake education and information programmes, particularly for the benefit of low-income consumer groups in rural and urban areas.

Role of Voluntary Organizations in Consumer Education

There are more than 800 consumer organizations in India protecting and promoting their interest.

The role and functions of most of the voluntary organization in consumer education are as follows:

1. **Consumer Guidance:** They build up consumer awareness through periodical exhibitions, meetings, demonstrations, and through television, radio and such other mass media. They address students, women groups and social organizations.
2. **Consumer Education:** They bring out journals to educate consumers. Trained social workers educate the lower income groups through various programmes. The tricks and sharp practice of unscrupulous traders are exposed. Consumers buying power, credit and satisfaction are improved.

3. **Consumer Representation:** These voluntary societies represent consumers in advisory bodies such as the central council, state council and lobby in parliament and assemblies on behalf of the consumers.
4. **Consumer Protection:** These voluntary bodies act as the listening board for consumer grievances. They follow the complaints against shopkeepers, leaders and manufacturers. They file public interest litigations in consumer and regular courts.
5. **Consumer Resistance:** A strong consumer resistance movement is also being built up on the lines of Swadeshi movement. Goods, which are to be boycotted on some ground or other, are being listed and circulated. These voluntary bodies have achieved spectacular results. Hundreds of cases have been won in various consumer courts on behalf of the consumers.

Food Adulteration and Its Harmful Effects

An article of food shall be deemed to be adulterated if:
(a) The article sold by a vendor is not of the nature, substance or quality demanded by the purchaser and is to this prejudice, or is not of the nature substance or quality which it proposes or is represented to be.
(b) If the article contains any other substance which affects, or if the article is so processed as to affect, injurious by the nature, substance or quality there of.
(c) If the article had been prepared, packed or kept under insanitary conditions whereby it has become contaminated or injurious to health.
(d) If the article consists of wholly or in part any filthy, putrid, rotten, decomposed or diseased animal or vegetable substance or is insect infected or is otherwise unfit for human consumption.
(e) If the container of the article is composed, whether wholly or in part, of any poisonous or deleterious substance which renders its contents injurious to health.

Adulteration is quite common, in food article. It is a crime which cannot be pardoned. It spoils the health of the consumers.

Example:
(1) 300 grams of vanaspati is found in a 500 grams tin of ghee, but labelled as "Pure Ghee".
(2) One kilogram of sugar packet weighs only 970 grams, where as labelled as "**Net Weight One Kilogram**".
(3) 500 grams of chilly powder packet consists of 150 grams of red brick powder or coloured saw dust, where as labelled as "**Pure**".
(4) Chemicals are added to make the milk thick and white.

Adulteration causes a number of diseases, for example, respiratory track infection, lung cancer, a number of skin diseases and many more. Therefore, consumer must be aware of their rights and government should take appropriate measures to check adulteration.

THE RIGHT TO INFORMATION (AMENDMENT) ACT, 2019

The Right to Information (Amendment) Bill, 2019 was introduced in Lok Sabha by the Minister of State for Personnel, Public Grievances and Pensions, Jitendra Singh, on July 19, 2019.

This Act of Parliament received the assent of the President on the 1st August, 2019. This Act has replaced the previous Right to Information Act, 2005. It shall come into force on such date as the Central Government may, by notification in the Official Gazette, appoint. This act proposes to give the Centre the powers to decide the salaries and service conditions of Information Commissioners at central as well as state levels. This act has amended section 13 and 16 of the earlier act. There may be three features of this Act:

(i) **Term of Information Commissioners:** According to the amended act, the central government will notify the term of office for the CIC and the ICs.

(ii) **Determination of Salary:** Salaries, allowances, and other terms and conditions of service of the central and state CIC and ICs will be determined by the central government.

(iii) **Deductions in Salary:** The Act states that at the time of the appointment of the CIC and ICs (at the central and state level), if they are receiving pension or any other retirement benefits for previous government service, their salaries will be reduced by an amount equal to the pension. But the present Act has removed such provision.

Comparison of the provisions of the Right to Information Act, 2005 and the Right to Information (Amendment) Bill, 2019

Provision	RTI Act, 2005	RTI (Amendment) Bill, 2019
Time period	The Chief Information Commissioner (CIC) and Information Commissioners (ICs) (at the central and state level) will hold office for a term of five years.	The Bill removes this provision and states that the central government will notify the term of office for the CIC and the ICs.
Salary	The salary of the CIC and ICs (at the central level) will be equivalent to the salary paid to the Chief Election Commissioner and Election Commissioners, respectively. Similarly, the salary of the CIC and ICs (at the state level) will be equivalent to the salary paid to the Election Commissioners and the Chief Secretary to the state government, respectively.	There is no such provision now. It will be determined by the central government.

| Deductions | The Act states that at the time of the appointment of the CIC and ICs (at the central and state level), if they are receiving pension or any other retirement benefits for previous government service, their salaries will be reduced by an amount equal to the pension. Previous government service includes service under: (i) the central government, (ii) state government, (iii) corporation established under a central or state law, and (iv) company owned or controlled by the central or state government. | No Provision |

PROCESS

Under the Act, all authorities covered must appoint their Public Information Officer (PIO). Any person may submit a request to the PIO for information in writing. It is the PIO's obligation to provide information to citizens of India who request information under the Act. If the request pertains to another public authority (in whole or part) it is the PIO's responsibility to transfer/forward the concerned portions of the request to a PIO of the other authority within 5 days. In addition, every public authority is required to designate Assistant Public Information Officers (APIOs) to receive RTI requests and appeal for forwarding to the PIOs of their public authority. The citizen making the request is not obliged to disclose any information except his name and contact particulars.

Constitutional Aspect of the Right to Information

Article 19(1) (a) of the Constitution guarantees the fundamental rights to free speech and expression. The prerequisite for enjoying this right is knowledge and information. The absence of authentic information on matters of public interest will only encourage wild rumours and speculations and avoidable allegations against individual and institutions. Therefore, the Right to Information becomes a constitutional right. This will help the citizens to perform their fundamental duties also.

Right to Information is not Absolute

As no right can be absolute, the Right to Information has to have its limitations. There will always be areas of information that should remain protected in public and national interest. Moreover, this unrestricted right can have an adverse effect of an overload of demand on administration. So the information has to be properly, clearly classified by an appropriate authority.

Areas of Non-Disclosure

- International relations and national security.
- Law enforcement and prevention of crime.

- Internal deliberations of the government.
- Information obtained in confidence from some source outside the government.
- Information which, if disclosed, would violate the privacy of an individual.
- Information, particularly of an economic nature, when disclosed, would confer an unfair advantage on some person or subject or government.
- Information which is covered by legal/professional privilege, like communication between a legal advisor and his client, and
- Information about scientific discoveries and inventions and improvements essentially in the field of weapons.

These categories are broad and information of every kind in relation to these matters cannot always be treated as secret. There may be occasions when information may have to be disclosed in public interest, without compromising the national interest or public safety. For example, information about deployment and movement of armed forces and information about military operations, qualify for exemption. Information about the extent of defence expenditure and transactions for the purchase of guns and submarines and aircraft cannot be totally withheld at all stages.

CASES RELATED TO CONSUMER EXPLOITATION AND RIGHT TO INFORMATION

Case 1

This case is related to Automobiles in general and Motor bikes in specific. And this was reported in a reputed newspaper of India. This case pertains to Bajaj CT 100 motorcycle where Vehicle dealer had promised a mileage of 100+ kms.

Since the customer could not get the promised mileage, he approached the dealer with his grievance and during the subsequent checking of the defective vehicle even by company service engineers, they could not achieve the promised figures. Hence, the customer demanded compensation. Since, they refused to entertain any claims for compensation the customer had no other option than approaching the consumer forum. The case was finally settled by the National Commission in favour of customer by awarding replacement of vehicle and monetary compensation alongwith court cost.

The legislation has made it mandatory for the manufacturers to print the cost of production and maximum retail price on packaging of consumer goods, so that the consumer could not get overcharged by the agents/dealers.

It is essential for the consumers to know the difference between the maximum retail price and actual price of the goods. The maximum retail price is inclusive of all taxes and a retailer can sell at a price below the MRP. In fact, consumers should always look for retailers who sell below the MRP because the MRP is the maximum retail price allowed for that commodity and not the actual price and a retailer can well reduce his margin built into the MRP. While on the other hand, the actual price could be about 10-15 per cent lower than the MRP. Sometimes, the printed MRP is so high that the difference between the selling price and the MRP can be as much 30-50 per cent. It is an offence to sell at a price higher than the market price. Whereas the actual price could be about 10-15 per cent lower that the MRP.

Case 2

A complainant filed a complaint case before the apex consumer court. The issue involved in the complaint was that the complainant went to purchase a product namely tarpaulin (Waterproofed Canvas), the price mentioned on the 'duckback baby sheet' purchased by him was ₹ 92, but the seller asked him to pay for ₹ 112 along with the statement that the price of the sheet was actually ₹ 124 but it had an old label indicating the MRP as ₹ 92. So after discussion, the price was settled between them (the seller and the buyer) at ₹ 112.

In the above said matter the State Commission held that if the old label on the product indicated ₹ 92 as the MRP, then charging more than what is mentioned on the packaging is illegal and the activity of the seller constitutes an unfair trade practice, and as a punishment for indulging in such a practice, the commission used the relatively new provision in the Consumer Protection Act to impose exemplary damage and asked the seller to pay the consumer punitive damages of ₹ 10,000.

The apex consumer court, before which the seller filed an appeal, said it fully agreed with the view of the State Commission. While doing so, it pointed out that if the price had been increased from ₹ 92 to ₹ 124 due to increased cost of production and transportation, then this would apply only to the new stock. The price of the old stock cannot change. In these circumstances, the old stock cannot be sold at the new price. Therefore, the State Commission was right in imposing exemplary compensation. (M/S Cargo Tarpaulin Industries Vs Sri Mallikarujun (B. Kori), revision petition number 2132 of 2018, decided on July 5, 2018). It is an offence to sell at a price higher than the marked price. It is for this reason that manufacturers provide a more than adequate cushion for dealer margins while marking the MRP. Whereas, it is specifically mentioned under the Consumer Goods (Mandatory Printing of Cost of Production and Maximum Retail Price) Act, 2006 that no person shall sell or caused to sell any consumer goods without printing the cost of production and maximum retail price of the product after the expiry of six months from the date of commencement of this act.

Case 3

A landmark judgment, the National Consumer Disputes Redressal Commission, New Delhi, has directed the Union Ministry of Petroleum and Ministry of Consumer Affairs to ensure that all LPG marketing companies issue necessary instructions to distributors to provide to every deliveryman, proper weighing scale for the purpose of weighing LPG cylinder in the presence of customers, before delivery.

The two member bench of the National Commission, comprising of Justice K.S. Gupta and Justice S.N. Kapoor, in their 28-page order passed on a petition filed by Consumer Protection Council, Rourkela. a voluntary organisation, further directed that the Ministries should also instruct the LPG marketing companies to give due publicity by publishing the same in the vernacular language of each and every state as well as in English and Hindi newspapers apart from giving similar type of advertisement in TV for information of the consumers.

The case was filed by the complainant Council in 2019 submitting that many consumers in the steel township Rourkela in Orissa's Sundargarh district were cheated by way of supply of LPG cylinders having less quantity of gas by Indian Oil Corporation. The organisation was represented through its Secretary, Sri B. Vaidyanathan.

A survey conducted subsequent to the complaint received from a consumer by the complainant Council, covering 48 households in June 2000 had revealed that as against the net weight of 14.2 kg of LPG, the consumers on an average were getting only 12.74 kg. Only 12.5 per cent of the refill cylinders weighed were within the tolerance range of 150 gms or less, as prescribed in 2nd Schedule of the Standards of Weights & Measures (Packaged Commodities) Rules.

The Commission, in its order passed on August 16th, also asked the Indian Oil Corporation to pay a sum of ₹ 50,000 to the complainant Council to meet the expenses incurred by it in protecting the interest of consumers and to continue to protect the interest of the consumers. Though the complainant Council had prayed for awarding 1 per cent of the estimated ₹ 750 crores loss inflicted on the consumers across the country, due to the under-weight deliveries, in a year, the Commission has not dealt this issue, in its directions.

LESSON AT A GLANCE

Consumer: Consumer is a person who has indicated his or her willingness to obtain goods and or services from a supplier with the intention of paying for them.

Consumer Exploitation: When producers cheat consumers of their hard earned money and hurt them either physically, mentally or financially by selling adulterated or defected goods or pool services to them is called consumer exploitation.

Ways in which a consumers gets exploited: (i) Under weight and under-measurement; (ii) Sub-standard quality; (iii) High prices; (iv) Duplicate articles; (v) Adulteration and impurity; (vi) Lack of safety devices; (vii) Artificial scarcity; (viii) False or incomplete information; (ix) Unsatisfactory after-sales services; (x) Unpleasant and rough behaviour and undue conditions; (xi) Hidden price component; (xii) Environmental hazards; (xiii) Other ways.

Reasons or Factors causing Consumer Exploitation: (i) Limited information; (ii) Limited supplies; (iii) Limited competition; (iv) Low literacy; (v) Lack of bargaining power; (vi) Irregular prices offered; (vii) Misleading advertisements; (viii) Lack of unity; (ix) Cumbersome and time taking legal proceedings.

Consumer Awareness: It is the knowledge of rights and duties of a consumer; so that he does not gets exploited. Consumer awareness can get promoted through consumer education.

Consumer Rights: (i) Rights to safety; (ii) Right to be informed; (iii) Right to choose; (iv) Right to be heard; (v) Right to seek redressal; (vi) Right to consumer education.

Consumer protection is very important to prevent consumers from getting exploited due to factors like: (i) Consumer dissonance; (ii) Unfair trade practices; (iii) Physical protection of consumer; (iv) Protection against environmental hazards; (v) Protection from deceptive advertising; (vi) Unorganized consumer; (vii) Growth of business.

Ways of Consumer Protection: (i) Self-regulation by business; (ii) Consumer self help; (iii) Legislative regulations; (iv) Business associations; (v) Consumer organisations.

Consumer Protection Act, 2019: Received the President's assent on 9 August 2019 and has replaced the Consumer Protection Act, 1986 to protect and strengthen the rights of the consumers by establishing authorities, imposing strict liabilities and penalties on product manufactures, electronic service providers, misleading advertisers, and by providing additional settlement of consumer disputes through mediation. It extends to the whole of India except the State of Jammu and Kashmir. The basic aim of the Consumer Protection Act, 2019 is to save the rights of the consumers by establishing authorities for timely and effective administration and settlement of consumers' disputes.

Extent and Coverage of the Act: The Act applies to all goods and services whether in private, public or cooperative sector.

Right to Information Act 2019: Rights to Information Act 2019 has replaced the previous Right to Information Act, 2005. It shall come into force on such date as the Central Government may, by notification in the Official Gazette, appoint. This act proposes to give the Centre the powers to decide the salaries and service conditions of Information Commissioners at central as well as state levels. This act has amended section 13 and 16 of the earlier Act.

QUESTIONS

A. Short Answer Questions

1. Who is a consumer according to the Common Protection Act, 2019?
2. What is consumer exploitation?
3. How does false and incomplete information be a way for exploiting the consumers?
4. What is meant by hidden price component?
5. How do advertisement cause consumer exploitation?
6. Write a short note on consumer awareness.
7. Consumer education is an important method to eliminate consumer exploitation. Explain.
8. What is meant by consumer protection?
9. How does 'consumer dissonance' forms a root cause of consumer exploitation?
10. How is consumer protection important for the growth of business?
11. Deceptive advertising costs hard on a consumer's pocket. Comment.
12. Explain the ways by which the consumer can be protected.
13. What is COPRA 2019 and when did it come into force?
14. What aspects do the provisions of COPRA 2019 cover?
15. What is the scope of the consumer protection act, 2019?
16. How many consumer protection councils are there? Explain them briefly.

17. Name the various redressal agencies under COPRA 2019.
18. What is meant by information?
19. What is RTI 2019 and when did it come into force?
20. What are the different rights assigned to the citizen of India to collect information?
21. What are main areas of Non-Disclosure of Information?
22. Leena purchased some household goods from a general store. After reaching home she found a body lotion which was not billed. After checking the date of expiry and other details she started using it. She had rashes on her body due to the use of body lotion. Can Leena file a complaint under Consumer Protection Act, 2019? Justify your answer.
23. Write down the scope of consumer education (any two points).
24. What do you mean by food adulteration?

B. Long Answer Questions

1. Explain 'Consumer' for the purposes of goods and services.
2. 'Consumer is the king of market', still he is exploited. Discuss the reasons.
3. Write a note on the ways in which a consumer is exploited.
4. Explain the factors causing 'consumer exploitation'.
5. What is consumer awareness and how has it grown in recent times?
6. What is the need for consumer awareness in the modern days world?
7. Why are consumer rights important and how have they become an important part of a consumer's life?
8. What is the need of consumer protection and what are the various factors responsible for consumer protection?
9. Explain the objectives of COPRA 2019.
10. What is meant by a 'consumer' according to the Consumer Protection Act, 2019?
11. Briefly describe the redressal agencies under the Consumer Protection Act, 2019.
12. What are the amendments made in the Consumer Protection Act, 2019?
13. Explain the features of the right to information act.
14. Differentiate between the provisions of the Right to Information Act, 2005 and Right to Information (Amendment) Act, 2019.
15. Explain the different ways and means of consumer protection followed in India.

17 Globalisation

GLOBALISATION

Globalisation in its literal sense is the process of transformation of local or regional phenomena into a global one. It can be described as a process by which the people of the world are unified into a single society and function together.

This process is a combination of economic, technological, socio-cultural and political forces. Globalisation is often used to refer to economic globalisation, that is, integration of national economy into the international economy through trade, foreign direct investment, capital flows, labour movement and the spread of technology.

It is a historical process and the result of human innovation and technological progress.

DEFINITION

Globalisation may be understood as the expansion of local markets to include the markets of other countries in terms of movement of goods, services, capital and labour with least or no barriers of tariffs and non-tariff barriers.

The worldwide movement towards economic, financial, trade and communication integration, thus, Globalisation implies to opening out beyond local and nationalistic perspectives to a broader outlook of an interconnected and inter-dependent world with free transfer of capital, goods, and services across national frontiers.

OVERVIEW

Globalisation is the new buzzword that has come to dominate the world since the nineties of the last century with the end of the cold war and the break-up of the former Soviet Union. The frontiers of the state had an increased reliance on the market economy and renewed faith in the private capital and resources. a process of structural adjustment spurred by the studies and influences of the World Bank and other International organisations that started in many of the developing countries. Also, Globalisation has brought in new opportunities to developing countries. Greater access to developed country markets and technology transfer promise improved productivity and higher living standard. But globalisation has also thrown up new challenges like growing inequality across and within nations, volatility in financial market and environmental deteriorations. Another negative aspect of globalisation is that a great majority of developing countries remain removed from the process.

Till the nineties the process of globalisation of the Indian economy was constrained by the barriers to trade and investment. liberalisation of trade, investment and financial flows initiated in the nineties has progressively lowered the barriers to competition and hastened the pace of globalisation.

However, it does not include unhindered movement of labour and as suggested by some economists, may hurt smaller or fragile economies if applied indiscriminately.

The United Nations ESCWA has written, "Globalisation is a widely-used term that can be defined in a number of different ways. When used in an economic context, it refers to the reduction and removal of barriers between national borders in order to facilitate the flow of goods, capital, services, and labour although considerable barriers remain to the flow of labour."

Factors Enabling Globalisation

Globalisation is a series of social, economical, technological, cultural and political changes that promote interdependence and growth. Globalisation raises the standard of living in developing countries, spreads technological knowledge and increases political liberation. The main cause of globalisation is shared improvement in the standard of living.

Globalisation also refers to the trend toward countries joining together economically, through education, society and politics, and viewing themselves not only through their national identity but also as part of the world as a whole. Globalisation is said to bring people of all nations closer together, especially through a common medium like the economy or communication.

Hence, globalisation means adopting a global outlook in manufacturing, marketing, financing, human resource management and all other areas of business. A truly global corporation views the entire world as a single market. It does not differentiate between domestic market and foreign markets. It conducts its operations worldwide as if the entire world were a single entity.

The main factors that led to the development of globalisation are as follows :

- Growing similarities of countries in terms of available infrastructure, distribution channels and marketing approaches.
- Growth of national capital markets into global capital markets due to the large flow of funds between countries.
- Technological restructuring *i.e.,* technological revolution, such as micro-electronics reshaping competition globally.
- Products becoming available to more global consumers due to reduced costs and global distribution systems.
- Widening of competition from domestic markets to global markets.
- Growing international competition. In order to survive in global markets, firms have to improve efficiency of operations, reduce costs and improve quality.

In all we can say that, there are two major types of factors, which lead to globalisation :

Pull Factors: Are the proactive reasons responsible for pulling business to the foreign markets and an economy to open up. This incorporates profit advantages, foreign exchange earnings and growth in overseas markets, which are the examples of pull force.

Push Factors: Are the reactive reasons which imply compulsions of the domestic market which prompt a country and business to globalise. The increasing trade deficit and foreign exchange crisis, limited domestic demand, the need to operate at optimum size, growing competition in the home market, government policies and regulations, etc., are the examples of push factors.

Steps Taken for the Globalisation of Economy

The changes in our economic policy since 1991 have contributed a lot to the globalisation of economy.

Raising Foreign Equity Participation: The foreign equity participation has been increased to 51per cent from 40 per cent.

Devaluation of Rupee: Rupee was devalued by 20 per cent in 1991-92. This was done to facilitate exports and discourage imports. It also aimed to promote the inflow of more foreign capital.

Convertibility of Rupee: Partial convertibility of rupee was granted through the budget of 1992-93 and full convertibility was aimed at encouraging export earnings.

Long Period Trade Policy: The foreign trade policy was announced for a period of five years, for liberalisation. It removed restrictions on external trade.

Encouraging Open Competition: With minimised government control the exports and imports were left to the market forces.

Customs and Tariffs were Changed: Customs and Tariff policies were modified to enhance foreign trade.

ECONOMIC LIBERALISATION

Globalisation may be seen as a major driving force of global economic integration and has the following main features: (i) Internationalisation of production, with very fast changes in the structure of production; (ii) Liberalisation and expansion of world trade *i.e.,* linking the domestic economy with the global economy.

The basic ideology regarding liberalisation is that the economic management has to be taken care of by the market forces of demand and supply *i.e.,* the major decision regarding the economy *i.e.,* factors of production and their allocation, etc., are controlled by the price mechanism. It actually means that the government has liberalized views towards the trade and industrial policies, etc. This helps to curtail the intervention of the state in economic activities as much as possible, thereby making all the economic decision guided by free market forces, thus, generating a free market economy. This free market economy results in the optimal and efficient utilisation of resources by competitive operation of markets. The associated advantages are:

- Demand generation by reducing product prices.
- Raising real income.
- Generating gainful employment.

All these specified advantages were first shown by Adam Smith. He also demonstrated how liberalised exchange and working markets produce output which maximise both individual and social benefits.

Economic Liberalisation in India

The process of economic liberalisation began in India in July 1991 when a package of economic reforms was announced. The central theme underlying these reforms has been an increasing reliance on the market mechanism. Economic liberalisation refers to deregulation and reduction of government controls, greater autonomy of private investment, less dependence on the pubic sector, more opening of the economy to international trade, less restrictions on the convertibility of the rupee and so on. The policy reforms carried out since 1991 have come to be known as economic liberalisation.

The purpose of economic liberalisation is to unlock the economic potential of the country by encouraging private sector and multinational corporations to invest and expand. This is expected to introduce much more competition into the economy creating incentives for increasing efficiency of operations. Imports have been opened to encourage technological upgradation of Indian industry. Economic liberalisation comprises of both privatisation and globalisation.

Objectives of Economic Liberalisation

- Generation of competitive environment in the industrial sector through expansion of private sector.
- Reducing government support to the defective public sector industries.
- Enabling free market forces to operate without any government intervention on the grounds of maximum or minimum price legislation. This results in achieving optimum allocation of economic resources.
- Regulating efficient utilisation of factors of production and achieve supply side efficiency.
- Removing trade barriers to facilitate international trade.
- Overcoming the macro economic crisis arising out of rising price level and growing fiscal deficit, unfavourable balance of payments situation, shortage in foreign exchange reserve, etc.

Steps taken to Liberalise Economy

Licence Free Industrial Development: A large number of industries were exempted by the government from any kind of industrial licencing *i.e.*, companies can be formed without any restriction.

Growth of Industries: Industries can easily expand themselves according to the needs of the market, not waiting for government approval.

Freedom of Production: Producers are free to produce goods of their choice.

Extension of Investment Limit of Small Industries : The investment limit of small-scale industries is increased to one crore, in order to enable them to modernise their industries.

Import Machinery and Raw Material were not Charged: Necessary foreign exchange can be exchanged from the market for current account transactions and the government permission is not required. This would generate competition and increase efficiency.

FERA (Foreign Exchange Regulation Act) which was considered to be an ineffective measure to control inflow and outflow of foreign exchange was replaced by FEMA (Foreign Exchange Management Act) in 2000 to attract more FDI and technology transfers.

Impact of Economic Liberalisation

- Growth in GDP (Gross Domestic Product).
- Fall in inflation rate.
- Growth in industrial production.
- Expansion of markets for the industry.
- Liberal choice of location and technology for production.

- Improved prospects for agricultural exports and other industrial sectors.

PROMOTION OF FREE TRADE

Globalisation is also achieved to a great extent by free trade practices due to removal of trade barriers. This is carried on in different ways.

- Reduction or elimination of tariffs; creation of free trade zones with small or no tariffs.
- Reduced transportation costs, especially resulting from the development of containerization for ocean shipping.
- Reduction or elimination of capital controls.
- Reduction, elimination, or harmonization of subsidies for local business.
- Creation of subsidies for global corporations.
- Harmonization of intellectual property laws across the majority of states, with more restrictions.
- Supranational recognition of intellectual property restrictions (*e.g.* patents granted by China would be recognized in the United States).

TECHNOLOGY

The most important feature is that of technology, that has rendered a lot to the development of globalisation especially through communication.

People around the globe are more connected to each other than ever before. Information and money flow more quickly than ever. Goods and services produced in one part of the world are increasingly available in all parts of the world. International travel is more frequent. International communication is quite common.

Technological innovation has contributed to globalisation by supplying infrastructure for transworld connections. In particular, developments in means of transport, communication, and data processing have allowed global links to become denser, faster, more reliable and much cheaper. Large-scale and rapid globalisation has depended on a host of innovations relating to coaxial and later fibre-optic cables, jet engines, packaging and preservation techniques, semiconductor devices, computer software, and so on. In other words, global relations could not develop without physical tools to effect cross planetary contacts.

We are living in the era of advanced communication which has converted the whole world to a 'global village' through the facilities of quick exchange of information with the help of electronic media. Various communication services such as telephone, telegraph, radio, television, satellite communication, fax, e-mail, etc., have transformed the modern society.

REGULATIONS

Next to technology, regulation has also played an enabling role for globalisation. Supraterritorial links would not be possible in the absence of various facilitating rules, procedures, norms and institutions. For example, global communications rely heavily on technical standardization. Global finance depends in good measure on a working world monetary regime. Global production and trade are greatly promoted by liberalisation, that is, the removal of tariffs, capital controls and other state-imposed restrictions on the movement of resources between countries. Tax laws, labour legislation and environmental codes can also encourage (or discourage) global investment. In short, globalisation requires supporting regulatory frameworks. This is possible when the global trade regulating body works strictly based on multilateralism.

CAPITALISM

Capitalism has been a facilitating force for globalisation. Already in the 1850's, **Karl Marx** said, that *"capital by its nature, drives beyond every spatial barrier"* to *"conquer the whole earth for its market"*. More specifically, global markets offer prospects of increased profits through higher sales volumes. In addition, larger production runs to feed global markets and promise enhanced profits due to economies of scale. Capitalists also pursue globalisation since it allows production facilities to be sited wherever costs are lowest and earnings greatest. Furthermore, global accounting practices enable prices and taxes to be calculated in ways that raise profits. Finally, global connections themselves (telecommunications, electronic finance, and so on) create major opportunities for profit making.

Impact of Globalisation

Globalisation is much like fire. Fire itself is neither good nor bad. Used properly, it can cook food, sterilize equipments, form iron and heat our homes. Used carelessly, fire can destroy lives, towns and forests in an instant.

"Globalisation can be incredibly empowering and incredibly coercive. It can democratize opportunity and democratize panic. It makes the whales bigger and the minnows stronger. It leaves you behind faster and faster, and it catches up to you faster and faster. While it is homogenizing cultures, it is also enabling people to share their unique individuality farther and wider." —**Friedman**

Globalisation has dangers and an ugly dark side. But it can also bring tremendous opportunities and benefits. Globalisation requires vigilance and the rule of law to keep it away from devouring societies.

Globalisation is good for the world economy. Globalised economies grow faster than inward looking economies, they can move more quickly to higher income levels where they can enjoy better environmental outcomes.

Achievements of Globalisation in Indian Economy
- Efficient and Professional Management of Services and modern technology transfers;
- Inflow of large amount of foreign exchange through inward investment;
- Promotion of Healthy Competition;
- Accelerated rate of growth of Indian economy;
- Increased country's exports, outward foreign investment;
- Helped to check inflation;
- Spectacular growth of IT sector through B.P.Os; and
- Improved quality of life or standard of living, etc.

Negative Aspects of Globalisation
- Outsourcing, while it provides jobs to a population in one country, takes away those jobs from another country, leaving many without opportunities.

- Although different cultures from around the world are able to interact, they begin to melt, and the contours and individuality of each begin to fade.
- There is little international regulation, an unfortunate fact that could have dire consequences on the safety of people and the environment.
- The countries lose sovereignty over decision-making regarding import and investment policies.

Implications of Globalisation

The implications of globalisation for a national economy are many. Globalisation has intensified interdependence and competition between economies in the world market. This interdependence is reflected in regard to trading in goods and services and in movement of capital. As a result, domestic economic developments are not determined entirely by domestic policies and market conditions. Rather, they are influenced by both domestic and international policies and economic conditions. It is thus, clear that a globalised economy, while formulating and evaluating its domestic policy cannot afford to ignore the possible actions and reactions of policies and developments in the rest of the world. This constrains the policy option available to the government, which implies loss of policy autonomy to some extent, in decision-making at the national level.

Comparative Impact of Globalisation on World Economies

Globalisation is good for the world economy. globalised economies grow faster than inward looking economies, they can move more quickly to higher income levels where they can enjoy better environmental outcomes.

Globalised Countries Growing Faster

Average annual GDP growth for rich, globalised developing and non-globalised developing countries.

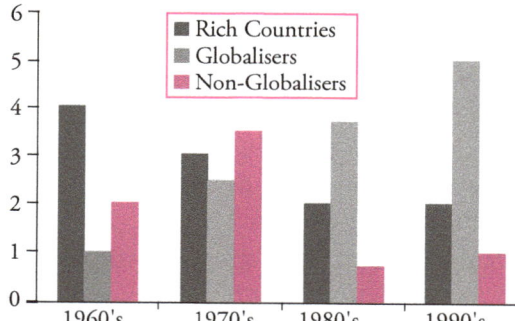

There is strong evidence that trade boosts growth especially for poor economies. A recent study of 72 developing economies found that since 1980 their ratio of trade to Gross Domestic Product (GDP) grew at an average faster than developed economies. The economies studied included China, India, Brazil, Malaysia, Mexico and Philippines.

In the 1990's the GDP of these economies grew at an average of 5.0 per cent annually up from 1.4 per cent in the 1960's. These economies have been closing the gap between their income levels and those of the world's rich economies.

Economies that did not increase their exposure to international trade reduced their average annual growth from 3.3 per cent in 1970's to 0.8 per cent in the 1980's and 1.4 per cent in the 2010.

LESSON AT A GLANCE

Globalisation: Is a process of increasing economic integration and growing economic interdependence between countries in the world economy. It involves not simply cross-border movement of goods, services, capital, technology, information and people, but also an organisation of economic activities which crosses national boundaries.

Factors Enabling Globalisation: (i) Growing similarity of countries in different areas; (ii) Development of global capital markets; (iii) Technological restructuring; (iv) Products are available to global customers; (v) Competition from domestic markets; (vi) International competition; (vii) Inflow of foreign capital; (viii) Increasing employment opportunities.

Pull Factors: Profit advantage and growth in overseas markets.

Push Factors: Trade deficit, foreign exchange crisis etc.

Steps Taken for the Globalisation of Economy: (i) Raising foreign equity participation; (ii) Devaluation of rupee; (iii) Convertibility of rupee; (iv) Long period trade policy; (v) Encouraging open competition; (vi) Customs and tariffs were changed.

Economic Liberalisation: The process in which the market forces of demand and supply manage the economy. The government has liberalised views on trade and industrial policies.

Economic Liberalisation in India: Started in July 1991.

Objectives: It refers to deregulation and reduction of government controls, greater autonomy of private investments, less dependence on public sector, more opening to international trade and flexibility in convertibility of rupee.

Steps Taken to Liberalise Economy: (i) License free industrial development (ii) Growth of industries; (iii) Freedom of production; (iv) Extension of investment limit of small industries; (v) Import of machinery and raw materials.

Promotion of Free Trade: Trade barriers were removed and tariffs were reduced.

Technology: Technological development and innovation like internet, cellular phone, fax, etc., have changed the way of business works. World is actually got transformed into a global village.

Regulation: Presence of facilitating rules, procedures and norms that have enabled globalisation.

Capitalism: Capital by nature drives beyond spatial barrier. It has enabled globalisation.

QUESTIONS

A. Short Answer Questions

1. What is globalisation?
2. When did globalisation begin?
3. Explain pull and push factors leading to globalisation.
4. What is meant by economic liberalisation?

5. Write a few advantages of liberalised economy.
6. Explain licence free industry generation.
7. What is the impact of economic liberalisation?
8. Differentiate between liberalisation and globalisation.
9. Explain the scope of globalisation.
10. State the various liberalisation measures undertaken by the Indian Government.

B. Long Answer Questions

1. What are the main factors that led to globalisation?
2. What steps are taken by Indian government for the globalisation of economy?
3. Explain economic liberalisation in India.
4. Explain the objectives of economic liberalisation.
5. What is meant by free trade?
6. How have technological developments transferred the world into a 'global village'?
7. What are the positive effects of globalisation?
8. What are the drawbacks of globalisation?
9. Globalisation is both boon and bane for Indian Economy. Give reasons to support your answer.

18
World Trade Organization (WTO) and Multinational Corporations (MNCs)

For the growth of International Business, the effective removal of trade and tariff barriers and to facilitate expansion and balanced growth of trade influencing liberalisation and globalisation processes different organisations were set up in different period of time which could deal with the promotion of economic and financial co-operation among nations (member countries). These organisations help in facilitating free flow of goods across international boundaries.

A few organisations are as following:

(I) GATT (GENERAL AGREEMENT ON TARIFFS AND TRADE)

GATT was formed on 30th October 1947, when a conference was held in Geneva. GATT came into real existence and started functioning from 1st January 1948. It is a multilateral treaty which till 1994 had been signed by 118 Governments who were called as "Counteracting Parties". Once 80 per cent of the world trade was influenced by the functions of GATT. It was neither an organisation nor a court of justice. GATT was an agreement and a decision-making body. It was a forum where the members could meet from time to time to discuss and solve their problems and to establish and maintain friendly relations among its members.

(II) UN CONFERENCE ON TRADE AND DEVELOPMENT (UNCTAD)

OVERVIEW

The Economic Policy of 1991 changed the scenario of business in India as it started spreading its wings beyond boundaries. There was a steep development of International Business, with which arose the need to administer it. To facilitate it, several organisations were formed to regulate the trade among different countries.

The World Trade Organisation (WTO) was formed in 1995 by about 77 countries of the World (including India) to facilitate multilateral trade arrangements between different countries to facilitate economic globalisation. Before the establishment of WTO, these countries followed a legal arrangement, viz., the General Agreement on Tariffs and Trade (GATT) to promote international trade. The GATT came into existence in 1947. India is one of the founder members of GATT. Since its inception, GATT has been concerned with the promotion of international trade in an environment where the trading partners put minimum restrictions on trade (in the form of tariff and non-tariff barriers).

This activity led to the development of MNCs (Multinational Corporations) in India which have rendered Indian Market and Economy with tremendous growth, competition and opportunities.

The United Nations Conference on Trade and Development (UNCTAD) was established in 1964, following the growing dissatisfaction among nations with the operation of such international institutes as the IMF and GATT, since these institutions favoured the developed countries and failed to tackle the special trade and development problems of the Least Developed Countries (LDCs). GATT, in particular, though, being committed to free trade, reduction of tariffs and abolition of preferences and import restrictions, did not pay any attention to proposals made to stabilize commodity prices and give preferential treatment to LDCs in trade with developed countries. So, the Third World Countries or LDCs had to resort to UNCTAD to promote trade among themselves.

(III) WORLD TRADE ORGANIZATION

The WTO is successor to the GATT. The GATT was a forum where the member countries used to meet from time to time to discuss and solve the problem of world trade. That's why it is often called as watch dog of international trade. There were 77 member countries of the WTO on 1st January, 1995 which increased to 127 by December 1996 and now has 164 members by 2016. India is one of the founder members of WTO.

Members of WTO

The WTO has 164 members, which represents more than 95 per cent of total world trade. The WTO is governed by a Ministerial Conference, which meets every two years; a General Council, which implements the conference's policy decisions and is responsible for day-to-day administration; and a director-general, who is appointed by the Ministerial Conference. The WTO's headquarters is in Geneva, Switzerland.

Objectives of WTO

- To eliminate discriminatory treatment in international trade relations.
- To facilitate the optimal use of the world's resources for sustainable development.
- To ensure the reduction of tariffs and other barriers to trade.
- To facilitate higher standards of living, full employment, increase in production and trade in goods and services of the member nations.
- To enhance competitiveness among all trading partners so as to benefit the consumers.

Functions: The following are the functions of WTO:

- It facilitates the implementation, administration and operation of the objectives of the Multilateral Trade Agreement.
- It administers the understanding of rules and procedures, governing the settlement of disputes of the agreement.
- It co-operates with the IMF and World Bank and its affiliated agencies, with a view to achieve a greater coherence in global economic policy.
- It provides the framework for the implementation, administration and operation of the Plurilateral Trade Agreements relating to trade in civil aircraft, Government procurement, trade in dairy products and bovine meat.
- It provides the institutional framework for the administration of the substantive code which encompasses a spectrum of norms, governing the conduct of the member countries in the area of global trade.
- It ensures the implementation of the substantive code.
- It acts as a forum for the negotiation of further trade liberalisation.
- It provides technical assistance and training to developing countries.

Role of World Trade Organization

World Trade Organization plays a very important role in the economic integration of different countries of the world. Many problems which are faced in international trade can be solved by this trade organization. The foremost among them are preferential tariffs, free trade zones, custom unions and above all financial problems.

The basic assumption of WTO integrating various countries is to enlarge the market for every country by facilitating the extension of trade beyond national boundaries of each country.

If the market is enlarged, two positive effects are likely to occur.

First, there will be an increase in efficiency because the pad of existing resources is reallocated. Second, there will be technological progress and a higher level of investment.

The principal aim of the World Trade Organization was to avoid the economic mistakes of the post-world war of non-formation of the International Trade Organization (ITO). The International Monetary Fund (IMF) was thus, established to promote economic and financial co-operation among its member countries in order to facilitate major expansion and balanced growth of world trade. The International Bank for Reconstruction and Development (IBRD) or the World Bank is a sister institution of IMF. It was established in 1945 to bring about a smooth transition from a war time to peace time economy. The Asian Development Bank (ADB) was set up in 1966 because it was strongly felt that there should be a bank for Asia like the World Bank to meet the developmental needs of this region. But the International Trade Organisation could not be formed due to participating countries' reluctance to free world trade. At the place of ITO, the General Agreement on Tariffs and Trade (GATT) came into being.

The General Agreement on Tariffs and Trade (GATT) emerged to call international conference to decide on trade liberalization, raise the standard of living, ensure full employment and to expand the production and exchange of goods at a global level. In 1964, the United Nations Conference on Trade and Development (UNCTAD) was established following the growing dissatisfaction with the operation of international institutions such as the IMF and the GATT, as these institutions did not favour the development problems of the Less Developed Countries (LDCs).

Benefits to Indian Companies

The World Bank and GATT Secretariat estimated the beneficial impact of the WTO regime. They had pointed out that this regime would lead to substantial increase in the volume and value of world trade. The largest increase was expected to be in the areas of textiles (about 60 per cent), followed by agriculture, forestry and fishery products (20 per cent), and processed food and beverages (19 per cent). Government of India was also optimistic in enlarging its share in these fields of trade, because of her competitive advantages in these lines of production.

India is also likely to benefit from the improved prospects of agricultural exports, because world price of agricultural products would be relatively higher than those in India, when the developed countries of the world would reduce the agricultural subsidy under the WTO regime. India experienced some disadvantages equally which are as follows :

1. Many of WTO rules are designed in the interest of developed countries at the cost of developing countries.

2. As per rules and regulations of WTO; India has to pay huge royalty to the patent holders of medicines, chemicals, etc.
3. Developed countries used WTO for non-trade areas to interfere in the management of domestic economy of a country.

MULTINATIONAL CORPORATIONS (MNC)

A Multinational Corporation refers to an organisation which is having its headquarter in one country and business operations in other countries. This means that this type of organisation has business across the countries. The country in which the MNC has its registered office is called home country and the country in which it carries its business operation is called host country.

U.N.O. has defined multinational corporations as *"Enterprises which own or control production or service-facilities outside the country in which they are based."*

In the words of **W.H. Moreland**, *"Multinational corporations or companies are those enterprises whose management, ownership and controls are spread in more than one foreign country."* Such companies are also called supernational or transnational companies / corporations.

For instance, Coca Cola is a company registered in the U.S.A and it has production and marketing facilities in many countries of the world. Some other popular multinational corporations include Pepsi (USA), Ponds (USA), Brook Bond (U.K.), Sony (Japan), Suzuki (Japan), Cadbury (U.K.), Proctor and Gamble (USA), GEC (U.K.), Gillette (USA), General Motors (USA), Honda (Japan), Johnsons & Johnsons (USA), etc.

Multinational corporations started about 25 years ago and have spread their operations all over the world. U.S.A. has the maximum number of multinational corporations in the world, some specialise in selected products only while others take up varied products. In India, MNC's operate in fields such as chemicals, electrical machinery, aluminium, metal and its products, pharmaceutical, heavy engineering goods, consumer goods, etc. IBM, Philips, Unilever Ltd., Ponds, DuPont, Siemens, Imperial Chemicals industries, Hyundai, Honda are some of the examples of multinationals.

FEATURES OF MULTINATIONAL CORPORATIONS

The significant features of most of the multinational corporations are as under:

They are a Giant Size Company: The assets and sales of MNCs run into billions of dollars and they make huge profits through their operations. For example, the physical assets of IBM are worth around 8 billion dollars.

They Carry Operations in Several Countries: MNC operates in many countries through a parent corporation in the home country. It runs its operations through a network of branches and subsidiaries in host countries. other operations, such as production, marketing are scattered in different countries.

They have a Centralized Control: MNC has its headquarters in the home country through which control is exercised over the branches and subsidiaries. The local management of branches and subsidiaries operate within the policy framework of the parent corporation, though the degree of decentralisation may vary depending on the local factors.

They Possess Oligopolistic Power: Through the process of merger and takeover of other firms, in course of time, MNC acquires a huge economic power. This coupled with its giant size makes it oligopolistic in character because of which it has a dominant position in the market.

They Provide Collective Transfer of Resources: A multinational corporation provides a multilateral transfer of resources. This transfer takes place in the form of a "package" which includes technical know-how, machinery and equipment, raw materials, management expertise, etc.

They Access International Market: MNCs have vast access to international markets as a result of vast resources and superior marketing skills. Because of this, MNCs are in a position to sell whatever product they choose to manufacture in different countries.

Advanced Technology: MNCs use sophisticated technology of production which give them an edge over other companies in host countries. They produce low cost world class product with innovative features which help in increasing the standard of living.

FUNCTIONS OF MULTINATIONAL CORPORATIONS

Multinational companies have many important functions in several developing economies including India. The benefits of MNCs to the host country are as follows:

Investment of Foreign Capital: MNCs can help the developing economies to secure capital from the developed countries. They facilitate transfer of capital from countries where it is abundant to countries where it is scarce. Thus, MNCs can help to increase the investment level and thereby the pace of development of the host country.

Transfer of Technology: The developing countries have old and obsolete technology. MNCs can be used as vehicles for the transfer of superior technology to the developing countries.

Creation of Job Opportunities: The MNCs help to increase the investment level and thereby employment opportunities in the host country.

Utilisation of Idle Resources: The MNCs help in the utilisation of idle resources in terms of labour force, minerals, other raw material, etc., of the host country and thus, generate income for the country.

Creation of Healthy Competition: MNCs increase competition and break domestic monopolies. The inefficient firms are forced to either improve or withdraw from the market.

Professional Management: The MNCs kindle a managerial revolution in the host countries by professional management and the employment of the latest management techniques. The host countries are thus, able to develop a culture of professional management.

Research and Development Activity: Developing countries lack investment in research and development areas. Multinationals can survive in the international markets only if they spend some of their resources in these activities. These companies spend some part of their research budget in developing countries. Secondly, the new improvements in their methods of work helps the host countries.

Benefits of Multinational Corporation in Indian Context

Multinational companies have been entering India in a big way for the last 26 years. The liberalised economic environment has helped in the entry of many multinational companies into the country in one form or the other. Some companies have started wholly owned subsidiaries, some have made joint ventures while some are taking important projects. Indian business is helped by the entry of multinational companies in the following ways:

- Multinationals are bringing more and more capital into the country. It is supplementing the efforts of Indian business.
- These corporations are bringing better technology in all the formats of business.
- Indian industry is facing a lot of competition from multinational organizations. This has compelled and helped the domestic industry to improve the quality of their products so that consumer is not reluctant to buy their products. Now the organisations who don't care for the liking of the consumer, have to compete with multinationals, then either there will be an improvement in their performance or they will face closure.
- Foreign companies are taking up many projects in India in the infrastructural area. Many power projects are being set up by multinationals. This will ensure infrastructural growth in the country.
- The inputs in India are relatively cheaper. The agricultural output forming raw material content and abundance of labour have attracted multinationals to meet their international commitments while producing in India. This increases exports from India and a favourable balance of trade will emerge in due course of time.
- The foreign exchange needs of Indian industry are met by multinationals. It helps in importing better technology and also enables expansion and diversification of production activities.
- MNCs through their giant size and international operations break domestic monopolies. They compel the domestic companies to improve their efficiency or withdraw from the market.
- MNCs acted as a dynamic force in development of Indian economy by generating employment opportunities, producing innovative and technologically superior goods, providing high pay packages, thus enabling Indians to purchase quality products and improving their standard of living.

LESSON AT A GLANCE

GATT (General Agreement on Tariffs and Trade): It is a decision making body, which maintains friendly relations between members.

UNCTAD: UN Conference on Trade and Development was formed to promote trade among Third World Countries or LDCs.

World Trade Organisation: Formed in 1995 with 77 members (including India) to facilitate multilateral trade arrangements between different countries in the light of economic globalisation.

Multinational Corporations: A multinational or transnational corporation is the one which extends the area of its operations beyond the country in which it is incorporated. Its headquarters is located in one country and it carries on its operations in its home country and also in a number of foreign countries known as host countries.

Features of Multinational Corporation: (i) They are a giant size company; (ii) They carry operations in several countries; (iii) They have a centralized control; (iv) They possess oligopolistic power; (v) They provide collective transfer of resources; (vi) They access international market; (vii) Advanced technology

Functions of Multinational Corporations:

(i) Investment of foreign capital; (ii) Transfer of technology; (iii) Creation of Job opportunities; (iv) Utilisation of idle resources (v) Creation of healthy competition (vi) Professional management (vii) Research and development activity.

QUESTIONS

A. Short Answer Questions
1. What is GATT?
2. What is UNCTAD?
3. When and with how many members did WTO start?
4. What are the objectives of WTO?
5. What benefits have the Indian Companies obtained from the WTO?
6. Define MNC. Give few examples.
7. Write full form of IMF and GATT.
8. How is India likely to benefit from the agricultural exports under WTO regime?
9. Why is WTO regarded as 'Watch Dog of Foreign Trade'?

B. Long Answer Questions
1. What are the functions of WTO?
2. How has WTO influenced the economic integration of different countries of the world?
3. What are the features of an MNC?
4. Explain any five functions of an MNC.
5. What benefits have been brought about in Indian Economy or business Scenario with the advent of MNC's in India?

Case Study

CASE STUDY 1

GLOBALISATION

Globalisation is the process of rapid integration or interconnection between countries. Rapid improvement in technology has been one major factor that has stimulated the globalisation process. The past fifty years have seen several improvements in transportation technology which has made much faster delivery of goods across long distances possible at lower costs. Even more remarkable have been the developments in information and communication technology. In recent times, technology in the areas of telecommunications, computers, internet has been changing rapidly. Mobiles are used to contact one another around the world to access information instantly which has been facilitated by satellite communication devices. As we know, computers have now entered almost every field of activity. We are in the world of internet now where we can obtain and share information on almost anything we want to know. It also allows us to send email and talk across the world at negligible costs.

Many people gets benefit from all such developments and it enhanced the process of globalisation. For instance, A news magazine published for London readers is to be designed and printed in Delhi. The text of the magazine is sent through internet to the Delhi office. The designers in the Delhi office get orders on how to design the magazine from the office in London using telecommunication facilities. The designing is done on computer. After printing, the magazines are sent by air to London. Even the payment of money for designing and printing from a bank in London to a bank in Delhi is done instantly through (e-banking) internet. In such a manner, life of people has changed drastically. Employment opportunities has increased and so the economic growth of the countries.

India controls at the present 45 per cent of the global outsourcing market with an estimated income of $ 50 billion) As per the Forbes list for 2007, the number of billionaires of India has risen to 40 (from 36 last year) more than those of Japan (24), China (17), France (14) and Italy (14) this year) The services sector acts as the engine of growth of the economy with a contribution of more than 60 per cent of GDP. India is ranked 18th among the world's leading exporters of services with a share of 1.3 per cent in world exports.

Q.1. What is Globalisation?

Q.2. Identify the words describing the use of technology in production in the example of news magazine.

Q.3. How is information technology connected with globalisation?

Q.4. What are the benefits of globalisation?

CASE STUDY 2

Consumer Awareness

Arya, a student of Mayur Vihar, joined a two year course at a local coaching institute for professional courses in New Delhi. At the time of joining the course, she paid the fees of ₹ 61,020 as lump sum for the entire course of two years. However, she decided to opt out of the course at the end of one year as she found that the quality of teaching was not up to the mark. When she asked for a refund of the fee for one year, it was denied to her.

When she filed the case in the District Consumer Court, the court directed the Institute to refund ₹ 28,000 saying that she had the right to choose. The Institute again appealed in the State Consumer Commission which upheld the district court's direction and further fined the institute ₹ 25,000 for a frivolous appeal. It also directed the institute to pay ₹ 7000 as compensation and litigation cost.

The State Commission also restrained all the educational and professional institutions in the state from charging fees from students for the entire duration of the course in advance and that too at one go. Any violation of this order may invite penalties and imprisonment, the commission said.

Q.1. What was the duration of the course which Arya joined?
Q.2. Why she asked for refund?
Q.3. Which right has been used by Arya?
Q.4. Where did she file the case first?

CASE STUDY 3

Bhopal Gas Tragedy

Bhopal is known for its historical records, artificial lakes and greenery but most of all, the city is remembered across the globe for the worst industrial mishap of the world.

Post midnight on December 3, 1984, poisonous gas that leaked from the factory of Union Carbide in Madhya Pradesh capital killed thousands of people directly. The incident is now known as the Bhopal disaster or Bhopal gas tragedy.

As per official records, this tragedy killed 3,787 people. The figures were updated by the Madhya Pradesh government later as the immediate official estimate had put the death toll due to gas leak from Union Carbide factory at 2,259.

However, activists fighting for justice for Bhopal gas tragedy victims put the figures of death between 8,000 and 10,000. In an affidavit, submitted in 2006, the government said that the Bhopal gas leak caused 5,58,125 injuries that included approximately 3,900 severely and permanently disabling injuries.

Bhopal had a population of about 8.5 lakh back in 1984 and more than half of its population was coughing, complaining of itching in eyes, skin and facing breathing problems. The gas caused internal hemorrhage, pneumonia and death. The villages and slums in the neighbouring areas of the factory were the worst affected.

Q.1. What is the other name of Bhopal gas tragedy?

Q.2. When was affidavit submitted?

Q.3. What were the problems faced by the population?

CASE STUDY 4

Chernobyl Disaster

The Chernobyl disaster was a nuclear disaster which occurred on April 26, 1986 at the Chernobyl nuclear power plant in Pripyat, Ukraine. At that time, Ukraine was part of the Soviet Union.

This event was one of the worst accidents in the history of nuclear power. Because the RBMK reactors used at the plant had no containment building to keep the radiation in, radioactive fallout drifted over parts of the western Soviet Union, Eastern Europe, Scandinavia, the UK, and the eastern United States. Large areas of Ukraine, Belarus, and Russia were badly contaminated. About 60 per cent of the radioactive fallout landed in Belarus. About 360,000 people needed to be moved to other places, where they could live after the accident. In addition, many people suffered from long term illnesses and some people were even diagnosed with thyroid cancer and acute radiation poisoning.

Before the accident, there was a planned power reduction. By the beginning of the day shift, the power level had reached 50 per cent. Following this, randomly, one of the regional power stations went offline. It was then requested that the further power reduction would be postponed. Despite this request, the reduction and preparations for a test that was to happen continued.

The accident occurred when the fourth reactor suffered a huge power increase. This led to the core of the reactor exploding. Due to this explosion, large amounts of radioactive materials and fuel were released. This caused the neutron moderator, made of graphite, to start to burn. The fire caused more radioactive fallout to be released, which was carried by the smoke of the fire into the environment.

Reactor 4 was covered by a "sarcophagus", made from steel and concrete to stop the escape of more radiation from elements such as corium, uranium and plutonium, as well as radioactive dust. The sarcophagus was covered in 2016 with the New Safe Confinement structure.

The accident raised concerns about the safety of the Soviet nuclear power industry. The Soviet Union slowed down the process of making its nuclear industry bigger for some time. The Soviet government also had to become less secretive as a result of the accident. Since then, Russia, Ukraine and Belarus have become separate countries. Those countries have been burdened with continuing costs for decontamination and health care because of the accident.

Q.1. What type of disaster was this?

Q.2. What was the consequences of this disaster?

Q.3. When was the accident occurred?

Q.4. What did Soviet Union do after this disaster?

Project Work

PROJECT WORK-1

Identify 100 consumers of major brands of edible oils in a locality where you live. Draw up the pattern of their monthly expenditure on this product and compare it with the other household expenditure. Make a presentation of your findings in the class.

   (i) Visit a nearby shop of consumer products. With the help of the shop-keeper of that shop, prepare a list of major brands of edible oils which are demanded by the consumers.
   (ii) Interact with any 100 consumers who come to the shop for purchasing edible oil of major brands as selected above.
   (iii) Try to gather information from the selected consumers about:
      (a) Their monthly household expenditure on edible oil.
      (b) Their monthly expenditure on the other household items.
   (iv) Use the information as collected above in the following manner:
      (a) Find out the per centage of expenditures incurred on edible oil to the total household expenditures:
         - Consumer wise, and
         - Overall.
      (b) Find out the total consumption of edible oil for a month:
         - Consumption of each brand separately, and
         - Total consumption of all the brands.
      (c) Whether any specific brand is preferred by the consumers, if yes, why?

Make a summary report of your findings.

PROJECT WORK-2

Identify the major brands of bathing soap that are available in the market in your area. Select a sample of 10 shops/departmental stores that sell these brands and collect the sales of these brands over a period of one week at these shops. Identify the brands that sell the most and present your findings in way of presentation in your class.

   (i) On the basis of a data as collected above, draw a table showing name of shops, name of brands and sales figure collected in respect of individual brand of soap.
   (ii) Identify the best selling brand and draw the following conclusion:
      (a) Per centage of sale of this brand to the total sale of all the brands available.
      (b) Variation in the sale of this brand in this week as compared to sale of last week.

(c) Why this brand is preferred to the other brands of soaps available in the market? The reason may be either economy in use or any specific advantage, which may be highlighted in your report.

PROJECT WORK-3

Make a presentation on the central problems an economy faces. Explain these with reference to the Indian Economy.

(i) Identify the basic problems of an economy.
(ii) Analyse these problems as they exist in a mixed economy; as India is an example of mixed economy.

PROJECT WORK-4

Take a developed country such as USA and a developing country such as India. Analyse the main characteristics of these economies.

(i) Prepare a detail note of the main characteristics of the USA, a developed economy.
(ii) Prepare an another detailed note of the main characteristics of India, a developing economy.
(iii) Compare both the economics on the basis of characteristics as noted above.
(iv) Stress on those characteristics of Indian economy which seems as weaknesses in the development of an economy.
(v) Give your suggestion on the basis of the detail you have collected above what characteristic India should achieve to become a developed economy.
(vi) Make an emphasis on the most significant features of economy of USA which are not found in the Indian Economy.

Prepare a summary report. The help of your subject teacher is very essential for this project.

PROJECT WORK-5

Outline the main modes of transport in the district/city you live. What problems do you and other citizens face pertaining to the availability of public transport?

Analyse:

(i) Draw a table showing main modes of transport available in the district/city with their utilisation in per cent and numbers.
(ii) Interact with 20 to 30 people who use different modes of transport and try to known their problem, they feel while travelling.
(iii) With the information gathered as above prepare a note showing the problem pertaining to availability of transport.

PROJECT WORK-6

Take a table of food grain production in India from any textbook on Indian economy or any other secondary source such as internet. Interpret the changes in the production over a given period of time.

(i) Prepare a list of the years in which food grains have registered a rise in their production and the years in which the food grain production has declined taking the present year as the base year.

(ii) Identify the reasons for the fluctuation in the food grain production in India.
(iii) Give your suggestions for improving the agricultural productivity and the level of food grain production in India.

PROJECT WORK-7

Collect the information regarding population growth for the period between 1971-2001 in India and also the contribution of agriculture, industry and services sector for the same period, compare the two tables and present your findings in the form of a presentation.

On the basis of the information collected, make a presentation showing:
(i) Difference between the growth rate of population and rate of variations found in the table showing contribution of agriculture, industry and service sector.
(ii) Your comments whether these rate of changes as collected above are favourable or non-favourable.
(iii) A brief detail of causes responsible for the growing population.
(iv) Whether the contribution of agriculture, industry and service sector is not sufficient for the growing population ? If yes, why is it not sufficient ?
(v) Your suggestions for the betterment of agriculture, industry and service sector, to cope up with the requirements of increasing population.
(vi) Your suggestion on the population problem.
(vii) Conclusion of your overall findings.

PROJECT WORK-8

Make a presentation of the major trading partners of India in the last 15 years. Specify the major changes that have taken place in the last five years.

Collect the information as required for the above mentioned project and on the basis of statistics collected:
(i) Prepare separate lists of major trading partners of India before 15 years, before 10 years, before 5 years and at present.
(ii) Prepare separate list of major importers and exporters of India during the last five years.
(iii) Prepare separate list of major importer and exporter of India fifteen years before.
(iv) Compare the list prepared at step (i) and step, (ii) to find out the changes occured during the last five years. Give reasons also.
(v) Give your comments on the changes that have taken place during the five years.

PROJECT WORK-9

What are the major items of export and imports from India in the last five years? Use secondary data sources and highlight the changes that have taken place in that context.

Collect the information as given above from the sources like books, magazines and internet etc.

Use the information as collected above in the following manner:
(i) Prepare a yearwise table of items of import during the last five years.
(ii) Prepare a yearwise table of items of export during the last five years.

(iii) Make an interpretation of both the list to draw the outline as given below:
  (a) Whether the number of items of export is increasing or decreasing.
  (b) Whether the number of items of import is increasing or decreasing.
  (c) Whether contribution of export in the total foreign trade is increasing or decreasing.
  (d) Whether contribution of import in the total foreign trade in increasing or decreasing.

In the above tabulation, the item imported/exported should be mentioned in both quantities and value.

Glossary

B

Balance of Trade: The difference between the value of imports and exports of goods (*i.e.,* visible items) for a particular year. When visible exports are higher than visible imports, the Balance of Trade is said to be favourable. On the other hand, when import exceed exports, the balance is adverse or unfavourable. Sometimes the latter situation is referred to as the trade gap or deficit.

Bank Rate: The rate at which the Central Bank of any country is willing to discount first class bills. It is the rate of the discount of the Central Bank.

Bill of Exchange: A written instruction by one person (the drawer) to another (the drawee) to pay a named amount on demand or on a future date. Before a bill has any value it requires to be accepted by the drawee. If the latter is willing to carry out the instruction, he writes '*accepted*' across the bill and signs it. The bill is now described as an '*acceptance*' whereas until this stage it was merely a 'draft'.

Budget: An estimate of government expenditure and income for the financial year placed before the parliament on the last day of February.

Budget Deficit: If the proposed expenditure in the Government budget exceeds the anticipated income, there arises a '*deficit budget*'.

C

Capital: A factor of production comprising those material sources, other than land which are used in the production of goods and services, e.g., factory buildings, industrial plant, power stations, transport facilities. Thus, capital is wealth used for production.

Capital Formation: Change in the stock of capital in any country during any particular time period.

Credit Control: The activities which are associated with the attempt to regulate the extent of money outstanding to a business through its trading operations. Such activities include the initial determination of a potential customer's ability to meet debts, the establishment of credit limits for customers and the securing of prompt payment of money due.

D

Devaluation: A term meaning the reduction in valuation of a currency in terms of others, either by fixing its exchange value at a lower level or by allowing it to be depreciated by market forces.

E

Extensive Cultivation: An attempt to increase the production of foodgrains by increasing the area of cultivable land.

F

Fiscal Policy: A policy under which the government uses its expenditure and revenue programmes to produce desirable effects and avoid undesirable effects on the national income, production and employment.

G

Gross Domestic Fixed Capital Formation: Investment in fixed assets, *e.g.,* expenditure on buildings, vehicles, plants and machinery for replacing or adding to the stock of existing fixed assets, expenditure on maintenance and repair being excluded.

Gross Domestic Product (GDP): An estimate of the output of the factors of production in a country. It measures the value of goods and services produced in a year. These are usually valued at market prices, so if any indirect taxes such as value added tax are deducted and any subsidies are added, the result is GDP at factor cost. Gross means that depreciation has not been deducted. If has, then the result is net domestic Product.

Gross National Product (GNP): The Gross domestic product plus the income from property abroad less the income from property in Britain going to foreigners abroad.

H

Human Capital: Refers to the education, experience and skills possessed by a workforce.

I

Indirect Tax: Refers to tax that is not assessed on and collected from those who are intended to bear it. Examples are value added tax, sales tax, payroll tax and excise duties.

Inflation: Refers to a situation in which the generated level of prices is steadily rising or, in other words, the value of money is falling. There are several types of inflation:

(i) Creeping Inflation: Describes a rise in the price level at a rate of 2 to 3 per cent per annum. This type of inflation does not do very serious harm and it may, in fact, stimulate investment.

(ii) Moderate Inflation: Describes a rise of 4 to 5 per cent per annum and this rate is high enough to have undesirable effects.

(iii) Rapid Inflation: Describes a rise of 6 per cent or over and it is positively harmful and has undesirable effects on incomes, imports and exports, savings and consumption.

Infrastructure: A term used to describe those forms of capital which help investment in producer goods to be fully productive, *e.g.* roads, railways, water supplies, educational facilities etc. A sound infrastructure is pre-requisite of rapid economic growth.

Intensive Cultivation: A process of increasing foodgrains production through multiple cropping (*i.e.,* a given area is sown more than once in any year).

M

Monetary Policy: Measures taken by the Central Bank and the national treasury to manipulate the money supply with the intent to influence the output of goods and services, employment, the price level, the rate of economic growth, or the balance of international payments.

Money Supply: The total quantity of money in circulation at a given moment.

Monopoly: A single seller of any commodity which has no close substitute in the market. The monopolist has substantial control over the market price of such a commodity.

N

Net Domestic Product (NDP): When the depreciation cost of capital is deducted from the Gross Domestic Product, we get NDP.

Net National Product: A term used in connection with calculation of the national income. It is the amount of gross national product less depreciation.

O

Occupational Structure: The distribution of the work force in a country according to their occupation in agriculture, industry and service activities.

P

Per Capita Income: The income which is earned per individual; calculated by taking the total income of a group and dividing it by the number of individuals in the group.

S

Secondary Sector: Sectors consisting of manufacturing industries, construction work, electricity, gas and water supply in the Indian economy.

Small Scale Industry (SSI): Industrial Units which require relatively less amount of capital and labour than the large and medium scale industrial units. The Industrial Policy Statement (1997) of the Government of India shows that, if the investment in plant and machinery is up to ₹ 3 crore, then that unit will be treated as SSI unit.

T

Tariffs: Duties imposed by the Government of any country on imported items.

Tertiary Sector: The sector consisting of banking and insurance, transport and communications, defence and administration, hotels and tourism, and other types of services in an economy.

U

Underemployment: Those who do not get full time employment and, even if they are engaged in any full time activity, their earnings are insufficient to fulfil their minimum needs.

Unemployment: The stock of all those individuals who are not in employment and who are either in the process of moving to a new job or who are unable to find work at the prevailing wage rate.

V

Vicious Circle of Poverty: A situation where low per capita income of less developed countries results in low savings, low investment, low capital accumulation, low productivity, low production and again ends with low per capita output and income. Thus circular causation explains the perpetuation of poverty in these countries.

W

Worker Participation Rate: This shows the proportion of main and marginal workers in the total workforce in India consisting of people within the age group 15-59 years.

www.ingramcontent.com/pod-product-compliance
Ingram Content Group UK Ltd.
Pitfield, Milton Keynes, MK11 3LW, UK
UKHW050417240426
12048UKWH00014B/678